MW01136661

The
Educational Philosophy
of St. John Bosco

The Educational Philosophy of St. John Bosco

By JOHN MORRISON

SALESIANA PUBLISHERS
New Rochelle, New York

The Educational Philosophy of
Saint John Bosco - *First American Edition*

Reprinted from the Australian original
with permission of the author

© 1979 Salesian Society, Inc.
Reprinted 1997

Library of Congress Catalog Number 79-54817
ISBN 0-89944-050-9

Typeset at the Salesian Technical High School in Kowloon, Hong Kong
Printed in U.S.A.

FOREWORD

The educational ideas of John Melchior Bosco[1] are relatively unknown in Australia: the combined libraries of the Universities of Sydney and N.S.W., together with the N.S.W. Public Library and the shire libraries of Sutherland, have only two references to him: one, a version of Bosco's *History of Italy*[2] by a J.S. Morell; and the other, some thumb sketches in two encyclopedias,[3] giving no details of his educational system.

Yet John Bosco's theories are put into practice in some seventeen Catholic educational institutions[4] spread over three states of Australia: South Australia has five centres, Victoria eight, N.S.W. and Tasmania two each. These Bosconian centres have literature on their founder, so that over seventy different works have been made available for research purposes.[5] The largest single collection came from Boys' Town, Engadine, N.S.W., and the two Bosconian schools in Engadine were opened to inspection, teachers there volunteering information. The Rector of Boys' Town,[6] and the Parish Priest of Engadine,[7] were interviewed in their official capacities; the Provincial[8] provided additional literature on the subject; and conversations were held with a priest[9] who has recently had access to additional primary source material from the Don Bosco archives in Italy.

Although this bibliography on Don Bosco is fairly extensive in terms of what is known to be available on the subject, and includes volumes written in Italian, French, and English, it is pertinent to point out that this material, with very few exceptions, has been written by Catholic clerics who look at the man both as a saint and legendary figure.

It has been the writer's task, therefore, while accepting this overview on Bosco, to cull from a largely apologetic fund of biographical literature those aspects from Bosco's life and works which relate to his pedagogy, and then place them in the general framework and context of Catholic education.

John Morrison

CONTENTS

CHAPTER 1

JOHN BOSCO IN PERSEPCTIVE

Part I: John Melchior Bosco in Historical Perspective.

John Bosco's birth in 1815 saw Napoleon defeated at Waterloo; the Congress of Vienna; and temporary peace restored to Europe. In 1820, with rebellions in Naples, and revolution at Palermo, John Bosco, when only five, was already teaching catechism to his friends at Becchi. When six, his native Piedmont saw the abdication of Victor Emmanuel in favour of Charles Felix, and heard of the death of Napoleon in 1821. When nine, John Bosco had a dream which was to illumine his pedagogical purpose to educate poor and deprived children. Frederick Froebel wrote *The Education of Man* in 1826 by which time John Bosco was learning Latin, and when he was twelve, there died in 1827 the renowned Swiss educator, Pestalozzi.

From 1828 to 1830, whilst Ferrante Aporti[1] founded the first children's hospice in Italy, and with revolutions in Poland, and the declaration of Belgium independence imminent, with the deaths of two succeeding popes, Leo XII and Pius VIII, John Bosco was struggling to gain, despite poverty and adversity, an education to fit him for his life's work. In 1831, at the age of sixteen, with Mazzini in exile at Marseilles and the 'Young Italy' movement under way, while Charles Felix was being succeeded by Charles Albert in Piedmont, young Bosco, amid widespread social and political uncertainty, decided to enter the priesthood and so began his secondary studies in Chieri, a town near Turin. Having finished his schooling, he entered the seminary at Chieri on 30th October, 1835, at a time when Ferdinand I had become Emperor of Austria. From 1835 to 1840 he studied for the priesthood, was ordained and said his first mass in 1841, the same year in which G. Frederick Herbart, the German pedagogist, died.

By 1843, Don Bosco[2] had begun his first evening classes for poor boys; the next year saw the beginnings of his first Festive Oratory, which in modern parlance means boys' club, or, youth centre, in Turin and from 1844 to 1847 Don Bosco began regular evening schools, and organised catechetical instruction. He put into practice methods of education which gained university recognition. Professor G.A. Rayneri, Department of Pedagogy, Royal University of Turin, when lecturing to his students in education, often told them: "If you want to see pedagogy in action, go to the Oratory. . . . and watch Don Bosco."[3] Elsewhere, Mazzini founded the 'Giovane Europa' in 1844; Pope Gregory XVI was succeeded by Pius IX in 1846; while in 1847 the gathering forces of liberalism were being expressed in terms of liberty of the press, and in subtle forms of anti-clericalism in Don Bosco's native Piedmont.[4] Yet in this atmosphere of change Bosco founded his first sodality, the Sodality of St. Aloysius, took in boarders at Valdocco,[5] opened another Oratory at Porta Nuova in Turin, began his first retreats for boys, and found time to publish his *Il Giovane Provveduto*[6] (The Companion of Youth).

There were vast changes in Church and State in 1848 in most of Europe,[7] and popular opinion hardened against the Church,[8] some priests being openly attacked in the streets. In Turin, for example, in 1848 Don Bosco narrowly escaped death by musket fire[9] and in the same year survived a severe beating at the hands of a gang of toughs[10] in the backstreets of Valdocco. During this period it was Don Bosco, who said: "The revolution will proceed step by step and will carry out its program to the smallest detail."[11]

He had already shown political acumen in refusing to take part in political demonstrations. Earlier, in 1847 he had decided on a policy of non-political alliance whereas the Archbishop of Turin, Monsignor Fransoni, had become unpopular because of his alleged interference in politics.[12] This political policy of Bosco's was to come to his aid when the Church, largely due to the rising forces of liberalism, was to suffer severe losses in power, status and followers.

During this time Don Bosco increased and expanded his Oratories and works[13] despite a mounting fever of revolution in Turin.[14]

From 1849 to 1853 there were further changes in the political structures in some of the kingdoms of Italy. In 1849 the Roman Republic was proclaimed, Charles Albert abdicated in favour of Victor Emmanuel II in Piedmont; the Bourbons returned to Sicily; the French occupied Rome. By 1850 Pius IX had returned to Rome;

while in December 1851 the Napoleonic coup d'etat occurred; in 1852 Cavour,[15] who admired Bosco's educational methods, headed the Piedmontese ministry; and 1853 saw the insurrection in Milan. During this time of upheaval, 1849 to 1853, Don Bosco steadily consolidated his Oratories; erected a new church and hospice for his Oratory boys; and the professional schools for boarders were begun, despite personal threats, disappointments, and attempts on his life by anti-clerical factions. In 1853 he wrote the first of his apologetics, the *Letture Cattoliche*[16] (Catholic Readings) which were often effective in answering, sometimes silencing, the popular anti-clerical newspapers of Turin.

Between 1854 and 1859 the struggle continued between Church and State in parts of Europe. In Piedmont, religious Orders were suppressed, church property confiscated by the State at a time when, in the Balkans, the Crimean War broke out. In 1855 there was an alliance between Piedmont, France and England; 1856 saw the Congress of Paris, while in 1858 the Catholic world was hearing of the apparitions at Lourdes. By 1859 there had been another war between Austria and Piedmont, revolutions in Modena, Parma and Bologna; the Battle of Villafranca on 11th of July; annexations of Tuscany and Bologna, and by November, the Peace of Zurich.

Bosco, despite further inroads of anti-clericalism, founded another three sodalities,[17] published three works,[18] enlarged his Oratory and began woodworking classes at Valdocco. He gained encouragement from Urbano Rattazzi, an anti-clerical, to found a religious society. Rattazzi[19] was impressed by Bosconian educational methods and he urged his government to adopt them. A year after a visit to Rome for his first audience with Pius IX, Don Bosco, in December 1859, announced the foundation of the Salesian Society,[20] and in the same year completed plans for the running of a secondary school course at the Oratory.

From 1860 to 1864 political turmoil continued in most parts of the Italian peninsula. In 1860 alone: Savoy and Nice surrendered to France; Cavour returned to office in Piedmont; there were plebiscites in Tuscany, Emilia, Romagna; Palermo capitulated to Austria; Garibaldi entered Naples with resultant plebiscites in Naples, Sicily and Umbria. Cavour was dead by 1861, Garibaldi made his attempt on Rome in 1862.

It was during periods of upheaval and change that Don Bosco was expanding his educational system to include provinces outside Turin, and crystallizing his pedagogical ideas.

In 1860, for instance, he had added a directorship, that of the seminary at Giaveno, to his growing educational responsibilities; by 1861 he had installed the first printing press in the Oratory at Valdocco; in 1862 he had added a blacksmith's shop. In 1863 there was established his first school outside Turin, at Mirabello. In the same year he built a new church: Mary, Help of Christians. Another school outside Turin was opened at Lanzo in 1864.

In 1865 Don Bosco was fifty years of age; in 1867 he visited Rome for the second time, and in the same year he opened a new college at Mornese, some ninety kilometres to the east of Turin. In 1868 the new church of Mary, Help of Christians was consecrated, and in 1869 he began a series[21] of edited classics to be used in his schools. In the same year Don Bosco widened his educational horizons to provide for the education of young girls (under the tutelage of the confraternity of the Daughters of Mary, Help of Christians) who were taught by the same methods as those applied in his Oratories in Turin and elsewhere.

In 1870 he declined the Cardinal's hat, an offer from Pius IX, on the grounds that his work would be hampered if he were raised to the hierarchy: his educational ideas largely depended on a simple approach, a cardinalship could only hinder the rapport he already had with his charges. His request was that he remain plain Don Bosco. In 1870 he began his first school outside Piedmont, at Alassio in Liguria, some 120 km to the SSE of Turin. In 1871 he pioneered a federation for some of his past pupils.[22] Later, this idea of keeping in touch with ex-pupils became one of the features of Salesian pedagogy. By 1872, the Institute of the Daughters of Mary, Help of Christians was founded, and Mother Mary Mazzarello[23] became Superior of the Order which was to become a counterpart[24] to Bosco's Salesians. In the same year Don Bosco took over the college at Valsalice and began his methods there. By 1874 the Constitutions of his Society were approved;[25] in 1875 the first Salesian missionaries departed for the Argentine, and closer to home, in Nice, France, another Salesian school was founded.

In the next two years Don Bosco put the Salesian Co-operators,[26] members of the laity who were prepared to co-operate with Salesians in extending the work of charity among those in need, on a firm basis. Meanwhile, a second Salesian missionary contingent gathered in Rome in preparation for field work in South America. The first *Salesian Bulletin*[27] was published in 1877, the year in which the First General Chapter of the Salesian Order was held. Today, the bulletin appears in over thirty different countries and in twenty-five languages other than English. This was the year, too, of the third Salesian missionary venture to South America and the first for the Daughters of Mary, Help of Christians.

Don Bosco held his first conference with the Salesian Co-Operators when in 1878 Umberto I became monarch of Piedmont upon the death of Victor Emmanuel II, and Pius IX was succeeded by Leo XIII. Later, in 1880, while Don Bosco was journeying through France, at a time when religious Orders were being restricted there, the Salesians received assurances that their work in France would not be interrupted. A Second General Chapter of the Salesian Society was also held in 1880, the year in which Leo XIII entrusted to Don Bosco the building of the church of the Sacred Heart in Rome.[28]

Bosco, again in France in 1881 received enthusiastic receptions, and in 1883, spoke with Victor Hugo, who described the priest-educator as a "legendary figure".[29]

By 1884 a Salesian House[30] was in Spain; but in 1885 Don Bosco formally handed over the reins of Salesian government to Michael Rua.[31] Now deteriorating in health, in 1886, Don Bosco was welcomed in Spain; he made his last journey to Rome in 1887, to consecrate the church of the Sacred Heart; in 1888 he died. He was buried at Valsalice, Turin.

Part II: The Global Dissemination of Salesian Pedagogical Methods.

Since Don Bosco's death, the growth of the Salesian Society and the dissemination of their educational methods have been on an international scale. When their founder died, the Society numbered 1,015 members spread over 62 Houses in six Provinces;[1] in 1900, there were 4,372 Salesians, 359 Houses, 34 Provinces; sixty years later, 16,364 Salesians, 1,071 Houses, 51 Provinces;[2] and, in 1966, some seventy-eight years of Salesian enterprise had realised 22,560 Salesians, 1,384 Houses, and 73 Provinces.[3] The Daughters of Mary, Help of Christians, who use Bosconian pedagogical methods, today have 18,600 Sisters working in 1,450 Houses throughout the world.

Don Bosco's methods are used, too, in mission schools. Today,[4] sixteen mission areas are entrusted to the Salesians: five in India, four in Brazil, and one each in Thailand, the Congo, Paraguay, Ecuador, Venezuela, Colombia, and Mexico.[5] These mission territories cover an area of 1,696,950 sq km and include over 20,000,000 people. Altogether there are 267 Mission Centres housing some 2,990 Salesian missionaries[6] who are using the pedagogical methods of Don Bosco.

Salesian educational centres have been established in Italy, Austria, Belgium, Czechoslovakia, France, Germany, England, Yugoslavia, Holland, Poland, Portugal, Spain, Israel, China, the Philippines, Japan, India, Burma, Thailand, the Dominican Republic, Argentina, Tierra de Fuego, Bolivia, Brazil, Guatemala, Chile, Colombia, Ecuador, Mexico, Paraguay, Peru, the United States of America, Uruguay, Venezuela, Central Africa, South Africa, Canada, Ireland, and Australia.[7]

The Daughters of Mary, Help of Christians are also widely established. They have 56 Provinces of which eighteen are in Italy, eleven in Europe, twenty in the Americas, six in Asia (Australia being included in the Asia region), and one in Africa.[8]

As a combined force in the spreading of Bosconian pedagogical methods, the Salesians and the Daughters of Mary, Help of Christians exercise considerable influence in the education of infants, children, adolescents, and adults. The Oratory, which commands an important place in their system, has in Italy, for instance, 676 establishments; the rest of Europe and Africa have 281, Asia and Australia 93, the Americas 751; making 1,801 Oratories in all.[9] They run 663 professional schools which cater for vocations in mechanics, electrical trades, electronics, printing, book-binding, tailoring, carpentry and joinery, sculpture, agriculture, floriculture, and many others.[10] Between them the two Orders have 75 agricultural schools, 1,610 grammar and high schools, 843 kindergartens, 687 primary schools, 131 evening schools, 108 tertiary institutions, 262 missionary schools, 690 workrooms, 362 works of assistance, mainly orphanages, 283 Houses of formation, and 127 publishing houses[11] which further Don Bosco's ideas.[12]

Notes to Part I of Chapter 1

1   J.B. Lemoyne. *The Biographical Memoirs of Saint John Bosco*, Vol. II, p.311.   Ferrante Aporti, 1791-1858, noted Italian educationist who knew Don Bosco and praised his work, particularly his *Storia Sacra* (Bible History) which, according to Aporti in 1846, greatly benefited the cause of popular education in Italy.

ibid., pp.165-167: Aporti became the first teacher, in the Turin Method School, in 1844.

2   After his ordination John Bosco was always referred to as 'Don' Bosco. The title 'Don' is an abbreviation of the Latin 'dominus' meaning 'master'. In Italy 'Don' is used as a title for priests; it stands for 'Father'.

3   Lemoyne, *op. cit.*, Vol. III, p.21.   Today, in Italian Universities, the pedagogy of Don Bosco is a study in its own right.   As early as 1925, Bosco's ideas on education were officially incorporated into Italian tertiary curricula. See Fascie, D.B. *Del Metodo Educativo Di Don Bosco.*

4   Lemoyne, *op. cit.*, Vol. III, pp.1-5: In 1847 Liberalism was not yet openly opposed to the Church, but was espousing causes of Unification.   In Switzerland, there were early signs of anti-clericalism.

ibid., pp.164-168: Inspired by Vincenzo Gioberti's writings, especially his *Gesuita Moderno*, Italian revolutionaries offered clerics prominence if they took part in their affairs.

5   Don Bosco's first Oratory, the Oratory of St Francis de Sales, was

located at Valdocco, an unsavoury quarter of Turin.

6   Lemoyne, *op. cit.*, Vol. III, pp.6-7: In 1847 Don Bosco published his *Il Giovane Provveduto (The Companion of Youth)*. This book fulfilled a need and became very popular.

   ibid., pp.9-15: A description of the above book's contents are given here.

7   In 1848, in central Europe, Constitutions were granted in Palermo, Naples, Florence, Turin, and Rome.   There were: revolution in Vienna, risings in Venice and Milan, revolts in Hungary, revolutions in Berlin.   Charles Albert, of Piedmont, declared war on Austria, 23rd of March, with the subsequent occupation of Milan by the Austrians.   Pope Pius IX left Rome for Gaeta; Karl Marx issued his *Manifesto* on the class struggle.

8   Lemoyne, *op. cit.*, Vol. III, p.276: Due, to a large extent, to influences of an anti-clerical Press.   In Turin, for example, the popular paper *Gazzatta del Popolo*, repeatedly wrote against the Church and its ministers.

9   *ibid.*, p.211: Don Bosco was shot at by a fanatic when the former was instructing older boys in the catechism in the St Francis de Sales Oratory. Fortunately, the shots missed both Bosco and his boys.

10   *ibid.*, pp.275-283.   An account of Bosco's encounter with hooligans has been recorded.

11   *ibid.*, pp.164-168.

12   *ibid.*, pp.190-196: Don Bosco's wisdom of non-political alliance; Fransoni's objections and unpopularity.

   ibid., pp.208-211: Mob violence in Turin against the Jesuits; Fransoni's closing of the seminary in Turin; mobs outside the Convitto Ecclesiastico threatened its inhabitants.

13   In 1849, Don Bosco opened a third Oratory at Vanchiglia in Turin. In 1850 he obtained a subsidy for the Oratory from the Ministry of the Interior. By 1851 he had the first stone laid for his new church of St Francis de Sales, and the following year saw its inauguration.

14   Lemoyne, *op. cit.*, Vol. III, pp.302-303: Charles Albert's defeat by Austrians in 1848 brought the populace of Turin to the brink of revolution.

15   *ibid.*, p.289: As early as 1848, both of the Cavour brothers, Marquis Gustavo and Count Camillo, were admirers of Don Bosco's educational methods, paid frequent visits to his Oratories and seldom missed important functions there.   Count Camillo, who later headed the 1852 Ministry, openly praised the Festive Oratories.

16   From 1853-1884, Don Bosco kept up, in his *Letture Cattoliche (Catholic Readings)* a steady volume of apologetic literature which was acknowledged

as being erudite and relevant in theological matters, education, faith and morals. Altogether the number of volumes during this period amounted to over 150.

17   The Immaculate Conception Sodality, 1856; The Blessed Sacrament Sodality, 1857; The Sodality of St Joseph, 1859.

18   1855: *The History of Italy;* 1857: *Lives of the Popes;* 1859: *Life of Dominic Savio.*

19   Lemoyne, *op. cit.,* Vol. V, pp.34-39: In 1857 Bosco visited Urbano Rattazzi who was Piedmont's Minister of the Interior, and later, Prime Minister. Rattazzi, although hostile to the Church, was an admirer of Bosco's educational methods and a frequent visitor to his Oratories in Turin.   It was Rattazzi who, impressed with the discipline of Bosco's schools, urged the government to use his methods.

ibid., pp.281-283: In 1856, Rattazzi claimed that the government had an obligation to retain Bosco's Oratories; they cut down the juvenile delinquency rate in Turin.

ibid., pp.459-461: It was during Bosco's 1857 visit to Rattazzi that the latter, because of the eminently humanitarian nature of Bosco's Oratories, decided that there should begin a new Congregation, with Bosco as head, and that it would get support from the Turin government. Don Bosco's policy of non-intervention in politics was paying him dividends at a time when generally the Church was being suppressed by the Government.

20   The term 'Salesian' is derived from St Francis de Sales.   Don Bosco had a special devotion to this saint who was an ecclesiastic and charitable pastor. His writings although intellectual are filled with subtle humour.   Bosco was drawn to the humane nature of this Doctor of the Church who has been called by modern Catholic theologians as the Churchman for all times.

21   *La Biblioteca della Gioventu Italiana.* This work, founded by Don Bosco, amounted to 204 small volumes.

22   A section dealing with past pupils is to be found in *Don Bosco in the World.*   Igino Giordani (et al), Elle di Ci, Turin, Leuman, Italy, 1968. pp.131-135.

23   *Centenary 1872-1972, Daughters of Mary, Help of Christians:* Mary Domenica Mazzarello, 1837-1881, co-foundress of the Salesian Society's counterpart, in religion and education, the Daughters of Mary, Help of Christians.   Mary Mazzarello, with Don Bosco's help began a community of Sisters at Mornese, Piedmont.   The aim of this community was a dedication to the service of the young according to the method and in the spirit of Don Bosco. Mazzarello's community grew and today they are in every Continent, have a working force of 18,600 Sisters in 1,450 schools and Houses.   Further information on the history and achievements of this Order: the above book, is listed in the Bibliography.

24 *Don Bosco in the World, op. cit.*, p.117: The system is based on kindness, meekness, sacrificial joy, and love, and is, in essence, the Preventive System of Don Bosco. (See Chapters 4, 5 and 6).

ibid., pp.200-201: The scope of their education is wide: they run nurseries, primary and secondary schools, orphanages, and even have a University in Lins, Brazil. In 1954 they opened, in Borgata Lesna, Turin, their International Advanced Institute of Pedagogy and Religious Sciences of the Daughters of Mary, Help of Christians.

25 *Constitutions and Regulations of the Society of St Francis of Sales:* pp.69-132; pp.5-64: The first reference applies to the Constitutions of the Society; the second to Don Bosco's comment on the approval of the Constitutions.

26 The Pious Union of Salesian Co-Operators, founded by Don Bosco, was officially approved by Pius IX in May, 1876, and was known as the Third Salesian Family (the First Family being the Salesians; the Second Family, the Co-Adjutors).

J. Aubry. *The Salesian Co-Operator: A Real Vocation in the Church.* This book offers a concise history and evaluation of the Salesian Co-Operators.

27 *Don Bosco in the World, op. cit.*, pp.179-180: Originally entitled *The Catholic Lover of Books*, this Monthly booklet, printed at the Oratory, was one of Don Bosco's methods of disseminating information, both religious and cultural. Its final form appeared in 1877 and in 1878 bore the title: *Salesian Bulletin.*

28 Leo XIII was of the opinion that Don Bosco was the person who alone had the necessary influence and popularity to raise the funds for the building of this huge church.

29 *Don Bosco in the World, op. cit.*, p.47.

30 The term 'house' in Salesian terminology means an establishment whose primary aim is to educate the young in the ways of religion and to a healthier and meaningful Christian life.

31 Lemoyne, *op. cit.*, Vol. VII, p.329: Fr Michael Rua, 1837-1910, became the successor to Don Bosco and the Society's second Rector Major (Head) in 1888, the year of the founder's death. Rua, who had known Bosco since 1845, was carefully prepared by the latter to carry on the educative work of the Salesians. In 1863, when Don Bosco sent Rua to take over the school at Mirabello, the latter carried out Bosco's requirements to the letter.

Notes to Part II of Chapter 1

1 *Don Bosco in the World, op. cit.*, p.241: The Salesian Society is divided into Provinces, each dependent on a Head who is known as the Provincial.

In 1966, the world tally of Provinces amounted to 73: Italy 13; Europe 23; Americas 27; Asia 9; and Australia 1.

2 *ibid.*, p.89.

3 *ibid.*, p.76.

4 *Centenary 1872-1972 Daughters of Mary, Help of Christians, op. cit.,* p.1.

5 *Don Bosco in the World, op. cit.,* pp.377-382.

6 *ibid.*, p.377.

7 *ibid.*, pp.242-345.

8 *ibid.*, pp.346-376.

9 *ibid.*, pp.389-390.

10 *ibid.*, pp.389-391.

11 *ibid.*, pp.389-390.

12 *ibid.*, pp.383-384.

CHAPTER 2

THE FORMING OF AN EDUCATOR

Don Bosco was a man of unusual character, his particular personality influencing to a large extent, his pedagogy; his methods were associated with his talents, which had been developed deliberately to further his educative mission: the preparing of poor and abandoned youths to take their place in society.

He would use his personality and skills to attract people's attention, he would even act the fool to arouse their interest; then, by showing concern for their welfare, he persuaded them to work and learn, not only for themselves, but for him. His followers, both in his time, and today, felt that his trust had been placed in their hands: they could not fail him.

He used different kinds of experiences to forge lessons from which his students could become, in his view, better persons; nothing was ever wasted: despair could be turned to hope, futility to aspiration, failure to a sense of fulfilment. In a sense he was a pragmatist;[1] using his talents to yield consistent results, which were concerned primarily with preparations for living and for life.

His personality was an attractive one. People from all walks of life have admired him—churchmen, politicians, academics, writers, journalists, educationists have expressed their admiration both for the man and the part he played in the development of modern education.

The London *Times*, for instance, described Bosco as "the Saint Vincent de Paul of the twentieth century,"[2] while Huysmans, French man of letters, stated: "Don Bosco was, together with Saint Vincent de Paul, the one most alive with love for abandoned boys".[3] Joseph Zoppi, the Swiss poet, wrote: "If ever there existed a method of education adapted to inspire confidence and love, it is the method of Don Bosco".[4] Franklin D. Roosevelt said of him: "A real educator ....a master in the direction of vocations, and a pioneer of professional and agricultural schools",[5] while Giovanni Giolitti, an Italian politician, wrote:

> I value most highly the Salesians and their prodigious educative activity which shows itself in terms of a most praiseworthy contribution to the nation, producing excellent professional men and upright workmen. It is not easy to shape Italians: Don Bosco has succeeded. It is a great triumph for him and a great piece of good fortune for the nation....[6]

I. Joergensen, too, Danish man of letters, said: "Don Bosco is one of the most complete and outstanding men that the world has ever known",[7] and Hug Wast, the Argentine academic, who also admired his work, wrote: "Don Bosco is one of the great builders of the culture of the Argentine";[8] while Daniel-Rops, a French writer, stated:

> Don Bosco is truly the type of a great founder idealist and realist at the same time; a man who knew how to dare all and yet to exercise prudence, seeking nothing for himself; not an agitator, nor still less a man of intrigue, but a builder of solid reality.[9]

From Columbia, Jose Franciso Socarras, an educator in his own country, remarked: "Don Bosco penetrated into the spirit of youth by the only way permissable. He loved boys as only mothers and saints know how to do it."[10] And Pope John XXIII wrote of him: "....he has carried the glory and the successes of the charity of Christ to the farthest ends of the earth",[11] and, "....Don Bosco still lives in the charm which he excercises over young souls. He, in fact, has the rare capacity of being able to welcome and to understand the aspirations of youth."[12] These two themes: admiration for the man himself, and appreciation for what his educational methods had achieved, are reflected in members of the Catholic hierarchy, laymen, and students from many parts of the globe.

When Archbishop Richard Pittini was asked to write a foreword to Forbes'[13] work on Bosco, for example, he wrote, in part: "He did not talk much: he acted. He did not write long and elaborate educational treatises: his example is the best one. When asked about the secret of his immense success with youngsters, he simply answered: 'love....'."[14]

E. B. Phelan, in her book, *Don Bosco. A Spiritual Portrait*, explained, in more personal terms;

> He was never domineering. He never gave commands. He
> invariably worded his requests politely; he never imposed his
> counsels—he also requested permission to suggest advice.
> When circumstances forced him to be stern or even threatening,
> he was calm and in control of himself.[15]

Similarly, Henri Gheon, a French authority on Don Bosco,
was impressed that Bosco, when near death, was more concerned with
the welfare of others, than with himself.[16] Gheon later admitted
that the Bosco personality was so unusual that he felt inadequate, as
a writer, in trying to capture the true nature of the man; that he had
"delivered to the reader his shadow only, and not his substance."[17]
Auffray, another historian noted for his works on Bosco, reflects a
similar feeling, when he writes about the "phenomenal moral magnetism"[18] of the pedagogist, fascination for which drew all kinds of
people to him.

His particular personality, then, appears to have had what modern
writers sometimes attribute to some of our own leaders: a charisma;
which was as essential to his individuality as it still is to an understanding of what he came to demand from those who were to accept
his ideas and methods—both in his own time, and today.

Contemporaries of Don Bosco who had opportunities to see him
at close range, first followed the man—only then the ideas. Michael
Rua, a pupil of Don Bosco's, who later succeeded him, becoming the
second Salesian Rector Major in 1888, for example, has left this 1845
impression of the teacher:

> I remember that, on Sundays, when Don Bosco came to say
> Mass for us and often also to preach, as soon as he entered the
> chapel.... something like an electric shock seemed to run
> through all the children. They would jump to their feet and
> leave their places to mill about him until they had succeeded
> in kissing his hand. It took quite some time before he could
> get through to the sacristy. There was nothing he good
> Brothers could do to prevent this apparent disorder and so
> we had our way. Nothing of this sort happened when other
> priests came, even pious and renowned ones.[19]

On the other hand, by 1847 there were high officials in Piedmont who believed that Don Bosco was dangerous, capable of inciting a revolt in Turin. These rumours about the priest-educator came to the ears of Marquis Cavour, father of Gustave and Camillo Cavour, the latter being he who played an important role in the unification of Italy. The Marquis, after having Don Bosco's educational activities investigated by the Carabinieri, was heard to conclude: "Don Bosco! Well, he's either a lunatic or a candidate for the Senate."[20]

While few contemporaries seemed able to specify what it was, in particular, about the educator that made him stand out from his fellows, and while references to him are either from Italian or French sources, or from sympathetic—perhaps even activist—members of his church throughout the world, there do appear to have been certain elements in his approach to people, in his manner, or address, his attitude, or expressions, which had a lasting effect. For instance, Professor Francis Maranzano[21] wrote in 1893 of the powerful influence Don Bosco had on children, particularly those who were running wild and seemingly beyond help:

> What mysterious power could attract hundreds of boys, formerly accustomed to run at will through the streets, over the fields, and along the banks of the river, who had known no other law but their own animal instincts? What miraculous power could have gathered them all around one poor priest? What self-interest, what advantage did they hope to get from following him, in ever increasing numbers, what joy, when he was obliged .... to move from place to place, from one building to another, even into a meadow under the open sky?[22]

Maranzano was of the opinion that Don Bosco's way of speaking could have had something to do with his popularity with children; apparently he spoke in such a way that even the most disobedient boy felt personally encouraged to "banish all boredom.... to transform even the most uninviting spot into a lovely and beautiful place."[23]

Charles Tomatis, who first met the pedagogist in 1847 while attending his evening classes held at the St. Francis de Sales Oratory in Valdocco, and who later as a young man helped Don Bosco in his educational work among boys, went a little further to explain:

> Most of my companions were of a happy, carefree nature, though they studied and worked hard. There were regular

evening classes during which Don Bosco taught us arithmetic and penmanship. His presence alone filled us with an indescribable joy.

What we all admired in him, in these and in many other circumstances, was the blend of firmness and gentleness of manner, of patience and of inexhaustible forebearance with which he overcame or forestalled difficulties, and his ability to pursue all things to a successful conclusion. Above all, his humility appealed to us. One evening, while he was teaching us the metric system, he made a mistake while making some calculations on the blackboard, and thus he could not solve the problem correctly. Though the large class was paying attention, they did not see the difficulty. Detecting the error, I arose and, as best I could, corrected it. Other teachers might not have welcomed such a public correction, but Don Bosco not only graciously accepted it, but thereafter held me in such high regard that I was overwhelmed.[24]

Father Joseph Cafasso, however, director of the Turin Convitto Ecclesiastico,[25] a theological college which Don Bosco attended for three years after his ordination in 1841, viewed the man as somewhat of an enigma. In 1853 Cafasso wrote: "As for me, the more I study him, the less I understand him! He is simple, but extraordinary; humble, but great; poor, but at the same time engaged in seemingly unrealizable projects of vast proportions. He is sorely tried—I might even say that he could be considered unsuited to his tasks—and yet he succeeds splendidly in everything he undertakes. He is a great mystery to me! I am convinced, however, that he works for God's glory and that God alone is his guide."[26]

Hyacinth Ballesio first met Don Bosco in 1857 at the Oratory in Valdocco and stayed on there, for eight years. During this time, and thereafter, Ballesio recorded many anecdotes about Bosco. This approach, through anecdotes, was to become one of the means by which Bosco's followers were both to perpetuate his memory as a person-to-be-emulated, and to inculcate his pedagogy. Rather than a series of treatises or works of a theoretical nature to teach others about Bosco's philosophy of education, or about his educative methods, his Salesians recounted incidents, examples, situational problems dealt with, difficulties handled, responses to people and events. They attempted to describe, rather than analyse, the effect of the man himself, often blurring the distinction between educator and theory, as if each were, essentially, the same. The communication of Bosconian educational ideas was a personal, experiential encounter, descriptive, intimate and confident in tone. Canon Ballesio's testimony shortly after the pedagogist's death, for example, is a personal account:

> Don Bosco's life and work belong to history, and history will eloquently make clear to coming generations that for half a century he was the apostle of good. What history will neither be able to tell in full nor make us fully understand is his innermost life: his constant, quiet, sympathetic, invincible, and heroic self-sacrifice; his deep love for us, his sons; the confidence, esteem, reverence, and affection he inspired in us; the way we looked up to him and the regard we had for his authority, saintliness, and learning. To us he was the symbol of moral perfection. History can hardly portray or describe the soothing comfort that a word, glance, or even a nod of his could bring to our hearts! One would have to have seen or experienced it! The spell exercised by a saint over his contemporaries or intimates cannot be described even in the best written biography. The fragrance of his words and virtuous deeds wanes as the years go by. But we have seen and heard Don Bosco. In those years, when his works were concentrated in the Oratory, the impact of his personality was even more striking. His powerful energy, talents, and love were entirely at our disposal from early morning to late at night. I can still see him hearing confessions, saying Mass and giving us Communion. He was never alone, never with a minute to himself; he was constantly besieged by boys or visitors seeking advice in the sacristy, on the porticoes, in the playground or refectory, on the stairs, and in his room. This went on, morning, noon, and night; it is so today, and it will be thus tomorrow and always. He looked after everything and knew each of the hundreds of boys by name. He kept in touch with everything and gave advice and orders. Without the help of secretaries he maintained a correspondence that would have kept several people busy fulltime. Singlehandedly he planned and provided for the material and moral needs of the Oratory.[27]

Later, Canon Ballesio attempted to explain, in his *Vita intima di Don Giovanni Bosco*;[28] Bosco's dealings with his followers and students: "he was friendly and affable, avoiding a formalism and a rigorism which erect a wall between superior and subject. His authority inspired respect, confidence, and love. Our hearts went out to him with intimate, joyful, and total abandon. We all wanted to go to him for confession. For countless years he devoted sixteen to twenty hours a week to this.... fatiguing apostolate in addition to his many other absorbing occupations. This was a mode of operation more unique than rare between superior and dependents....that enables an educator to discover his pupils' temperament, wield it prudently, and unlock its hidden energies."[29]

Father Paul Albera,[30] attempted, too, to describe the sway Don Bosco had over his pupils: his use of the glance was often more effective than speech; he would often communicate without the use of words: facial expressions, apt gestures, sufficed. At other times "the harmonious cadence of his words—all these acted on us, as a powerful magnet, exercising an influence which we all accepted with joy—an influence we would not forego for all the gold in the world."[31]

Not unlike the more appealing performers today, whose images are familiar to young people, and whose influence appears to be powerful, Don Bosco early developed skills in entertaining to attract people. Some of his stunts and exhibitions of strength could almost be labelled 'gimmicks'. But, by excelling in spectacular physical feats, he would attract the attention of those whom he wanted to educate.[32] While still young he added to his repertoire of athletic skills, achievements proper to the entertainment world of his day. He became adept at sleight-of-hand tricks and a convincing magician.[33] Apparently he believed he had to excel in order to gain attention.

Fortunately, for his purposes, he was an extraordinarily strong person: he could crack peach and apricot seeds between his teeth and "crush walnuts, hazelnuts, and almonds between the thumb and index finger of either hand."[34] He was seen snapping wrought-iron railings into small pieces, and many a boy felt the strong grip of his arm during physical education lessons.[35] This strength helped to take him through a lifetime's labour of love in the education of poor and abandoned youth. Not all his followers, however, have had his robust physical fitness, his athletic prowess, or unusual strength. To emulate these characteristics could be an impossible, despressing task for the would-be educator. It was not the physical qualities, as such, that were to be sought after, but the involvement, determination, and time-spent-with youth that were to characterize a Salesian educator.

Morand Wirth, for example, in his book *Don Bosco et les Salesians, Cent Cinquante Ans D'Histoire*,[36] writes about how, while Bosco was aware of the importance of physical exercise in the educational program of youth, it was to be more than just exercise: it was an exuberance, inspired by the teacher, which infected his students and encouraged them to joyously participate in the games he devised for them. Although, because Bosco was so magnificently endowed in a physical sense, few educators, claims Wirth, profited as he did from recreational involvement with youth, Don Bosco had developed these qualities through regular exercise for the greater part of his life. He could leap, somersault, walk on his hands, juggle, walk the tight-rope, and regularly challenge the school to a race in the playground: his last victory was in 1868 when, at the age of 53, he came in first, ahead of 800 noisy students. He played with, and encouraged them, to enjoy themselves in an uninhibited way.

Much of the pedagogist's inspiration was derived from an unquenchable enthusiasm, an enthusiasm which was to be an essential for all Salesian teachers: youthful, persistent, and buoyant. He did not hesitate to use unusual methods, for instance, in getting boys to attend his Oratory. He often walked the streets of Turin looking for prospective students. He would sit down on the footpath and join in a game of cards with dishevelled youths who would eye him suspiciously. Unexpectedly, he would snatch the takings and sprint down the street, hotly pursued by the enraged card players. Heading straight for the Oratory, he would dash into the church which would be full of Oratory students who, by now, were used to their teacher's methods, and would look on with amusement at the impending fate of the new arrivals. In no time their money was returned, a laugh shared, and the Oratory had enrolled yet another group of boys who were then to begin to learn by Bosco's more usual methods.[37]

The boys themselves regarded Don Bosco as the Oratory's inspiration and centre. At one time, in 1846, he had to go to Becchi for health reasons. After two weeks had passed, the impatient Turin boys walked to Becchi to visit their teacher who had been sorely missed. They presented him with the proposition that either he had to come back to join them in Turin, or, they would move the whole Oratory to Becchi and join him there instead.[38]

Don Bosco was not, however, always the entertainer. John Filippello, a lifelong friend of Don Bosco, related how he held the respect and admiration of those whom he had contacted: "He moved among us as one having authority."[39] Bosco was also admired by the police who witnessed many an attempt by the priest-educator to stop brawls between warring gangs of youths in Turin. "The police, who watched from a distance, had to admit that only Don Bosco had the courage to throw himself into the middle of those brutal brawls, and that he alone knew how to pacify those wild youngsters."[40] Don Bosco was hated and feared, too: attempts were made on his life, but people came to his rescue.[41] He forgave his attackers, helping many of them afterwards.[42]

Extremely popular among his fellows, he did not however, seek popularity. When studying in the Chieri seminary, his free time, on Thursdays, was taken up by his friends who would invade the place asking for coaching. The following incident, for example, was recorded by Father James Bosco (no relation): "On Thursdays the seminary parlour was filled with young students who came with notebooks and school papers to be examined. John willingly corrected, pointed out mistakes, explained doubtful points and went over their lessons with them. He never let them go without some uplifting thought."[43] On other occasions, Bosco's appearance "would elicit outbursts of joy: the boys would crowd around him and listen to his stories, always new, varied and edifying. He spoke so engrossingly that an hour seemed a minute."[44]

His students, too, needed him: they craved his physical presence, the personal relationship. This constant companionship with youth has become one of the most demanding, for modern Salesian teachers, of Bosco's ideas. It is not an authoritarian and removed supervision that his students came to demand, it was a continuing and personal sharing with the educator of all the day's activities. On one occasion, for example, some three hundred boys went looking for him when he did not appear at their school to hear confessions. The sight of this crowd of boys "soaked in perspiration, bespattered with mud, so tired and hungry that anybody would have felt sorry just to see them"[45] must have moved Don Bosco when they finally found him at Sassi, a suburb of Turin.

Politicians, on the other hand, who had few affiliations with the Catholic Church, admired Don Bosco for his bluntness when he attacked the 1854 Confiscation Laws[46] which threatened the existence of religious Orders in Piedmont. "Don Bosco's brave outspokenness did not lessen the benevolence of the civil authorities toward him.... They soon became convinced that he nursed no grudge against anyone, regardless of political affiliation. For this reason no one ever took offence when he—uncompromisingly but without acrimony—took a stand opposed to theirs."[47] This aspect of the Salesian educator has been handed down to his followers, too. Dealing with authorities in many different nations with differing regimes, educators are often expected to handle, with directness and tact, sometimes with boldness and outspokenness, situations not directly concerned with the classroom or playground. At times teachers have been responsible for both the building and maintenance of schools; responsibilities which many find too heavy, when combined with teaching and regular school administration.

Don Bosco came to attract attention, as he became well known. Those who accompanied him in the streets noticed his popularity with the ordinary people. "Priests or young clerics who happened to go with him were amazed to see how much people liked him."[48] His popularity with children has been handed down by a Chieri townsman named Brosio who recalled:

> "....when I was still a boy at Chieri, Don Bosco, who was then a seminarian, was highly esteemed as a cleric of great virtue not only by us young boys, but also by men and older people. He was liked by all because he cared so much for youngsters. He was forever in our midst charming us with his affability and warm affection. One might say that he literally lived for young people. Whenever the seminarians passed on their way to the cathedral for religious services, everyone would stop to catch a glimpse of him and people

would point to the curly-haired seminarian, 'curly' for short, the nickname we boys had given to John. His pleasant and easy manners encouraged me to try and get to know him better."[49]

Traditions such as these have come to constitute the personal and intimate view of education that the Salesian teacher follows. It is an almost biographical approach, based on the living-out of educational ideas by Don Bosco himself, and later by his followers. A story, for instance, retelling what the priest-educator did under certain circumstances, gives a proved-by-experience background to the already accepted Catholic philosophy of life as applied to the Christian teacher. Better to base action on an actual real-life experience than, say, on a fictional character, such as Rousseau's Emile, for example. In the face of tragedy, disaster or terror, a precedent has been made.

An emergency arose in Turin in 1852 when a huge gunpowder arsenal, in the heart of the Dora district, blew up, causing widespread damage. Bosco came quickly to minister to the blast victims and "gave shelter and comfort to many terror-stricken youngsters from other institutions.... When night came, Don Bosco called all the boys around him. They were still afraid of some new disaster during the night, but Don Bosco exhorted them not to worry, to be calm, and to trust in God. He was so convincing that they finally went to bed fully reassured."[50] Reassurances, comfort, assistance are all dependent upon personally being there, staying there.

Don Bosco demanded of his teachers, too, professional competence, and scholarly application to study. Bosco himself was a successful student and an accomplished scholar. Father Calosso, young Bosco's first teacher, remarked on his memory[51] which he described as "prodigious".[52] Later Bosco, a voracious reader, placed great importance on training the memory through wide reading. He urged his students to study hard and to memorize extensively. "If you'll increase your knowledge," he told them, "you will be able to do much good, especially to the young people under your care. But it's no use learning if you can't retain what you learned through the training of your memory. You will forget all too easily."[53] He was convinced that the memory could be trained through practice at reading and that it would be beneficial to oneself, and to others in the teaching of children, if one's memory were retentive.

J.B. Lemoyne[54] has recorded that Professor Lanteri who, in 1834, was examining Bosco in Latin classics, was astounded at his remarkable memory and skill in translation.[55] Later, Don Bosco drew on his memory innumerable times when, because of his many teaching duties he could not regularly visit libraries to consult texts he had read years before and now needed for manuscripts he was preparing. He could quote whole chapters verbatim according to reliable witnesses.[56]

Perhaps it was partly due to his extraordinary memory that he had an "unbelievable ability to tell a story with an amazingly contagious charm. He could spin a yarn with such exuberance that his audience often doubled over with laughter."[57] Again, however, not every aspiring teacher can hope to achieve the confidence in presentation that a man like Bosco, with a retentive memory, could experience. This is, nevertheless, an integral part of the Bosconian educational approach, and confidence with subject-matter was to be an attribute of the Salesian teacher.

Bosco himself had a great capacity for intellectual work, and encouraged his students to work as hard as they could. As a youth his "intelligence and memory, his discernment and aptitude for studies" was commented upon,[58] and while a seminarian he instigated a scholastic circle of students in 1846 who discussed the more difficult philosophical, mathematical, and theological problems raised during lectures. He insisted on one basic rule for his circle: all discussions were to be in Latin.[59] A capable student, he once wrote an Italian composition so skilfully that the local pastor, who had read it, was of the opinion "that among the educated people in the area no one was learned enough to write such a fine composition and that consequently it was impossible for young Bosco to have done so...."[60] He later became so adept at Latin and Greek that he could translate easily and fluently in both, and in 1886, Lemoyne claimed, he had heard Don Bosco recite "entire chapters from St. Paul's epistles both in Latin and Greek...."[61] while "Monsignor Pechenino.... declared that Don Bosco was admirably versed in every branch of Italian and Latin literature."[62]

Competence in classical education was the basis of education at the time, but Lemoyne related, too, that in 1884, in Rome, he was surprised to hear Don Bosco discussing Hebrew syntax and Old Testament translations with a priest who taught Hebrew.[63]

Professor of Hebrew, Joseph Ghiringhello "had such respect for Don Bosco's learning that on occasions he consulted him on questions of hermeneutics and certain biblical narratives that needed clarification."[64] This was during 1850 and 1851, when the pedagogist was lecturing to seminarians in geography and church history.[65]

In theology Don Bosco covered the five year seminary course in four years "because of his keen understanding of theological matters".[66] Much later, in 1853, his theological training stood him in good stead when he engaged the Waldensians, a militant Protestant group in Turin, in a day-long debate in theology, and won.[67] From this type of response to challenge, the Salesian emphasis on the use of scholastic achievement comes. Learning is to be put to use when the situation demands. Conversely, however, it is not to be paraded; as another anecdote has come to recommend, it is sometimes more charitable to remain silent, speaking up only when asked, and then responding in honesty.

At Stresa, near Lake Maggione, in 1850, Don Bosco at a dinner with eminent scholars, some of whom were to play prominent roles in the Italian revolutions, including the poet Niccolo Tommaseo; novelists Tommaso Grossi and Ruggiero Bonghi; and the statesman and historian, Dr. Carlo Farini, who had just published a history entitled *Storia dello Stato Romano*[68] which was being acclaimed by some of the scholars at table. After a time, Don Bosco was asked to give his appraisal of Farini's work, unaware that the author was present in the company. Reluctantly, he evaluated the work, and in doing so, exposed some glaring inconsistencies in Farini's thesis. Those at the table were surprised that Bosco had even read the book; their surprise turned to interest as he logically but charitably, pointed out the errors, then volunteered the amendments. It was then made clear to Don Bosco that Dr. Farini was one of the guests at table. To everyone's surprise, Farini, in front of the select company, said to the priest-educator: "It's obvious that you know the subject very well and that you are an expert on history; I like your frankness. No one has ever yet pointed out these things to me."[69]

Don Bosco was, however, essentially a practical, hard-working person who had experience in many different trades. As a boy he became proficient in farming: "spading the ground, weeding, tending cattle, planting vines"[70] were all familiar to him. By 1831, at the age of sixteen, he had learnt to sing Gregorian chant, was a member of a choir, and began playing the violin, spinet, and organ. His teacher, John Roberto, "was delighted with his pupil."[71] About this time, Bosco interested himself in tailoring. "In a short time he was able to sew buttons, master hemming, as well as simple and complex stitching. Then he learned to cut out undergarments, waistcoats, trousers and jackets."[72] His will to learn next plunged him into blacksmithing: "Under the guidance of Evasio Savio, the local blacksmith .... John learned to work at the forge and handle the sledgehammer and file...."[73] Next, came woodworking: "....he learned to use the plane, the square, the saw and other tools. Soon he was able to make articles of furniture...."[74] While in his fourth year at high school, he served as a waiter in a cafe, helped in the running of a billiards saloon, became a skilled cook and mastered "the recipes for making all kinds of sweets, pastries, ices and mixing liqueurs and cold drinks...."[75] By 1833, he had added shoemaking to his list, "a craft he had picked up in Chieri...."[76] Don Bosco's all-round ability in practical skills prepared him for his educational work in evening schools in 1843 and in his first Oratory at Valdocco, in 1846. Joseph Buzzetti, one of Don Bosco's pupils, later described his teacher at work in the Oratory in 1848 depicting Bosco in the various roles of priest, teacher, choirmaster, music teacher, cook, barber, cobbler, cleaner, domestic, carpenter, tailor, launderer, and, nurse.[77]

This development, almost the exploitation, of his personal resources, led Don Bosco to develop his perceptiveness of other people: their responses, their attitudes and mannerisms. In his earlier years he "instinctively studied the personality of everyone he met."[78] When an adult, he could often "anticipate a need, chide a friend at an opportune time for faults unnoticed by others, or support decisions as yet unspoken."[79] Together with this perceptiveness, Bosco exhibited an observant eye for detail in all his undertakings.[80] These qualities helped him in his counselling work[81] and in his dealings with people and officialdom in varying situations and capacities. He became, probably unbeknown to himself, a sound psychologist. He had a special talent for gaining the confidence and co-operation of others, even those initially opposed to him:

> His affability and deep knowledge of the human heart enabled him to win over to his point of view even those who were antagonistic, stubborn, discouraged or just difficult. When he realised that appealing to propriety, charity or duty would be ineffectual, he would very subtly set about enlisting the other person's self-love but without a trace of either flattery or deceit. He played upon this chord until he achieved the desired result. A word of praise from him, a fond reference to some former praiseworthy deed, a gesture or a word of esteem, confidence, trust, and respect, invariably overcame any obstacle or hostility, and he was thus able to obtain what he wanted from either his confreres or from strangers.[82]

In 1851 he silenced rough-tongued workers who were labouring on the building site of his new church project, simply calling them together and promising them drinks at the end of the week if they refrained from their blasphemy. His plan worked.[83]

It was because of this keen insight into human nature that Archbishop Fransoni sent the priest-educator to Viu, a village in the Lanzo Valley, to look into claims there about a woman who was performing extraordinary deeds and claiming to be a saint. Her "sanctity" was revealed as a sham. About this time, Don Bosco showed, too, how he handled young adults.[84] In 1876, he gladly took into his services a young cleric who, it was claimed by the Turinese clerics, was too boisterous and full of high spirits to become acceptable in parish work. Bosco believed that this young man's energy was just what was needed in educational work.[85]

In business matters he would often negotiate terms at a loss[86] to achieve his purposes, always related to the education of poor and abandoned youth. He did not hesitate to take risks, or to speculate.

He once sold property for a handsome profit to extend his plans,[87] and on another occasion, in 1851, contracted to buy property, which he sorely needed, well aware of the fact that he had no money with which to negotiate; his gamble paid off.[88] In 1852 he had a new three storey school project built in such a way that its austere architecture would not make it attractive enough for official appropriation in times of war,[89] realizing that other Orders had had their more spacious properties requisitioned during emergencies. His action[90] allowed his work to continue,[91] when in 1859 "after the Battle of Solverino, the Turin municipal authorities asked Don Bosco, as a patriotic gesture, to turn his new building over to them as an emergency hospital. Don Bosco agreed, but when the inspectors found that the staircases, corridors, and doors were too narrow, they thanked him but declined his offer."[92]

In order to protect his schools further, "he shunned politics, whether speaking in public or writing for the press, lest he be suspected of leaning one way or another and risk being hindered from doing good. . . . He knew how to keep silent when, to voice his thoughts would have caused harm. . . . He was always ready to be of assistance even to his opponents: he defended them if unjustly accused, and he praised them for their good deeds or for their knowledge and talents . . . . In all his doings there was the natural ease of one who has formed a habit of prudence by constant practice."[93]

In 1847, for instance, he had his Oratory boys follow a policy of non-involvement in the political demonstrations which were raging in Turin.[94] In 1848, too, at a time when revolutionary fever in Turin was at its peak, and when Bosco's refusals to associate with political marches did not go unnoticed; he was summoned to appear before officials at the Turin town hall for questioning. This time prudence took another form: he acted the simpleton: "He. . . . arrived. . . . looking like a simple fellow, unshaven, in hand-me-down clothes, discoloured shoes, and with a deliberately ungainly gait. He looked like the curé of some very remote mountain village. The officials, who at that time knew him only by name, finally decided that he was not anyone worth bothering about and, perhaps, even slightly deficient mentally. By behaving as a non-entity Don Bosco dispelled their fears...."[95] In both instances, he had used whatever methods seemed most likely to succeed to advance his educational causes in the midst of political unrest.

Again, in 1860, at a time when official government policy was against the financial support of Catholic schools, and aware of the importance of his schools in government eyes, Bosco made all parents enrolling their children at his Oratories first seek official recommendation for application to enrol; thereby gaining the necessary funds from the government, which had unwittingly granted approval for Bosco's institutions.[96] Shrewdness, even a certain ruthlessness in dealing with those who wanted to impede the educational movement by resorting to officialdom, was shown in Bosco's handling of another incident reported by Lemoyne, in which a government employee tried to confuse the issue by arguing on a religious matter. Bosco, in this situation acted quite differently from usual. He confused and demoralized the official until he admitted ignorance of the problem, then left him with a suggested reading list on the subject in question.[97]

This shrewdness was often exhibited in down-to-earth practical attitudes towards education. He insisted, for example, in 1848, during a crucial time in his career when some seniors who had previously abandoned him, wished to return, that the condition for their readmission was a personal interview with him. In this interview he welcomed them back and reinstated them to their former positions.[98] Because of his personal concern and friendliness towards them, they became useful helpers at the Oratory. They had not, however, just come back when things were not so difficult; they had experienced moments of uncertainty before the interview which they could not forget, and their return had been a personal encounter with their leader. This personal relationship with him was, in fact, to be the basis for future loyalty.

In dealing with one of the most personal aspects of religious life, prayer, Bosco was equally practical: he never became a slave to the forms of prayer; prayer was to be flexible, varying; the impetus of his work was not slowed down by pedantic patterns of devotional show. Thus he taught, by example, the young to think of prayer as something ongoing and natural, not as a timetable ritual of dumb show.

He was down-to-earth too, about examinations and conduct. He told his pupils in 1864: "No one is to look for favours. There will be no undue severity, but no leniency either. Examiners will be fathers, but judges too. There will be even less chance of leniency in matters of conduct...."[100] He believed that any evaluating procedure in education, to be of any worth, had to have a characteristic of objectivity tempered with justice and love.

He expected, however, courage and persistence, even fortitude, from his Salesians. He believed that the weak should be protected, and as a youth had not hesitated to defend weaker children from the more belligerent;[101] he persisted, later, too, in declaring his allegiance to the King at a time of political agitation,[102] and insisted on visiting the exiled Archbishop Louis Fransoni,[103] "displaying his courage to those who had ordered the Archbishop's banishment."[104] Again, in 1854, despite a summons and reprimand, he refused to blindly follow the attractive liberalism of those with whom he had to deal in an official capacity.[105] His courage was the inspiration his teachers and students were to recall; whether it was in the alleyways of the Valdocco district,[106] or, as in 1848 when he had been shot at, it was closer to home:

> Not in the least disconcerted, he showed such calm and presence of mind as to allay the fear gripping the boys. He reassured them with a smile, "What? Are you afraid of a joke in poor taste? It's only a joke. Some scoundrels don't know any better. Look, they've ripped my cassock and damaged the wall! Oh, well.... let's get back to our catechism".[107]

To be able to show a sense of humour at times of difficulty or distress came to be associated with the encouragement of a calmness in the face of disappointment or setback too. Another anecdote, illustrating this quality, shows how Don Bosco reacted in front of his students on the occasion of a musico-literary prize-giving day. A serious setback to the Oratory had occurred, some feared there would be no program, but rather than disappoint invited guests and the boys who had been so eagerly looking forward to the event,[108] Bosco invited his boys to turn misfortunes into something humorous. It was the spectacle of their teacher accepting "adversities with a smile"[109] that inspired them to take an optimistic view, and go ahead:

> Don Bosco had always endeavoured to accept adversities with a smile and look for the comical side of things. If he had to introduce changes in routine, he always did so with a certain air of gaiety that seemed to guarantee that it would be all for the better. By this method the boys always gladly welcome any new arrangement, no matter how unusual or inconvenient it might be. Following his example, they too formed the habit of looking for the funny side of things in their misfortunes.[110]

Humility, as well as a sense of humour, was a characteristic which many people observed in the priest-educator. As a young man he faced the humiliation of having to go begging to raise the necessary means to continue his education,[111] learning very early that pride could be a major obstacle which could obstruct the causes and aims of his educative mission.

In a way, lack of pride was one of Bosco's means to reach people. He had learned early to accept criticism, even unwarranted criticism, and "as a result, John's classmates not only admired his talent, but very highly regarded his humility and dignity" while he, meanwhile, "increased his influence among them."[112] On more than one occasion Don Bosco was heard to say: "I always needed the help of everybody!"[113] In this sense, his humility was the key to his successful relationships with people. From his "unassuming demeanour" few realised his knowledge, "only in some casual discussion, when necessary or opportune, it would flash like lightning in the sky, dazzling the unsuspecting. But these flashes were rare; due to the whirl of daily activity that engulfed him, he had little time for scholarly discussions ...."[114] Yet John Cagliero[115] wrote:

> During our friendly conversations he would recite eloquent passages from Horace, Virgil, Ovid, and other Latin and Italian authors in order to encourage us to study. Yet he never paraded his knowledge of the classics or even hinted at it in his books by quoting them. Anyone who did not know him very well, even though living under the same roof, would never have suspected his vast classical erudition in Italian, Latin, and Greek....[116]

In 1852, when Bosco tactfully withdrew the title of Chevalier[117] and substituted its equivalent in an annual subsidy for his Oratory boys instead,[118] he indicated his attitude towards honours bestowed.

Fathers Reviglio, Turchi, and Rua, have testified to this, Reviglio saying: "His manner and speech, his care to shun unnecessary honours, and his habitual and sincere conviction of his own nothingness afforded us a splendid lesson in the virtue of humility."[119] Turchi wrote: "Humble as he was, he acted amiably with both rich and poor. He refrained from giving orders even to his boys. His usual approach was: "Would you please do this or that?...."[120] while, according to Rua, "Don Bosco could have attained high church positions; as a matter of fact, several times they were offered to him, but he always declined.... Almost every day he reminded us of St. Augustine's advice: 'Do you want to be great? Start by being humble. Do you plan a great structure? First make sure that it is founded on humility'."[121]

When his name became an Italian household word, he would address those who usually approached him in awe, with the words: "I'm just plain Don Bosco!",[122] and to other fellow priests, who did not understand his theological, educational motives, he once said: "Examine my undertakings and my writings, and you will find the spirit that moves me; check my public life and all I do. If you find anything reprehensible, point it out, and I shall be grateful to you and do my very best to correct it. But please be specific."[123]

The dual characteristics of singlemindedness, and of serenity of spirit, so often dichotomies, were to become, characteristically, aims of the Salesian teacher.

In 1848, Don Bosco had shown that he could stand against those co-workers of his who were more interested in political agitation than in education.[124] His singlemindedness forced him to dismiss practically all staff on this issue but he successfully carried on with his work, despite the setback. His "great self-control",[125] and his philosophy of calm helped his growing educational commitments to continue during the 1848 Revolutions in his own homeland:

> He realised that, in the turmoil aroused by national aspirations, the course to follow was to approve what was good and patiently moderate what was bad, and of that there was much. He

saw how the revolutionary tide was swelling and how eventually it would become so devastating as to overthrow and sweep away all obstacles. Direct opposition would have been humanly impossible: not only ineffective but also self-defeating. So he decided to walk along the bank of the torrent, taking care lest he himself be swept away by those waters.[126]

In 1855, when repeatedly insulted in the streets by anti-clericals "he simply endured their jibes and resignedly went his way,"[127] retaining his self-control, patience and calm in the face of adversity.

To be serene, relaxed and at ease with individuals or groups of people is another aim for the Salesian educator. As a young student, Don Bosco's relaxation took the form of conversation with others,[128] whilst his self-assurance in front of crowds could be traced back to his schoolboy days at Becchi where he juggled and performed conjuring tricks in front of the villagers to attract them, prior to his educating them in their religion.[129] He gained many friends in high places, in later life, too:

> Whenever a new cabinet minister, prefect of a province, or mayor was appointed, he would never fail to call on him. This naturally made a good impression on the person singled out for such attention, bound him in friendship and brought good results.[130]

When asked by a fellow teacher the clue to his relaxed disposition, especially in front of important people, Bosco replied: "Just be yourself. Act naturally." His ease made him a popular table companion who "brought up interesting and edifying topics that delighted his hosts and guests".... and "he always managed to work in some pertinent religious thought or to stir his listeners to make some charitable contribution to help him in his undertakings."[132]

Friendly, confident, outgoing and kind approaches were to be made to the young, too. When in Marseilles, in 1877, Don Bosco was asked by some De La Salle teachers the secrets of his educational methods, he replied: "Boys should be guided and corrected but not by aloof superiors."[133] He believed that a friendly, charitable approach to educating the young was a necessary and sufficient condition of teaching. Friendliness and affability, based on patience, self-control, self-denial,[134] and love of his fellow man, were to be characteristics of the Christian educator.

Don Bosco, himself, developed his patience and tolerance to the point where, it is claimed:

> Whether as a seminarian or as a priest, whenever he was a guest.... he never betrayed any dislike, annoyance or fastidiousness. As far as he was concerned, everything was always fine. Rudeness forgetfulness, lack of foresight, neglect, inconveniences, stifling rooms in summer or unheated ones in winter, delays in serving meals, disagreeable food, long drawn-out conversations when he was overcome with weariness, all these things he accepted without ever showing annoyance or impatience or permitting himself a complaint....[135]

He had little patience, however, with rumour-mongerers, and the happiness of his schools was often largely due to his insistence, both to staff and pupils, that the reputation of others, regardless of popular opinion, was to be preserved at all costs.[136] He ruthlessly opposed backbiting and slander;[137] realizing that these could quickly bring down the reputation of a school, Yet, he could be gentle and tolerant to those who were often the target of rumour, fallen priests: "In dealing with them after a lapse, Don Bosco never tried to humiliate them, but rather showed them such kindness and compassion that the hearts of these poor men were deeply touched. Never did he let a word slip that might reflect on their sacred duty."[138]

Friendly, affable, and kind towards his fellows, he once said: "....a warm welcome, is what, above all, attracts boys. To obtain good results in educating youngsters, one must find a way first to win their love; then they will fear to displease him."[139] Lemoyne claimed that Don Bosco "knew them all individually by name and surname.... even though the number of boys he dealt with, whether boarders or day students, ran into the thousands."[140]

In 1861, when invited to give a retreat at Bergamo, Don Bosco's down-to-earth friendliness towards the seminarians there, gained their respect, but, at the same time, the local Rector's displeasure.[141] For priests, in those days, were supposed to be removed and aloof; Bosco, the visiting lecturer, who should have set an example, was being familiar with the students. But this was Bosco's method. Earlier, as a seminarian himself, he had shown, on many occasions, his personal concern for students:

> ....whenever John saw his fellow seminarians in the depths of gloom and doubt or plagued with difficulties in their studies, he assumed the triple role of adviser, friend and tutor.... He generously lent his books to anyone who wished to borrow them.... He often wrote sermonettes for seminarians who had been invited to preach in their parish church during the vacations, but lacked either time or ability....[142]

A natural friendliness towards children,[143] and the capacity to share his joy with them,[144] could be used for disciplinary measures as well. In 1859, he did not hesitate to dismiss the Oratory band because of their disobedience. He handled the problem calmly and with friendliness towards the offenders, who were given some sound, practical advice, and who did not go away empty-handed,[145] but he still dismissed them.

As a successful teacher Don Bosco was a realist: learning from others, being adaptable, reasonably open-minded, and in touch with current trends in education; and accompanying his research by sweat and labour.[146] In 1864, for instance, after 25 years of teaching experience, he consulted prominent educationists, physicians, and lawyers, before opening a boarding school at Lanzo.[147]

Some of his less orthodox approaches, however, had their beginnings in the methods of entertainers and charlatans Bosco had observed as a youth. He saw that they had "no qualms to meet the public face to face, without fear or embarrassment and thus win over people to exploit them for their own advantage."[148] He decided that he had more to offer than confidence men or tricksters, but he was adaptable enough to learn from their methods. At another time, Don Bosco was quick to use a popular tune of his day for more serious ends:

> "....while walking across Milano Square, he saw a troupe of young performers surrounded by a crowd. They were singing a worldly but respectable song to the accompaniment of a guitar and violin. One youth sang the verses and the others joined in chorus to sing the refrain. Don Bosco was much taken by the melody, for it had a lilt which would certainly make it popular. Taking out pencil and paper, he leaned against the door post of the Prefecture Building in a corner of

the square and set down the notes. He then searched for a
sacred poem which might fit the catchy tune and found a highly
suitable one, *Noi siam figli di Maria* (*We are Mary's Sons*).[149]

This eclecticism in educational practice, tending towards an open-
mindedness of approach, probably accounts for the rapid extension
of his educational methods from his death, in 1868, to the present
day.

Don Bosco's wit and a sense of fun also helped, creating in his
followers a tradition of humour and lightheartedness. A story told
of his own student days deals with an oral examination[150] which he
attempted in theology in 1841. He was asked a question on Canon
Law which, in Bosco's view, was irrelevant. "Unruffled, John im-
provised a non-existent canon of the Council of Trent, with random
phrases that came to his mind. 'Is that really what the Council
said?' queried Gastaldi, astounded at his straight face. Don Bosco
chuckled, and the examiner could not help joining in."[151]

Other anecdotes illustrate what has become a characteristically
Salesian attitude to humour in educating the young: humour in moments of crisis, on outings, in the classroom, or playground. For
instance, in 1852, part of a new school building construction collapsed
during a particularly heavy downpour; the Mayor and two engineers
came out to the Oratory to commiserate with and offer help to Don
Bosco:

> While the members of the municipal commission together
> with Don Bosco and several boys.... were standing there,
> staring at and deploring the enormous damage, one of the
> boys noticed that the pillars were swaying, and shouted:
> "Watch out!" Immediately all ran from the area toward the
> centre of the playground. As they were doing so, the wall
> came thundering down with an awesome din; rafters, bricks,
> and stones fell in a wide radius. Everyone was aghast. The
> impact made the ground tremble like an earthquake, and more
> people came running from all sides. For an instant the stunned
> Don Bosco grew pale, but he immediately regained his calm.
> Turning to one of the bystanders, Mr. Duina, he remarked
> with a smile: "We've been playing bricks!"[152]

Don Bosco often took his boys on excursions into the countryside,
and his sense of humour could not be denied, when, in 1855 during

one of these outings, he found himself in front of his humble birthplace at Becchi. With a generous sweep of his arms he exclaimed: "Behold, the feudal estate of Don Bosco!" The boys roared with laughter.[153]

Humour in dealing with the official functions associated with education and the raising of money for education, is also suggested in the following encounter that took place in Rome, 1858, when Don Bosco and his friend Count de Maistre, attended a glittering diplomatic gathering where etiquette demanded that the guests should only converse in Spanish, French or German. Undaunted, Don Bosco and the Count exchanged pleasantries in Piedmontese. Upon being asked by puzzled diplomats as to the language they were using, Don Bosco answered: "Sanskrit!"[154] Often, to avoid answering a particularly embarrassing question, he would fall back on a formula of "Otis Botis Pia Tutis",[155] which was meaningless nonsense designed to bring home to the petitioner the incongruous nature of his question.

It was, however, no accident that when a boy at school, young Bosco was nicknamed "the dreamer".[156] His first plans for the education of poor and abandoned boys came to him in dreams. Later, as a young priest, his dreams continued. "After a day marked by many worrisome problems, plans, hard work, he would not sooner rest his weary head on his pillow than he would enter a new world of ideas and visions that would exhaust him till dawn."[157] Lemoyne remarked that "Don Bosco said to us many times: 'Call them dreams, call them parables, call them whatever you wish, I am sure that they will always do some good.' "[158] The Paradox of the dreamer who was principally a practical man of action was the essence of Don Bosco, the educator. Both vision and application were complementary.

To the Salesians of his day, dedicated enthusiasts among both clergy and lay people, Bosco's personality was the focal point of their teaching careers. Lemoyne, for instance, recorded the words and actions of his leader for posterity, convinced that Bosco's place in history was assured. He had lived with the educator for 24 years at the Oratory, noting down details and anecdotes, comments and reactions concerning Don Bosco. After Don Bosco's death in 1888, he devoted the rest of his life, some twenty-eight years, to gathering further material on the man he revered as a saint. His enthusiasm, perhaps even awe, is reflected in his effusive, adulatory style. Almost apostolic in his zeal to commit to writing the mission of Don Bosco, his intimate yet ornate, subjective yet sincere, accounts are often sentimental in tone, yet sensitive and refined in their unapologetically personal way. He writes with a flourish, his involvement and his love expressed with a sort of wondering candour. For the modern-day Catholic, particularly in the Anglo-Saxon tradition, Lemoyne's subjectivity, selectiveness, and enthusiasm in amassing his evidence, could present difficulties in response, associated with the romanticism of his approach. His emphases are always on those positive aspects of character which made Don Bosco a charismatic personality, rarely commenting on other aspects perhaps less attractive. Don Bosco's attitude towards women, for instance, was based on the Italian village-life environment which had to preclude even a hint of scandal, and tended to make him aloof with women. The education of girls and young women, for instance, he left to the care of Mary Mazzarello and her nuns, who, although following Bosconian educational methods, were a separate development from the Salesians.

Lemoyne, on the other hand, did not intend his biographical memoirs to be read by any other than those dedicated successors to Don Bosco who would, like him, devote their lives to his way. His work was for religious. It is largely his work, nevertheless, that is the basis for Don Bosco's life. Nine volumes were written by Lemoyne himself, and sufficient numbers of anecdotes, recorded sayings and notes on Don Bosco remained after his death for two subsequent Salesian writers to complete another ten volumes: Angelo Amadei, who taught in the Oratory, wrote number ten, and Eugenio Ceria wrote volumes eleven to nineteen.

To look for the educator in records essentially for religious, has meant that, as once was done with other Catholic thinkers such as St. Augustine, the standpoint of both the clerical writers and of the educator himself, has to be acknowledged. Committed to Christian education, Don Bosco's life has influenced, and, through his modern Salesians, is influencing thousands of people. While it has first been within the Catholic Church, again as in St. Augustine's case, that records and comments were kept, the broad field of the Salesian educative works continues to develop within both pluralist and predominantly Catholic communities. Some Australian children for instance, are being educated by Salesians, the pedagogy of Don Bosco being interpreted and followed by both clerics and lay teacher staff.

Although, therefore, Don Bosco's biographies are the works of clerics, the information in them could be looked at from a secular, educational point of view. Similarly, although most commentaries on his work have come from Church sources, schools and teachers in those schools are established throughout the world. Basing their work on Bosconian pedagogy, Salesian teachers, though within the stream of Catholic education, are no more identical with other religious in their methods than are Catholic teachers within secular schools. And it is in the person of their founder, Don Bosco, that Salesians' pedagogy begins. As Father Thomas Carroll, of South Caulfield, Australia, is reported to have said: "....I saw a spirit; that of Don Bosco still happily living in the midst of his Salesians and boys";[159] and, as Father J. Ayers, another modern Salesian puts it: "....How does one define a spirit? Or how does one formulate a charismatic life-style—elusive yet distinctive—left as a legacy by Don Bosco....?"[160]

In an attempt to answer, in part, his own question, Fr. Ayers suggests that it is only by an "existential" experience "in the field" that, as "sons of Don Bosco", the spirit of the man can be caught.[161] This type of experience appears to be based on both a religious conviction and an almost personal encounter with the Salesian "spirit", traditions, stories and atmosphere, so that the viewpoint is not necessarily understandable in scientific terms. Committed to a personalist religion and educational method, Salesian clerics and nuns number, nevertheless, over forty thousand throughout the world, and their contribution to education is still based on "the biographical genre and anecdotal style"[162] of their founder's first followers.

Notes to Chapter 2

1 J. Ayers, 1974. *A Salesian Education.* p.20.
2 *Don Bosco in the World, op. cit.,* p.47.

3   *ibid.*, p.47.

4   *ibid.*, p.47.

5   *ibid.*, p.48.

6   *ibid.*, p.48.

7   *ibid.*, p.47.

8   *ibid.*, p.47.

9   *ibid.*, p.48.

10   *ibid.*, p.48.

11   *ibid.*, p.47.

12   *ibid.*, p.425.

13   F.A. Forbes. *Saint John Bosco.* Salesian Press, Tampa, Florida, 1941.

14   *ibid.* Foreword by Richard Pittini, Archbishop of Santo Domingo, Primate of the West Indies.

15   E.B. Phelan. *Don Bosco. A Spiritual Portrait.* Doubleday, New Yor, 1963, p.260.

16   H. Gheon. (Trans. F.J. Sheed), *The Secret of St John Bosco,* Sheed and Ward, London, 1954, p.190.

17   *ibid.*, p.202.

18   A. Auffray. *Saint John Bosco.* Isag-Colle Don Bosco, Asti. Italy, 1964, p.245.

19   J.B. Lemoyne. *op. cit.*, *B.M.* Vol. II, p.248.

20   *ibid.*, Vol. II, p.313. The word "senate" was a derogatory term for one of the city's gaols.

21   Professor Francis Maranzano spent his boyhood observing the educator at work, and for years afterwards, witnessed many of the unusual performances of Don Bosco.

22   Lemoyne, *op. cit.*, *B.M.* Vol. II, p.413.

23   *ibid.*, p.413.

24   *ibid.*, Vol. IV, p.11.

25   This was an ecclesiastic college of post-graduate status and was established so that priests after ordination, if they so desired, could continue their studies at a more advanced level. It was here that the director, Father Cafasso, came to know Don Bosco personally, and was able to give testimony to his character.

26   Lemoyne, *op. cit.*, *B.M.* Vol. IV, p.411.

27 *ibid.*, Vol. V, pp.486-487.

28 H. Ballesio. *The Innermost Life of Don Bosco.*

29 Leymoyne, *op. cit.*, *B.M.* Vol. VI, p.214.

30 Father Paul Albera, 1845-1921, succeeded Fr Michael Rua, as Rector Major of the Salesian Order, in 1910 and held this position until his death in 1921.

31 Angelo Franco. *A Lamp Resplendent.* Salesiana Press, N.J., 1958, p.36.

32 Lemoyne, *op. cit.*, *B.M.* Vol. I, pp.80-81.

33 *ibid.*, p.107.

34 *ibid.*, pp.99-100.

35 *ibid.*, p.100.

36 Morand Wirth. *Don Bosco et les Salesians. Cent Cinquante Ans D'Histoire.* Elle Di Ci., Torino-Leumann, 1969, pp.91-92.

37 Lemoyne, *op. cit.*, *B.M.* Vol. III, pp.82-84.

38 *ibid.*, Vol. II, p.395.

39 *ibid.*, Vol. I, p.157.

40 *ibid.*, Vol. III, p.235. More detailed account of these fierce brawls, and the part played by Bosco: pp.231-235.

41 One person who came to Bosco's aid, when the latter was being attacked by thugs, was a ruffian armed with a knife. He persuaded Bosco's assailants to go. See *B.M.*, Vol. III, pp.278-283.

42 Lemoyne, *op. cit.*, *B.M.* Vol. IV, pp.488-495.

43 *ibid.*, Vol. I, p.289.

44 *ibid.*, Vol. I, p.232.

45 *ibid.*, Vol. II, p.353.

46 Urbano Rattazzi, Minister of Justice in the Piedmont Government, submitted on the 28th November, 1854, a Bill for the Suppression of Religious Orders, to the Chamber of Deputies. He was supported by Count Camillo Cavour who was Minister of Finance. Don Bosco knew both of these men who in turn respected and admired the educator's work among the delinquent boys of Turin.

47 Lemoyne, *op. cit.*, *B.M.* Vol. V, pp.124-125.

48 *ibid.*, Vol. V, p.126.

49 *ibid.*, Vol. I, p.307.

50 *ibid.*, Vol. IV, p.277.

51 *ibid.*, Vol. I, p.135.

52 *ibid.*, p.137.

53 *ibid.*, p.240.

54 John Baptist Lemoyne, biographer of Don Bosco, first met the latter in 1864 and spent the rest of his life to 1916, recording the deeds of the pedagogist.

55 Lemoyne, *op. cit.*, *B.M.* Vol. I, p.245.

56 *ibid.*, pp.322-323.

57 *ibid.*, p.288.

58 *ibid.*, pp.151-152; p.208.

59 *ibid.*, pp.304-305.

60 *ibid.*, p.167.

61 *ibid.*, p.294.

62 *ibid.*, p.306.

63 *ibid.*, p.315.

64 *ibid.*, Vol. III, p.439.

65 *ibid.*, pp.434-435.

66 *ibid.*, Vol. I, p.365.

67 *ibid.*, Vol. IV, p.435.

68 History of the Roman State.

69 Lemoyne, *op. cit.*, *B.M.* Vol. IV, pp.89-93.

70 *ibid.*, Vol. I, p.155.

71 *ibid.*, p.174.

72 *ibid.*, p.174.

73 *ibid.*, p.175.

74 *ibid.*, p.193.

75 *ibid.*, p.217.

76 *ibid.*, p.209.

77 *ibid.*, Vol. II, p.254.

78 *ibid.*, Vol. I, p.104.

79 *ibid.*, p.104.

80 *ibid.*, Vol. III, pp.17-18.

81 *ibid.*, Vol. I, pp.262-267.

82 *ibid.*, p.321.

83 *ibid.*, Vol. IV, p.182.

84 *ibid.*, Vol. II, pp.370-372.

85 E. Ceria. *Memorie Biografiche di D.G. Bosco.* Vol. XII, p.409.

86 Lemoyne, *op. cit.*, *B.M.* Vol. II, pp.364-365.

87 *ibid.*, Vol. III, pp.327-328.

88 *ibid.*, Vol. IV, pp.169-172.

89 Many church buildings, convents, friaries, monasteries, were ideal for conversion into military hospitals during war emergencies when casualties could not be accommodated in existing hospitals.

90 Prudence in business matters was one kind of foresight. However, Don Bosco was gifted with another kind of foresight which helped him progress in his educational work, at a time when liberalism in Italy was impeding most Catholic educational advancement: "He was fearless in upholding the rights of God and His Church, but, while he was an open enemy of error, he respected and loved those who erred, and they became convinced of his sincere regard for them and knew there was no deceit in him.

"His simplicity suggested a good-natured temperament, and this attracted all kinds of people to him, great and small, learned and ignorant.... Thus, little by little, Don Bosco was able to begin his undertakings, to the benefit of Church and country, winning the esteem and help of all those who, unprejudiced and endowed with good sense, understood the importance of his plans. This was a fruit of his remarkable foresight." Lemoyne, *op. cit.*, *B.M.* Vol. II, pp.174-175.

In 1845, Don Bosco's foresight led him to repeatedly ask bishops "to meet the challenge of the times" and look into new educational methods, using those techniques which would be to the advantage of Catholic schools. See Lemoyne, *ibid.*, *B.M.* Vol. II, p.170.

91 *ibid.*, *B.M.* Vol. IV, p.328.

92 *ibid.*, Vol. IV, p.328.

93 *ibid.*, Vol. II, pp.173-174.

94 *ibid.*, Vol. II, p.193.

95 *ibid.*, p.207.

96 *ibid.*, Vol. IV, pp. 276-277.

97 *ibid.*, Vol. VII, p.132.

98 *ibid.*, Vol. III, pp.306-307.

99 *ibid.*, Vol. I, p.271.

100   *ibid.*, Vol. VII, p.409.

101   *ibid.*, Vol. I, pp.252-252.

102   *ibid.*, p.356.

103   Archbishop Louis Fransoni, Bishop of Turin, who because of his stand against the forces of liberalism, was removed from his See by Marquis Massimo d'Azeglio, and finally exiled to Lyons in 1850.

104   Lemoyne, *op. cit.*, *B.M.* Vol. IV, p.77.

105   *ibid.*, Vol. V, p.4.

106   See Note 40. Another episode on this theme: Lemoyne, *op. cit.*, *B.M.*, Vol. V, p.192.

107   *ibid.*, *B.M.* Vol. III, p.211.

108   *ibid.*, Vol. III, p.304.

109   *ibid.*, Vol. IV, p.360.

110   *ibid.*, pp.360-361.

111   *ibid.*, Vol. I, p.183.

112   *ibid.*, pp.172-173.

113   *ibid.*, pp.274-275.

114   *ibid.*, p.296.

115   John Cagliero, 1838-1926. Pupil of Don Bosco, who took Salesian educational methods to South America in 1875. Later, as Cardinal Cagliero, he helped to further Bosconian pedagogical methods in Europe.

116   Lemoyne, *op. cit.*, *B.M.*, Vol. IV, pp.451-452.

117   A medallion presented by the government to those who excelled in humanitarian endeavours. The title of 'Chevalier' was an honour and could be likened to a British O.B.E.

118   Lemoyne, *op. cit.*, *B.M.* Vol. IV, pp.339-340.

119   *ibid.*, Vol. IV, p.455.

120   *ibid.*, p.455.

121   *ibid.*, pp.456-457.

122   *ibid.*, Vol. V, p.432.

123   *ibid.*, Vol. VI, p.188.

124   *ibid.*, Vol. III, pp.293-296.

125   *ibid.*, Vol. I, p.314.

126   *ibid.*, Vol. II, p.175.

127   *ibid.*, Vol. V., p.191.

128 *ibid.*, Vol. I, pp.218-219.

129 *ibid.*, p.254.

130 *ibid.*, Vol. II, p.349.

131 *ibid.*, Vol. V, p.199.

132 *ibid.*, p.203.

133 Ceria, *op. cit.*, *B.M.* Vol. XIII, p.716.

134 Lemoyne, *op. cit.*, *B.M.* Vol. I, p.296.

135 *ibid.*, p.371.

136 *ibid.*, Vol. VI, p.604.

137 *ibid.*, Vol. II, pp.95-96.

138 *ibid.*, Vol. V, p.433.

139 *ibid.*, Vol. II, pp.198-199.

140 *ibid.*, p.199.

141 *ibid.*, Vol. VI, p.496.

142 *ibid.*, Vol. I, p.287.

143 *ibid.*, Vol. V, pp.506-507. Don Bosco was often seen in village squares, mobbed by laughing children. People could pinpoint his whereabouts by looking for a swarm of boisterous children, gathered around someone.

144 *ibid.*, Vol. V, pp.97-99. Don Bosco would often transfer his happiness to his pupils by having special assemblies of singing, poetry, drama, to celebrate some special, joyous occasion.

145 *ibid.*, Vol. VI, pp.165-166.

146 *ibid.*, Vol. II, p.328.

147 *ibid.*, Vol. VII, p.440.

148 *ibid.*, Vol. I, p.85.

149 *ibid.*, Vol. II, p.105.

150 Father Lawrence Gastaldi was the examiner in charge of the questioning.

151 Lemoyne, *op. cit.*, *B.M.* Vol. I, p.382.

152 *ibid.*, pp.358-359.

153 *ibid.*, Vol. V., p.224.

154 *ibid.*, p.593.

155 Ceria, *op. cit.*, *B.M.* Vol. XI, p.243.

156 Lemoyne, *op. cit.*, *B.M.* Vol. I, p.190.

157   *ibid.*, p.190.

158   *ibid.*, p.191.

159   Ayers, *op. cit.*, Foreword p.1.

160   *ibid.*, p.3.

161   *ibid.*, p.3.

162   *ibid.*, p.4.

CHAPTER 3

MAXIMS AND METHODS

Part I: Maxims

Throughout his long pedagogical career Don Bosco developed a number of maxims, resolutions, and norms based on his experiences, which he disseminated among his teachers and followers. Because his pedagogy was based on practical items of distilled thought, positive plans for action, and actual situations experienced, those who followed his methods did so with confidence, feeling they could operate along guidelines laid down from experience.

The motto Don Bosco adopted throughout his life: "ama et fac quod vis"[1] was characteristic of his approach to education. "Hence, his easy manner, free of anxiety and marked by the full freedom of the child of God."[2]

As early as 1835 he wrote down some resolutions which were to guide him in his priestly life. One such resolution read: "Every day I shall tell some example or some spiritual maxim to my companions, my friends, my relatives, or at least to my mother."[3] Perhaps the most productive of these was derived from St. Francis de Sales' saying: "Ask for nothing, refuse nothing",[4] in the educative mission. Bosco's energy, capacity for work, demanded voluntary suppliers of material and intellectual gifts which, when offered, were never refused. Together with kindness and a belief in the dignity of man, this response to life's opportunities was largely responsible for his successes and pedagogical achievements: nothing was wasted because nothing was refused.

In 1841, prior to saying his first Mass, he wrote down that he would be "very rigorous" in the "use of" his time; to "suffer, work, humble" himself "in all things whenever it is a question of saving souls"; and to use as a "guide" the "charity and gentleness of St. Francis de Sales." He also resolved to "set aside some time every day for meditation and spiritual reading."[5] This recognition by Bosco of the importance of the uses of his time, and of timing,[6] were to be used to advantage in preparing himself for a pedagogical task which was to last a lifetime.

On the other hand, such an attitude to time, often allowing little or no privacy in recreation, and rarely permitting that relaxed sense of leisure time uncomplicated by responsibilities which is generally demanded by the modern teacher, presupposed a dedication and determination extraordinary rather than the norm. Coupled with the Bosconian emphasis on the teacher's continuing presence among students, it is, indeed, "rigorous".

According to Lemoyne,[7] another maxim followed by Don Bosco which largely accounted for his successes in diplomacy, was that of Christ who told his followers: "Remember, I am sending you out to be like sheep àmong wolves; you must be wary, then, as serpents, and yet innocent as doves."[8] This advice, too, demanded, in the word "wary", watchfulness which left the Salesian educator with little personal time. It was in another of Bosco's mottos, however, that an understanding of this attitude could be found. On the wall of his room was inscribed St. Francis de Sales' motto: "Give me souls; away with the rest".[9]

In 1847, the first boarders he took in at Valdocco, were to read on their dormitory walls, the inscription: "God sees you"[10] which, no doubt, had an effect on them. This inscription was the only written guideline they had; there were no formal rules laid down by the priest-educator. However, Professor Joseph Rayneri, Department of Pedagogy, Royal University of Turin, who frequented Bosco's Oratory from 1846 to 1853, recorded some of the educator's sayings which, in Rayneri's opinion, were ideally suited for the young: "Act today in such a way that you need not blush tomorrow"; "Do not put off till tomorrow the good you can do today. You may not have a tomorrow"; "Let us strive to fare well in this life and in the next"; "Be slow to pass judgement"; "Do you want your companions to respect you? Always think well of everyone, and be ready to help others. Do this and you will be happy."[11]

Don Bosco's custom of giving maxims to his staff and boys, however, was not always a blanket approach. He believed that some of these pieces of advice had to be tailored to suit the needs of each individual. They were not general rules to be followed: they were specific and particular, commensurate with the characteristics of the person concerned. His prescriptions were cherished and were called 'keepsakes':

> The....year was now ending. As he had done in the past on the same occasion, Don Bosco announced that he had a special keepsake for everybody. This custom offered him the opportunity of giving a personal piece of advice to each boy. One by one they approached him. Usually Don Bosco whispered a maxim or admonition taken from the lives of the saints, but occasionally he gave it on a slip of paper lest they forget it. These written momentos became a precious possession jealously guarded for years.
> He also gave keepsakes to the clerics, in Latin, that were drawn from Holy Scripture or the Fathers of the Church. Surprisingly, even when the Oratory priests and clerics numbered over fifty, he still gave each one a message, without notes and without repeating himself. The keepsake was so unerringly personal that all were amazed and said to themselves: "This is really for me!"[12]

One of his favourite maxims for his boys was that of St. Philip Neri:[13] "Run, jump, have all the fun you want at the right time, but, for heaven's sake, do not commit sin!"[14] Don Bosco himself regularly practised a similar attitude, expressed in his solgan: "Servite Domino in laetitia!" (Serve the Lord joyfully!). He served by cheerfully guiding, advising those who were in his care so that they knew they were wanted, needed, and loved, their Oratory being filled with joy. A feature of his schools was to become the joy that was found there:

> Oratory life was a blend of a reverent fear of God with untiring zest for work and study, all animated by holy cheerfulness. This admirable combination put almost everyone into an environment of joy, enthusiasm, and indescribable delight. Those who have not seen it can hardly imagine how noisy, carefree, and happy the boys were at their games, crisscrossing every square foot of the playground. Don Bosco—prime mover of that hustle and bustle—rejoiced no end. Knowing how he liked to join their games and conversations whenever he had time, the youngsters would often gaze up at his window and hope that he would come out on the balcony. If he did,

a joyful shout greeted him from every corner of the playground, and a rush of lads met him at the foot of the stairs to welcome him....[15]

Don Bosco's conversations with the boys "sparkled with witty remarks, wholesome sayings, and amusing anecdotes."[16] He eased the burdens of the worried, the depressed, the irritated, those feeling inundated with their schoolwork, by letting them know that it was normal to have these feelings. By identifying himself with their state, and then by giving them some practical guidelines to follow, he would restore them to cheerfulness. This continuing personal contact assumed the presence of educators at all times, even during students' recreation periods. It was not to be an interfering sort of supervision, but rather a familial and familiar presence. For instance, one of Bosco's favourite pastimes was to recite poetry aloud as he walked about the playground. It would often begin with a maxim "Tempora mutantur et nos mutamur in illis" (Times change and we with them).[17] He would amuse pupils by making up verses, using their names to improvise rhymes. Games were invented to reinforce rules of grammar, thus "even playtime was pleasantly turned into learning."[18] In 1850, Don Bosco was, in effect, already using an educational idea, that of learning through play activity, which was to become popular in the 1940's with the Percy Nunn school of educational philosophy.

Similarly, he would often ask for the real meaning of the algebraic expression "$a+b-c$". His ingenious explanation was that "a" stood for "allegro" (cheerful), "b" for "buono" (good), "c" for "cattivo" (bad); he would add: "So always be cheerful and good but never bad."[19] To the person lost in thought, or the daydreamer, he would ask: "When are you going to start working miracles?";[20] "To a little fellow who said nothing but just rested his head against his arm, he would jokingly say: 'Now you, keep quiet!' "[21]

Don Bosco's prescription, given in 1859, for good health and a long life was: 1. Clear conscience; 2. Moderation in eating; 3. An active life; and, 4. Good companions.[22] His formula, in 1860, for school spirit, he gleaned from St. Vincent de Paul[23] who advocated some time set aside during the day for the observation of silence. St. Vincent believed that "if everyone talks at will, there is a general disregard for all other rules as well."[24] People who observed Bosco's schools were struck with the way his pupils could, when called upon to do so, control themselves and maintain strict silence. This was possible because the Salesian teachers had come to know their students while teaching them: reciprocal love could be expressed in terms of silent as well as uninhibited behaviour.

> All these remarks and tricks of his generally ended with a confidential word that soon came to be called "la parola nell'orecchio"—a word in the ear—. . . . Thus, zealously and prudently governing the house by counsel, keeping in touch with everything, maintaining personal contact with each pupil, and knowing each by name and character, Don Bosco was able to give them advice. . . .[25]

The use of maxims, the "parola nell'orecchio", and other forms of easily remembered oral or written sayings, could approach prescriptiveness, particularly if they became specific advice to be accepted without question or discussion. Although Salesians worked within the boundaries of Catholic thought and action, Don Bosco had always eschewed the prescriptive in education; yet these words of advice or direction were given in such a way as to preclude discussion. Rather, they were to be reflected upon. Perhaps, however, since Bosco's methods relied so heavily on human relationships, particularly the difficult to analyse feelings of love and loyalty, he used terse admonitions and maxims in an effort to make practical the general lines of his code. Emphasis on moral education led to the development of outlines, or guideposts to moral behaviour, since Bosco's students often came from backgrounds without access to more detailed explanations. Simplicity and brevity, general instructions, set the tone as well as the direction. For a Catholic school or Oratory, little discussion on basic principles of morality could occur. It was, however, the manner in which authority was used that marked Bosco's schools as different; and it was the way in which the medium used came to be integrated with the maxim or advice given, that made the Salesian atmosphere unusual. The message was to become united with the method.

Part II: Methods

In 1883, Don Bosco took the chair at a St. Vincent de Paul meeting on the occasion of the opening of a new school. Whilst there he was asked: "What is your method of education?" Without hesitation, the pedagogist who by this time was 68 years of age and had behind him over 40 years of teaching experience, replied: "By means of affection, gain the heart of the youth."[1] Later, in 1886, two years prior to his death, a correspondent wrote to Bosco and asked how was it that he was so effective in getting people to learn? What methods inspired such application? Don Bosco replied: "My methods? I don't quite know myself. I always acted as the circumstances demanded. But I always had a purpose in view and held to hope. I was not hidebound or stereotyped; did not take away initiative of movement. I shunned the educational straitjacket and its narrowness."[2]

Salesians have tended to follow this fluidity of approach, not attempting to analyse in detail what their founder's theories were, but referring to particular instances of those 'circumstances' and 'initiatives', and describing his pedagogy in general terms, thus also shunning the prescriptivism of self-enclosed systems which have within themselves the seeds of their own decay. Peter Ricaldone, Rector Major of the Salesian Society from 1932 to 1951, and himself an educationist, for example, described Don Bosco's secret of the art of pedagogy simply as one "characterised by love and charity."[3]

Lemoyne has provided another clue: "He had a mathematical mind and in reasoning proceeded methodically, always starting with precise definitions drawn from the best authors."[4] When the educator introduced a topic "he began with its definition and then one by one cited his arguments for or against. Through this clear presentation, his teachings remained indelible in our minds."[5]

His teaching techniques were observed on occasions in 1845 when he visited Turin jails to help and comfort the inmates. He would select intelligent convicts, train them in dialogue discussion techniques, then use them as his assistants to further the Christian education of the others. Bosco trained these prisoner-assistants to ask those questions which would immediately arouse the curiosity of the other prisoners:

> "....as he was conversing with them or was beginning to teach them the catechism, one of his assistants would abruptly break in with a question or an objection arousing everybody's attention and curiosity. Don Bosco would then reply. Questions and answers were spiced with so many clever remarks, popular sayings, amusing or edifying incidents, that the truth, though presented humorously, would sink in, provoke thought and unfailingly lead some of them to turn over a new leaf.... [6]

Later, during a talk to Salesian Society members in May, 1864, Don Bosco suggested that his educational methods were based on forebearance, restraint, indulgence, and patience. It seemed that there were some present who had misgivings about these ideas: Don Bosco answered them in this vein: "Occasionally, you may think that we are too forebearing with certain boys, too indulgent, too easy. Be patient; payday will come. If superiors sometimes bide their time, they do so because of parents, benefactors, or even the boy's own good."[7] Bosco's implication that education takes time, that time must be provided for a gradual response from children, was in keeping with his emphasis on the ends, not the means, of education. Paradoxically, while his means were controversial, the ends, at least for Catholics, were not.

As early as 1849 Bosco's pedagogical methods were assuming a distinctive pattern. His teachers used clear, unambiguous classroom language: one point for each lesson, to be followed by reasoned explanations on that point by members of the class; Bosco often reversed roles: they became his teachers he their pupil. Texts were used for reference, or for clarification on some special point. They were aids, not props for the lesson. Lessons were interspersed with recreational activity which was always supervised: on family lines, not traditional ones. Don Bosco was their playground father, they his sons. Often lessons continued outdoors in, for that time, an innovative, relaxed manner. During walks in the countryside students would be encouraged to repeat some of the things they had learned days before. The point was that learning with Don Bosco was coming to be thought of as fun; and education a joyous outgoing experience.

Such an experience was, for the mid-nineteenth century, not surprisingly to be regarded with suspicion by many, and to become indelibly imprinted upon the memories of its recipients. In 1849, there was little joy in English public schools, for example, if we are to believe the writings of the Victorian novelists, Charles Dickens[8] and Thomas Hughes,[9] both contemporaries of Don Bosco. When many English methods were primarily based on the birch, fear, and aloofness, Bosco's pedagogy was centred in love, and respect for the individual:

> The discipline at the Oratory was not for show, it was individual —for the will. Don Bosco believed that boys should be allowed to make noise—as much as they liked at recreation. He believed in life and joy and movement. Sometimes he would line up his six or seven hundred boys, and march them off at a lively gait, singing a folk song of old Piedmont in which they lustily joined, keeping in step and marking the time by a vigorous clapping of hands. In and out they went, up a staircase, down a long corridor, round and round in serpentine twistings, delirious with excitement. The din was absolutely deafening, so was the tramping of hundreds of strong young feet; but when legs and voices were weary and they stopped for lack of breath, they had thoroughly enjoyed life. Even classes were enjoyable. The boys were expected to work seriously, but there were compensations. A theatre was one of Don Bosco's earliest enterprises. Plays were acted, historical episodes presented, and music was always to the fore. The choir of the Oratory was in demand for festive occasions all over the city. A choir of boys' voices was a novelty in Italy at that time and provoked much admiration.
> 'Without confidence and love,' Don Bosco would say, 'there can be no true education.' He himself was a living example. 'If you want to be loved.... you must love yourselves, and make your children feel that you love yourselves, and make your children feel that you love them.' Unwearying patience with the least responsive, a loving vigilance to defend them from themselves, a tenderness that persists in spite of all rebuffs, a trust that cannot but call out response—these were the principles on which he worked and taught others to work with him.[10]

Peter Ricaldone pointed out "that Don Bosco was using activity methods—often proclaimed as a twentieth century educational discovery—back in the 1840's when he insisted on active classes, that inductive methods of enquiry were best, that pedagogy consisted in the wholehearted participation of pupils in the work of their education and character formation. Moreover, Don Bosco had a psychological perspective on each pupil, conducted bright and happy classrooms, abolished "hateful punishments",[12] insisted on the liberty of the pupil and measured this liberty in terms of motivation and self-control. He used the high-light method of education: salient ideas were extracted and became focal points of interest. The "focusing of interest" game was already known and used by the priest-educator.

Ricaldone has suggested Bosco used methods[13] that could be considered quite modern when compared with today's standards. For example, the pupil's welfare was of primary importance: he was treated with kindness and respect; it was the educator's responsibility to place him in a happy, vigorous, enquiring educational environment where all were treated as equals, where all were encouraged to speak up, and out, to one another and to their teacher. Knowledge was adapted to the chronological age of the educand; classes were formed on the criterion of the pupil's age and not on ability. The indignity felt by an older student when sitting down in a classroom of younger pupils was not experienced in Bosco's schools. The pedagogist urged that his teachers show patience and understanding when pupils could not grasp essentials. And lessons, to be effective, had to be prepared by the teacher before they were given.

Topics were to be tailored to suit the needs and levels of understanding of the pupils: obscure terms avoided, verbiage outlawed, concinnity of style encouraged. Relevant examples were used to underline a point of learning, but not abused; Bosco believed that too many analogies were confusing and would defeat the purposes of the lesson. The aim was to give one salient point per lesson; the teacher was to hasten slowly when it came to the teaching of concepts.

Discipline was based on mutual trust between teacher and taught; if correction was necessary, there was, Bosco believed, a psychological moment for it. Above all, "the school was not the end; it was rather the instrumental means for improving the way of life."[14]

The primary objective of Bosconian pedagogy was to equip

Christian young people to take their places in corporate society. Don Bosco expected them to live their lives conscious of the needs and welfare of others. This demanded a positive rationale: the involvement in community and social welfare. "If one is to do good," he used to say, "he must have a little courage, be ready for sacrifice, deal affably with all and never slight anybody. By following this method I have always had significant success, in fact, marvellous success."[15]

This acknowledgement of his own success reflects an attitude close to pragmatic concern for results. He did not, when pressed for advice, attempt to detail specific methods, lesson plans, or educational programs. His approach was directed more towards the interpersonal relationship between educator and student. For example, in January, 1875, Don Bosco wrote a letter to Herminius Borio, a teacher at Borgo San Martino, about 70 km due east of Turin:

> You asked for advice. Here it is:
> 1. When you have to correct someone in particular, never do so in the presence of others.
> 2. When you give advice or counsel always try to send the person away satisfied and still friendly to you.
> 3. Always thank those who admonish you and take their corrections in good part....[16]

Braido[17] pointed out that Bosco was not concerned with any one educational idea, he chose what he thought useful for his purposes and imprinted on them his own particular style.[18] Bosco's method then depended, argued Braido, on a two-way process. His work was useless if he failed to win the confidence and love of the educand; education was a failure if the youth did not place his trust in the educator.[19]

Ricaldone, agreeing with Braido, stated that Don Bosco's successes were dependent on his utilization of the means made available to him, and that his outlook was never narrow, never biassed: he sought help from every quarter.[20]

Henri Gheon, in his Epilogue to *The Secret of Saint John Bosco*, reflects the attitude of those who still find his success an enigma:

A work founded upon authority has some chance of survival, for authority can be passed on. It descends from the great to the small in hierarchical order, each one using his power to keep the one below him in place. But a work founded upon liberty should, humanly speaking, engender only anarchy. And Don Bosco's was founded upon liberty.[21]

Don Bosco's methods, based on the principles of liberty rather than on those of authority, were aimed at a Catholic education, in which the element of authority is an essential. It was how this authority was gained and used, how a dialogue between those learning and those teaching was established, and how students could choose, or decide upon, their future, that mattered. The educator, therefore, while guiding and accompanying youth, while using every accomplishment or method he could to influence rather than compel, moved within the limitations of a Catholic philosophy of education.

Some of his means to this end were subtle and planned. For instance visitors to his Oratory in 1856 were surprised to see educational inscriptions painted on the walls of the porticoes of his new school building. The walls had been whitewashed and the letter work had been done by an artist, Peter Enria. Don Bosco remarked: "Now and then the boys rest for a while or stroll about these porticoes when they are tired of playing. Also outsiders who come here on business matters stand outside waiting to be received. Seeing these inscriptions, all will be curious enough to read them, if only to while away the time. Thus an inspiring thought will be etched into their minds and perhaps bear fruit."[22] Periodically, Bosco would take a theme from one of these wall inscriptions and use it for the subject of a good night talk to his boys. "Occasionally, while strolling through the porticoes with visitors, he enjoyed reading them aloud, referring to them as his private code of life, the secret for leading a good life and dying a good death."[23]

It could be said, then, that while his methods were innovatory and situational rather than theoretical, they were often based upon the ideas or theories of others. His innovations were extended to extra-curricular concerns, though always within the framework of the Catholic Church.

In 1859, for instance, Bosco was the first cleric to introduce into boarding schools Holy Communion on a daily basis.[24]   As was his wont, he did not compel the boys to go to the Eucharist: they freely went having made the choice themselves.   Later, in 1875, he set up a special "crash-course" for late vocations to the priesthood.[25]   This was an innovation which was looked upon with suspicion by the majority of the clergy of his day.   But his methods prevailed and his scheme gradually won acceptance.

In 1886, a journalist writing for the Turin newspaper *Cittabrino Brescio*, was impressed with a performance given by the Oratory Choir,[26] and when, at its conclusion, all the boys spontaneously went out and received Holy Communion, he concluded that the secret of Bosco's method was that he gave good example[27] without imposing any condition on the students.   He noted that Bosco's boys responded to this: the model was there to follow but the choice was theirs.   Don Bosco's methodology was therefore moral: it involved choice in an atmosphere free from constraints and conditions.

The educational methods were, however, closely connected with the personal qualities of the man.   Flexible and practical, extremely popular with children and youths, both relaxed and yet perceptive in his assessment of them, and at the same time maintaining a father-friend image, Don Bosco had adopted a technique compatible with these characteristics.

It would appear, then, that a certain type of person would feel free to follow him; that teacher training was to be more than the gaining of academic qualifications and classroom expertise; and that character-formation would become of importance.   The Salesian would be, for instance, capable of relating in a relaxed and friendly way to children.

Don Bosco was relaxed and friendly towards young people, he put children at ease and in a frame of mind to comply with his wishes. John Villa, from Ponderano, who attended the pedagogist's Oratory declared:

> I could not help comparing his friendly way with boys with that of other priests I knew.   None of them had ever been

as kindly and amiable. Nor was I the only one to feel this way. I learned that many other boys around him had exactly the same opinion.... I noticed that Don Bosco made a point of allowing the boys to be active and enjoy their games in order to attract them. The more noise they made at play, the happier he seemed to be. Whenever he saw us looking lonesome or not quite as lively as usual, he would leave no stone unturned until he had cheered us up again with new games and new ideas....[28]

He was more like a father than a priest, or a teacher. As an educator he had nothing of the policeman about him and everything of the father in his attitude towards children. His perceptiveness allowed him to shun the closed confessional; he understood that students would tell him more about themselves when outdoors than when inside a church: "Don Bosco had so long been accustomed to confess his children in the open air at the side of a ditch or on a grassy bank, that he had no devotion to the enclosed confessional, sometimes alarming to the very young. The boys knelt beside him, his fatherly arm around their shoulders, and told him all they had to tell. Then followed a little talk, heart to heart, and, with the grace of the sacrament on their souls, they would run off light-hearted and happy."[29]

Not all the early Salesians could cope with Bosco's students, however. For example, a young boy, John Cagliero, in 1852 was extremely troublesome at the Oratory, and because of his high spirits, drove Michael Rua, his teacher, almost to despair. It was suggested that Cagliero be sent away as he was so undisciplined. Don Bosco "who appreciated Cagliero's genuine qualities, would not hear of it.... discovered that Cagliero, among other talents, had great aptitude for music. He himself taught him the first rudiments and then entrusted him to the cleric Bellia for further instruction."[30] Due partly to Bosco's initial perceptiveness, Cagliero went on and became a Salesian missionary, educator, and finally a Cardinal of the Church.

What it was that made Don Bosco's methods work, Salesians themselves have tried to explain. Pietro Stella, a Salesian priest and author, for instance, saw Don Bosco as a practical man whose methods fitted a matrix, a configurational pattern of experiences dependent on circumstances:

Don Bosco had his absolute values and his constants but, working in the concrete, he had not become an absolutist, and while making his decisions he never delayed to dwell on an organic and theoretical systemization of his ideas. What he said, what he did, what he got others to do, was always inspired by circumstances; and even when he generalizes or theorizes, he is quick to base these on immediate experiences.[31] Rather than accomplish one thing at a time his differential nature had him attempting several things at once. His methods tended towards a calculus, a change within a change.

Lemoyne bore witness to Bosco's versatility. The educator's competence in various trades, his organizational ability, and academic accomplishments, presented a formidable picture for an educator to emulate. He could, for instance, cope with several things at once, remarking to Joachim Berto, his personal secretary in 1869: "This morning, while preaching on church history, I mapped out an entire issue of the *Letture Cattoliche* and also figured out a solution to a certain need of this house."[32]

For the less able, though perhaps equally dedicated, teacher, Bosco's example could have become an impossibility to imitate. He made clear, however, that the education of his priests was to be improved, and that the teacher as the Church itself, would have to move with the times.

When he saw the implications of 1848 and the awakening forces of liberalism for instance, he realised that the Church would have to change to meet the new demands. He recognised that if priests were not better educated they would be barred, by the state, from teaching literary or scientific subjects in public and private schools. "We must face facts," he said. "Times are bad and will not soon change. Within a few years we shall be forced either to have certified teachers or to close down our schools.."[33] Despite warnings that the moral climate of the University was "pestilential"[34] he insisted that his clerics take up courses in literature, philosophy, and mathematics at the University to meet the new requirements for the certification of teachers. Because his own nature was at ease with change, his methods followed suit: they were flexible enough to meet the new demands of liberalism and turn them to his advantage.

His purpose, nevertheless, was the same: the salvation, through the educative experiences of a Christian environment, of socially and spiritually deprived boys. Professor Casimiro Danna of the Royal University of Turin, then member of the government in power, wrote favourably about Don Bosco's work. He saw purpose in what Bosco was doing, and noted, in an educational journal,[35] that Don Bosco had "dedicated himself entirely to alleviating the sufferings of the poor through education."[36] He recognised, as did Bosco, that given a vocational education, the poor could at least be employed and earn enough to support themselves and their families. Hence Bosco's Oratories taught practical skills: tailoring, woodworking, metalworking, printing and bookbinding, and blacksmithing, as well as the basics of reading, writing, and number. Bosco, in effect, had provided a pedagogical method to combat poverty: an educational insurance policy for the deprived and under-privileged.

For this end, and because of the particularly demanding nature of his methodology, Don Bosco's followers have recognised the need for dedication to youth work as well as to the religious life, to young people with all their inconsistencies and problems, as well as to the profession of teaching.

Ricaldone for instance, has argued that Don Bosco took time and effort in the recruitment of teachers who were to work with him. Bosco personally selected and trained them in his teaching methods. Then they were invited to share with him in the responsibilities of his educative mission. He usually achieved this by using their self-love for constructive purposes.[37] In each person there were, he believed, strong qualities reflecting their abilities and personalities, which could be utilised for the collective welfare.

But his methods were as effective as the work, energy, and time he put into them and they, in turn, put into others. Education, for Don Bosco, was a full-time occupation, a life-long job. He worked himself hard, with ruthless determination to make every day count. Gheon wrote: "For never less than nineteen hours of each day he was on duty.... and he lived thus for 45 years. That was the price paid to keep the work going."[38] He succeeded. In the space of a century his pedagogy had become international.

This achievement has shown that, demanding as his educational ideas and methods are, there have been sufficient people to live them, and carry them forward, meeting needs as they arose, and adapting to different cultures and languages. Part of the Salesian tradition has become this growing, adapting, meeting-of-needs, developmental pedagogy, based on Don Bosco's actions in his meeting the needs of pupils and teachers. When, for example, in 1847, he realised that there were no suitable children's prayer-books because the existing ones were too obtuse theologically, he wrote *The Companion of Youth*[39] which cleared up existing difficulties and anomalies in this area: meeting their needs and furthering their religious education. Again, in 1846, Don Bosco found that he had insufficient teachers to cope with his expanding evening classes at the St. Francis de Sales Oratory. He met this emergency by selecting, from older boys who attended the Oratory, those who were intelligent and "desired a better education so that they could obtain more advantageous employment.... at the evening classes, both weekdays and Sunday,"[40] thus meeting his own needs as well as theirs.

The artisans[41] under Bosco's care were specially provided for, in a series of regulations issued in 1886, so that they could take their places in society and be able to provide for their families. He took pains to let them know that they were loved and held in esteem by their educators. Moreover, they were allowed to select the trade of their choice. He saw to it that they were taught, in addition to their trade, music and singing so that, in their leisure-time when they left the Oratory, they would be able to assist in their own parishes when they returned to them. Miscreant artisans were not dismissed; they were transferred to another Bosconian school so that their education and trade could be kept up. Bosco made sure in all circumstances that each artisan knew his trade thoroughly and not just superficially. All artisans who had finished their studies were placed with suitable employers and furnished with letters of introduction to the relevant parish priest. In these ways Don Bosco met the religious, intellectual, and professional needs of those artisans who were in his Oratories and under his care.[42]

To get to know the needs of students, Don Bosco advised his teachers to dialogue with them, both outside and within the classroom situation. The art of questioning was a part of the technique. He said in 1875:

> I also believe that pupils are to be questioned repeatedly so that, if possible, never a day passes without having the whole class interrogated. This has untold advantages. But I am told, instead, that some teachers enter the classroom, question one or two pupils, and then launch into their lesson without further ado. I would not endorse such a method even at university level. Question, question, question over and over again. The more the pupil is made to talk the more will he profit from his schooling.[43]

That the educator was to sustain a relationship of courtesy and understanding with his students, in order that they would learn the more readily in an atmosphere of love and respect, was not an easily accepted idea at the time, but in a reply to a request for advice, Bosco suggested that this relationship was the crux of the educational situation. In 1875, a philosophy lecturer, named Bertollo, dissatisfied with his students who had not met his expectations of them, wrote to Don Bosco seeking his advice on the matter. Bosco replied:

> I shall do all I can to enkindle love of study among your pupils; but you must also do everything you can to co-operate.
> 1. Think of them as your brothers; kindness, understanding and patience are the keys to their hearts.
> 2. Make them study only as much as they are able and no more. Make them read and understand what the book says without digressing.
> 3. Quiz them very often, ask them to explain and read, read and explain.
> 4. Encourage them at all times, never humiliate them; praise them as often as you can and do not belittle them; only show your displeasure when you wish to punish them.
> Try to follow this advice, and let me know the result.[44]

Bosco was suggesting to the lecturer that by showing concern for student welfare, he would develop in them a response, a readiness to learn; that by being relevent, and not too demanding, by using follow-up procedures to test their comprehension of concepts, he would gain their confidence, and develop their own confidence in what they did. Finally, by adopting a positive attitude, by praising his students whenever possible and never humiliating them in front of others, Bertollo would meet his students' needs, as well as satisfy his own requirements.

Another technique adopted by the pedagogist to satisfy both the needs of his teachers and pupils was that of the name-day. On a given day, each teacher was allowed to suspend lessons so that the pupils could meet socially with the teacher:

> On that day the teacher had the occasion to win over a hitherto unresponsive pupil, to clear up a misunderstanding, or to encourage a boy by a promise to help him. This custom was also a splendid opportunity for the teacher to forgive and put at ease those who feared the unpleasant consequences of their misdeeds at the end of the school year. On that day, the pupils, less guarded in their talk, unwittingly disclosed— and thus rid themselves of—their apprehensions, hurt feelings, and jealousies; even some acts of misconduct came to light which would have remained hidden and caused disorders or, possibly, spiritual harm.
> Don Bosco's aim in permitting these demonstrations of affection and gratitude was always the boys' eternal welfare.[45]

In seeking both to discover and to meet the needs of students, Don Bosco included the wider sociological environment in which his students moved, involving parents and employers as well as past pupils in his educational methodology. For instance, the priest-educator ran a petition-writing service for adults and their families, which in modern terms, would have been called a free legal-aid bureau. "Usually he lunched around noon; immediately afterward he set about writing petitions on behalf of needy people.... Later, when a room could be spared as a reception office, he arranged for one of his young clerics or another suitable person to sit there at certain hours and write petitions for those in need...."[46] When his artisans, in 1850, had to find employment in Turin, Don Bosco would make "careful enquiries beforehand about the integrity of the people to whom he was to entrust his boys; when necessary, he looked for more reliable employers. In addition he.... checked with the employers about the boys' deportment. Thus he showed both his interest in their diligence at work, and his concern lest the faith and morals of his young proteges be endangered."[47] In promoting both parent-teacher and employer-employee relations, Bosco was strengthening the bonds between his Oratories and the community at large.

The Festive Oratory program reflected this, as did the administration and organization of these institutes. As youth centres they afforded thousands of deprived and underprivileged youths an education and an opportunity to train for a vocation. These clubs also kept potential delinquents off the streets and helped promote their social rehabilitation, for those who came under his care were not the elite; they were not specially chosen from the ranks of the privileged classes, they were often, to the contrary, difficult social outcasts. His results were, therefore, all the more surprising, for he worked among the downtrodden, the socially deprived of Piedmont.

By 1846, Don Bosco's Festive Oratory program, for Sundays and holidays, was established. The gates opened at 8.00 a.m., confessions were heard, then followed Mass with Bosco giving an apposite sermon. Then there was recreation time with the boys playing the games of their choice. During this time, he would get to know the new arrivals and put them at ease. After play, music and reading lessons; lunch, after which, at 1.00 p.m. there were more games. Group work in catechism occupied them to 2.30 p.m., then followed hymn singing. In the late afternoon Don Bosco gave the boys a general talk which would always include lively and amusing anecdotes underlining some moral idea.[48] At sunset it was time for them to return to their everyday lives:

> This dismissal usually took place as follows: at a sound from the bell, they would assemble either in church or outside, depending on the weather, to recite the Angelus and night prayers. Afterwards, six of the stronger boys would hoist him up onto their shoulders as though on a throne, and Don Bosco would have to consent. They would then line up in several rows, and singing as they went, carry him as far as the circle known as the Rondo. There they would let him down, and sing a few more sacred songs.... Then a deep silence would ensue as he bade them all good night and a pleasant week, and invited them to come back the following Sunday. With all their might they would then shout in unison: "Good

night! Viva Don Bosco!" Finally, they would all go home, except for a few of the older boys who used to linger and escort Don Bosco to his home.... dead tired.[49]

By 1854 many of the methods employed by the priest-educator at the Oratory reflected those of a democracy. The prize-winners for outstanding behaviour were selected, by secret ballot, by the students themselves.[50] At the commencement of each school year, the duties and regulations for teachers and students were read out at an assembly attended by both staff and pupils. Each day, part of the first lesson was given over to a guidance lesson where "the teacher would give a short talk on the importance of study, the means to achieve solid, lasting progress, the necessity and nobility of an upright life, and the obedience required to co-operate with one's teachers."[51] The democratic atmosphere was developed thereby, with emphasis on reciprocal responsibility, with guidelines for the rest of the day, suggested early, staff and pupils alike being reminded of their responsibilities towards one another in a two-way pedagogical process.

The democratic spirit of Bosco's schools was reported by Father Ruffino, who lived at the Oratory, and observed the priest-educator at close range. Ruffino wrote:

> The boys were given all the freedom compatible with discipline and good conduct. When the bell summoned them to school, they were not required to line up; in the hot season they could remove coats and ties in the study hall. Assistants often reminded Don Bosco that order and decorum demanded otherwise, but he was loath to yield to this, so anxious was he to avoid all regimentation.[52]

Associated with this was Don Bosco's habit of delegating authority. When a suitable boy presented himself or when a citizen offered co-operation, Bosco would put him in charge of some work, make him feel responsible and important in the general running of the Oratory.[53] In 1848, for example, he delegated Joseph Brosio, an ex-serviceman, to form a cadet unit at the Oratory, and organize gymnastic displays involving military tactics and manoeuvres, which were very popular with the boys.

Concomitant with the principle of delegation was Bosco's system of centralization which allowed for things to be done by others but with the educator's knowledge. His paternalism led to an appreciation of what was being done and an overall awareness of how educationally effective the Oratory was at any given point in time.[54]

He attempted to share this information with his staff in what we might call regular staff meetings, which, by 1875, were held weekly. Department heads discussed the 'goings-on' of the Oratory, with a view to improving communication between subject departments, teachers, and pupils generally.[55]

Communication with the students on their grades and marks, although an extensive system of registration for the awarding of marks was established, led to a time-consuming procedure in case there were errors of judgement made by the teachers in pupil evaluation:

> The pupils.... aware that Don Bosco checked their grades and that the study hall marks for application were handed to him every Sunday, gave them great importance.... When the boys' grades were low, Don Bosco would check them against his application mark in the study hall and sometimes found that his teacher and the study hall assistant differed in their opinion of the student.... Don Bosco did not immediately pass judgement, but sought the cause which was sometimes beyond the pupil's control....Don Bosco would call these boys to his room, one at a time on different days.... To each he would give practical advice for using his time profitably.... Besides the official conduct register, he kept a private one with the names of all the pupils. Anytime he received an unfavourable report about a pupil or heard of even a slight fault of a kind to alert a prudent educator.... he would place a secret checkmark by his name according to his offence.... Only about ten percent of the pupils would have several checkmarks beside their names. He would then turn his attention to these, looking more minutely into their conduct, placing them under special supervision, observing the friends they associated with, having them questioned, or questioning them himself....
> Don Bosco also noted in this private register the students who were to discontinue their schooling and take up a trade or craft, the artisans deserved to be given a chance at studies, and those pupils who were to be taken back conditionally after the summer vacation.[56]

Communication, too, with the outside everyday world was maintained, and by 1860 Bosconian schools were publicly recognizable.

According to Canon Vigliotti for instance, who visited Bosco's new school in Giaveno, 30 km to the west of Turin, Bosconian schools were easily recognizable by their outside appearance. When Vigliotti saw the see-saws, parallel bars, and athletic equipment in the playground, he remarked: "It's obvious that Don Bosco was here."[57] Members of the community were often invited to view his work. Bosco realised that without benefactors, his educative mission would not succeed, and so community involvement in his enterprises was a financial necessity which led to close association with the commercial world. Many citizens were invited to participate in his ventures, and to visit the schools. These occasions also gave his boys an opportunity to display their knowledge and skills and impress the visitors with their efforts, furthering again Bosco's pedagogical methods.

In 1857 for example, Bosco organized an educational program to mark the laying of the cornerstone to his new church named after his spiritual mentor, St. Francis de Sales:

> After Father Moreno signed the document of the cornerstone blessing, there followed a musico-literary program which was truly delightful. James Bellia read a speech, several pupils recited brief poems, and six of the smaller boys put on a skit, written by Don Bosco, to accompany the presentation of a bouquet of flowers to the mayor.[58]

In May, 1852, in response to the community's overwhelming support in subscribing to a lottery run by Don Bosco to raise funds for educational evening class work by the Oratory, the following invitation was written by the pedagogist and sent to benefactors and to other prominent people; reflecting, perhaps inadvertently, some of his educational ideas:

> Turin, 14th May, 1852.
>
> Dear Friend,
> Your interest in the welfare of the Oratory of St. Francis de Sales prompts me to send you this invitation. Please honour us by your presence this coming Sunday, May 16th, from 2.00 to 5.00 p.m.
> The students frequenting our evening classes will give a demonstration of what they have learned. There will be nothing spectacular, but nevertheless it will be sufficient to show you that they have put their heart and soul into their work.

The demonstration will consist of:
1. Reading and writing, elementary arithmetic, the metric system, Italian grammar, vocal and instrumental music.
2. Elementary biblical geography, New Testament history, vocal and instrumental music.
3. Two dialogues: *Touring the Holy Land*, and *The Boy Who Didn't Win a Prize*.
Prose and poetry selections will be presented between numbers. I hope you will be able to accept this invitation. I welcome the opportunity to thank you again for all you have done and, I hope, will continue to do on behalf of my boys.

Your grateful servant,
Fr. John Bosco.[59]

Among the distinguished gathering at the Oratory to witness this performance were senators and aldermen from the government, Ferrante Aporti, the well-known educator, other prominent citizens, and the Bishop of Casale, Louis Calabiana. The efforts of the evening students moved the audience "to frequent and prolonged applause. The guests had come to the Oratory expecting to witness a recital by children; instead they saw sturdy young men who, unlike many others of their peers, spent their free time in completing their education."[60] Aporti, who in 1844 had directed Turin's Method School, declared that Bosco's evening class part-time students were as competent as full-time day students anywhere in Piedmont.[61]

There are still some educators who judge educational efficiency in terms of the pupils' silence: the quiet, orderly class is the functional one wherein positive work is being accomplished. In his own time, educators such as these did not hold with Don Bosco who believed that the business of education included those aspects of noise which were necessary and sufficient conditions of the learning process. There were given times, according to Bosco, when noise was natural and desirable. Strangely enough, visitors who examined Bosco's methods, were always impressed with the self-discipline of his boys and the control they exhibited, especially when left by themselves. Perhaps the attainment of self-discipline included their allowed, and therefore legitimate, use of noise which was an important expression of self.

A feature of Bosco's pedagogy was to become this understanding of a boy's natural noisiness and exuberance. In 1847, at the conclusion of catechism classes which were held in the body of the church for example, the boys would become boisterous and shout "Story! Story!" knowing that their teachers would indulge them in this regard. "The boys' shouting might have sounded irreverent in church, but Don Bosco knew that after sitting quietly for so long, they needed some outlet...."[62] and it was acceptable behaviour. On other occasions he used noises to advantage: hymn-singing was employed as a cover to "muffle the sound of shuffling feet"[63] and also to deter "the inevitable whispering of a large crowd of boys"[64] before evening prayers.

Nevertheless, there were occasions when noise—or lack of it —was an expression of rudeness and contempt. In dealing with rude recalcitrants who were reluctant to talk, Bosco was "unfailingly courteous and cordial"[65] but firm. The prudent educator made sure that he refrained from giving orders,[66] and that a word of reproach was to be phrased in such a way as to sound like suggested advice.[67] He rejected force: using time, love, forbearance, and outward concern for a person's welfare in order to induce co-operation. "Even the most callous boys have a soft spot. The first duty of the educator is to locate that sensitive spot, that responsive chord in the boy's heart, and take advantage of it."[68]

One method of dealing with a boy's indifference had been noted by Lemoyne, in 1855, while he was staying at the Oratory:

> ....During the first week, whenever the church bell summoned the boys to prayer, the youth would wander along the porticoes, sometimes humming popular songs. No one reproved him for doing so or tried to coax him to join the others. This apparent indifference annoyed him, and he began to feel a little bored at this self-inflicted isolation. Curiosity finally got the best of him and he decided to peek into the church. With no reverence for the sacred place, he walked to a corner and stood looking around. Some boys were praying, others crowding around a confessional; still others were receiving Holy Communion. "Idiots!" he muttered to himself, but loud enough to be heard by at least a few near him. He just wanted to assert himself, and perhaps he may also have been

trying to stifle a new feeling that he definitely wanted to resist. Things went on in this way for a while; he continued to go to church, but always in a manner showing indifference and contempt. By now several of the older and better boys belonging to the St. Aloysius Sodality[69] had made friends with him and coaxed him to play with them in order to keep him away from those boys on whom he might have a bad influence.... Then one day he approached Don Bosco's confessional and took his turn.[70]

Bosco's methods are known to have worked with young criminals. In 1855, for instance, the educationist received permission from a pessimistic, but curious Government Minister, Urbano Rattazzi, to take 300 prisoners from La Generala, a State prison in Turin, on a picnic into the countryside.[71] Bosco's condition, grudgingly granted by Rattazzi, was that no armed guards, or plainclothed policemen, were to accompany them, either there or back: the educator wanted to supervise them himself. Later, in the evening, when Bosco brought them all back to the jail, and had safely delivered them into the hands of the prison authorities, Rattazzi, now relieved, but still astonished at what Bosco had achieved, asked him to divulge the secret for the controlling of juvenile delinquents. Bosco replied: "Your Excellency ....our strength is moral. The State relies on commands and punishments, whereas we speak in God's name and appeal to the boys' hearts."[72] As recently as 1954 a similar situation was experienced by Salesian educators in Italy.[73]

When Don Bosco was in Paris, in 1883, a journalist asked him whether his educational system depended on punishments. Bosco assured him that he regarded repressive techniques as anathema. Discipline was fostered, he suggested, by a balanced program of work and play adequately supervized in an atmosphere of friendliness. The main idea, Bosco believed, was to maintain a family atmosphere with each member contributing to its welfare.[74]

In a similar atmosphere, Don Bosco's public sermons became uncomplicated and straightforward; with frequent use made of relevant, practical illustrations or examples. He had hit on this technique in 1837, after preaching at Capriglio where he was told by the local pastor Father Joseph Pelato, that his sermons, although theologically brilliant, were too academic and little understood by the local congregation.[75] Later, Bosco recalled this incident: "I kept this fatherly advice as a guide for the rest of my life. As things to avoid, I have saved those sermons in which I now see nothing but vanity and affectation. I am grateful to God for this merciful lesson, which bore fruit in my sermons, catechetical instructions and writings in which I busied myself even then."[76] Consequently, Bosconian sermons became well-known for their sincerity, simplicity, and relevancy,[77] while his lessons at the Oratory followed the methods adopted in the pulpit: plain language, clear explanations and illustrations accompanied by a pleasant disposition and a sense of humour.

In this atmosphere many young men were coming on weekends and evenings to learn to read and write. The simple lessons employed both to develop their confidence and to maintain their concentration after a day's work, were based on syllable sounds and on recognition. In 1841 Bosco hit on the idea of using the common diocesan catechism as a reader for them, this being a part of their lives and of their community:[78]

> For quicker and better learning, Don Bosco followed this system. He had them learn the alphabet and the formation of syllables for one or two Sundays. Then he took the little diocesan catechism and made them practise reading until they were able to read one or two questions and answers, which he then assigned to them as a lesson for that week. The following Sunday, after reviewing the assigned material, he went on to other questions and answers, and so on. Thus in the course of a few weeks, they were generally able to read and study for themselves whole pages of the catechism. This was a great step forward....[79]

Bosco's educational use of the catechism and the fact that his classes contained the most 'difficult' cases brought many curious visitors to the Oratory to observe his teaching methods. More often than not, these catechism classes were held outdoors:[80]

> One Sunday (in 1850) several Englishmen came to the Oratory to ascertain personally the truth of what they had heard about the priest of Valdocco.... After watching the unusual sight in amazement for several minutes, the Englishmen exclaimed,

"If all priests acted like that and taught catechism even in the fields, the whole world would be converted in no time at all!"[81]

The teaching of the catechism was an essential part of the content aspect of Bosco's work, and often dealt with difficult abstractions and concepts. He gave advice to his catechists,[82] teachers of religion, who were often young men finding it hard to handle boys little younger than they. From 1846 to 1866 for instance, he taught the older, and more interested young men, ways and means to effectively communicate religious knowledge to boys, many of whom were not particularly concerned with religion. He recommended that the teacher should stand during the lesson; in this way the boys' attention was more readily gained. Boys' answers to questions, he suggested, should be briefly commented on by the teacher who was to make sure not to digress, at this point, into areas beyond the scope of the lesson. He also advocated group work, in which some memorization of maxims, relevant to life, could be attempted. When the catechists themselves were to speak it was to be clearly and unequivocably, so that the class could grasp what was being taught. He advocated adequate lesson preparation, lest the teacher cut a poor figure in front of the class, and made the suggestion that catechists meet weekly to exchange ideas, improve techniques, and assess what they were trying to achieve. Lastly, catechists were reminded that to teach the boys to live in the world they should show them the value of good manners, deportment, proper speech; "how to act with superiors, fraternize with equals, converse with distinguished people, relax, and, in short, how to conduct oneself in different circumstances...."[83] above all, Bosco believed, effective catechetical teaching was by example rather than words. A catechist who was courteous, candid, and modest in his dealings with the boys, was worth more than thousands of words in any classroom.

Concerned as he was with his students' ease within the society in which they lived, Don Bosco was, nevertheless, alert to the need for a more global approach to communication. The study of languages, he believed, was vital to any educational program. He once said to his boys: "I urge you to take every opportunity to study languages. Every language that we learn removes a barrier between ourselves and millions of our fellow beings in other countries, and enables us to help a few and sometimes very many of them.[84]

In 1868, he broke away from traditional practice and included, in the language curriculum at the Oratory, the Latin classics of the Church Fathers.[85] His attitude towards the teaching of Latin was not, however, divorced from the boys' surroundings. By 1875, he had the works of Jerome, Augustine, Ambrose, Leo, and Seerus replace the time-honoured pagan ones because he believed that what the Church Fathers had to write was more relevant to the boys' needs.[86] This was no surprising decision on Bosco's part; he had, as early as 1853, urged the boys to study the Christian authors, as well as the traditional ones, for Latin style and content.[87] Bosco believed that the combination of Christian moral standards and classical style Latin would result in a better appreciation of the Latin language, and of the philosophy of the Church Fathers.

> "Do you really want to learn Latin?" Don Bosco would ask them.... "Do this: translate a paragraph from a classical author into Italian. Then, without looking at the original text, put your translation back into Latin, and then compare. Do this every day for a month. You'll be surprised how you'll begin to depend less and less on your dictionary."[88]

Don Bosco fostered a love and appreciation of poetry, too, in his schools. He would encourage the boys to write and recite[89] poems suitable for special Oratory celebrations: "....these events aroused and inspired budding poets. We still have hundreds of poems which we gathered as cherished souvenirs of happy days— some quite primitive, others truly elegant; through all beats a warm heart."[90] Linking creative writing with a momentous occasion in this way, gave immediacy as well as an opportunity for self-expression to students, so that the love of poetry developed naturally. Many present day English teachers are familiar with Brian Powell's *English Through Poetry Writing* (Ian Novak, Sydney, 1967) from the *Teaching Method Series* edited by W.F. Connell and W.H. Frederick, and improvements in students' command of language, as well as appreciation for poetry as a literary form, have resulted from what is claimed in the Foreword to be a "modern approach".

Don Bosco's methods in the teaching of music attracted the attention of professional music teachers Louis Rossi, Joseph Blanci, and Joseph Cerutti.[91] Don Bosco himself explained: "They, of course, had not come to learn music from me, but were interested in the method which is now in use in all our schools."[92] These music teachers had come, in fact, to see how the priest-educator taught boys to sight read music and how to take high notes in singing without straining for effect. They freely admitted having gained from the visit to Don Bosco, "whose method they later imitated."[93] Bosco's musical methods were successful because they were geared to cope with sudden changes in performances, loss of personnel, vagaries of temperament, and staff fluctuations within the school situation. Playing safe, he would teach solo parts to several boys at the same time; a group learning to read Vesper psalms would be taught to sing the antiphons the following Sunday. Meanwhile, a new group would be drilled in sight reading. Bosco had a policy that all his boarders were to learn Gregorian chant; no one was admitted to his singing classes until this was done. Newcomers to the Oratory were taught to read music; the others, meanwhile, were familiar with the working together "in singing psalms, antiphons and Masses."[94]

All this took place, according to Lemoyne, because Bosco believed "it would also perfect the moral and intellectual education of his pupils. The love and study of music was to become a permanent and distinctive feature of all his schools, because he considered it a necessary element of school life,"[95] as well as a means to self-expression and joy. Over the doorway leading into the music hall, Don Bosco had inscribed "Ne impedias musicam" (Forbid not music).[96] That few educators, at this time would have considered such a prospect for school students, is suggested by a journalist of the period, on Turin's *L'Armonia*. The enthusiasm and quality of singing of Bosco's choir at Susa had so impressed him that he wrote, on 8th June, 1854; "It is unfortunate that this aspect of educating the young is not more known and practised....."[97]

Games, singing classes, learning to play musical instruments, excursions, gifts to those who attended catechism classes, the putting on of plays, were some of the diversionary methods used by the pedagogist in 1848, to offset the war fever which was sweeping Turin.[98] Quick to respond to social and political changes, and to use student reactions to them for educational purposes, Don Bosco:

> . . . .adapting himself to the spirit of the times insofar as it did not conflict with faith and morals. . . . allowed the boys to engage in sham military drills in the Oratory playground. He even found a way to provide them with a good supply of mock rifles. As a condition for playing with them, he laid down the rule that the boys were not to come to blows as the Piedmontese and Austrians were doing, and that at the sound of the bell and were to put aside their arms and file into church. He also got them started on some new, less dangerous gymnastics. . . . and similar games. . . . he held sack races, and he presented short comedies and skits. In short, he stopped at nothing to provide diversion and amusement for all tastes. . . . Another very effective diversion was the singing class. To this he added piano and organ instruction and instrumental music, to the great delight of many boys. . . .Pride in their accomplishments, excursions to parishes where they were to sing, refreshments and even dinners tendered them soon made the boys forget the political turmoil around them.[99]

Don Bosco had a great use for games: they were a means to relaxation which, Bosco believed, was characterised by an atmosphere of exuberance and freedom, provided that the student was allowed to play the game of his choice. Bosco urged his teachers to submit to the wishes of their students during recreation time. Not only did games build healthy bodies, but they boosted morale. The priest-educator was convinced that there was a connection between the relaxation and enthusiasm of games and a good life. One of his favourite sayings, "be happy" was often only an invitation to play games.[100] But the greatest use of games, according to Bosco, was in the method of associating the teachers and pupils in a pleasant non-competitive atmosphere, then transferring that association to the classroom where the pleasantries of the playground would carry over into the less exciting business of schoolwork.[101] Having co-operated eagerly at play, they would now strive together at work, in a co-operative rather than competitive spirit, since the games played were not in any sense the type of competitive sports played elsewhere.

The simple, direct and entertaining mood of games was reflected in a book Don Bosco wrote as a sort of school textbook, in 1847.

His *Bible History*, (Storia Sacra), which was published in dialogue form, was "immediately adopted by many public and private schools, for which it was intended."[102] The method he used, which particularly appealed to younger readers, was to follow a biblical event with a corresponding and relevant maxim "expressed in terms which young minds could understand,"[103] accompanied by an appealing format: illustrations, maps, glossaries. Written in simple language, it was divided into eras, each chapter being confined to one basic subject. The educationist Aporti, among others, praised this publication.[104]

Another book written by Bosco which was to be publicly acclaimed[105] was :*The Metric System Simplified*, preceded by the four basic operations of arithmetic, for artisans and farmers.[106] Although Piedmont had until 1st January, 1850, to convert to the metric system, Bosco, anticipating the confusion this changeover would have in most people's minds, produced his book in 1846. In its Foreword he wrote:

> To forestall such mistakes and aid the public as well as I can, I have compiled this booklet with a view to rendering the metric system as simple and intelligible as possible, so that even people of limited education can understand it without the help of a teacher.[107]

The method he used to make the metric system easily understood by all involved the calculation of a conversion formula which, in its initial stages, proved difficult. Apparently, Professor Giulio, distinguished mathematician at Turin University, was also working on the Metric conversion problem, but could not readily arrive at a solution. Don Bosco, meantime, had left the Oratory and had sought the quietness of a friend's home, "determined to stay there undisturbed until he had found a solution."[108] Eventually he arrived at a method which Professor Giulio checked and used in his own work on the metric system.[109]

In writing these two books, Bosco had satisfied children's and citizen's needs in the areas of history, ethics, and mathematics. His methods were timely, relevant, straight-forward, pragmatic: they were aimed at producing results in social efficiency. At the same time, by "promoting something the government had at heart he was winning its goodwill and allaying the suspicions of those who opposed him",[110] thus ensuring the continuance of his educational institutions during troublesome times.[111] A tradition in Salesian work which has grown from these publications of Bosco's is in the printing houses scattered throughout the world. They are both training and producing institutions, serving educational purposes in several languages.

In 1864, during a series of talks[112] to the boys at the Oratory, Bosco suggested some methods of study which reflected his educational ideas. He advised wise use of time; working one step at a time; moderate and regulated eating habits; association with diligent students; regular recreational breaks; perserverance with difficult problems; no side-stepping of hard work. Reminding his boys that learning was not expected to be easy, he prepared them for those times when rigour as well as vigour was a student's lot, in this way honestly stating the situation so they would not be discouraged when they encountered difficulties.[113] On the other hand, he was prepared to go to great lengths to motivate children to begin and sustain their education. For example, in 1848, to off-set the materialism of prevailing social pressures, he introduced novelties to win lost boys back to his Oratory.[114] Non-boarders were provided with free meals; a cadet unit was provided with rifles and put under the instruction of Joseph Brosio, an ex-army N.C.O.[115] Again, in 1856, to keep hundreds of boys from harm,[116] during Constitution Day celebrations, Don Bosco hung confections and bottles of drink up on clotheslines in the Oratory playground and organised games with the food as prizes.[117]

Earlier, in 1855, Bosco had instituted an excursion to Becchi for a holiday, as a reward for good conduct at the Oratory, and as a means of keeping the boys interested and occupied, he formed a brass band which played at official functions in Turin, later becoming well-known for its concerts in the surrounding towns and villages of Piedmont.[118]

These methods, too, became a part of the Salesian tradition: excursions, outdoors work, games, novelties, and contests. The contests were not highly competitive, but were close to the spirit of a game in which "he offered them prizes and whatever other encouragement he felt to be necessary."[119] Don Bosco was prepared to use all types of incentives to gain the attention of youngsters, but these were always to be used in an atmosphere of friendly concern for the boys. Once, to convince Cardinal Tosti, a member of the Roman hierarchy, that real education could only begin by gaining the confidence and love of the educand, he went into a Roman park among young strangers to demonstrate how, by using motivational techniques, children could be won over to him. By being friendly, producing gifts, joining in with their games, speaking to each one in turn, offering encouragement and advice, the educator was accepted by this group of urchins, to the delight of the Cardinal who witnessed the scene.[120]

Bosco's methods of education were regarded by some critics, however, as being dangerous and revolutionary. Most Catholic educators of his time did not agree with boys being allowed "to indulge in every kind of uproarious activity" for the "system of education then dominant in the schools was symbolized by a teacher's sour look and a whip; consequently Don Bosco's new method seemed too liberal."[121]

His use of so many extra-curricular devices to gain the attendance of poor, deprived youths at his Oratories, his constantly devising new games for their recreation,[122] led to doubts about both him and his methods. He often spoke in public about his work, in the Piazza Emanuele Filiberto[123] for example, a favourite place where he could move up to groups of youths, talk, play cards, and gamble with them if necessary. Afterwards they would go back to the Oratory together for lunch. Often, standing on a chair, he preached a sermon to the crowds in the Piazza, using in this way, the methods of mass communication available to him at the time. He would comb the streets, cafes, hotels, and barber-shops of Turin, looking for needy boys,[124] and once he attracted their attention, would turn church sermons into witty and amusing dialogue discussions to gain the boys' interest and attention.[125] To encourage research, the questioning of accepted ideas, to spur on their quest for knowledge he would then give them puzzles to solve; or he performed sleight of hand tricks, offered food snacks, played instruments, and gave away boys' clothing.[126]

In times of compulsory schooling, such broadcasting or advertising on the part of the educator would conceivably be regarded as opposed to established methods of approach, and although education was not compulsory in Don Bosco's day, it is hardly surprising that his unorthodox methods met with resistance from some. Similarly, his boys' habit of questioning was regarded with suspicion; they were well-known for their repeated questioning. It was Bosco who encouraged this line of approach. Father Ghiringhello, a Turinese ecclesiastic, once called in on Don Bosco and requested that his boys give him—and his fellow theologians—a respite because they were exhausted by the continual bombardment of questions fired at them by the young members of the Oratory.[127]

In 1875, the acceptance of a multiplicity of motivational techniques was in evidence among his fellow Salesians when they attended regular conferences with Bosco in the chair. He acted more like a father than a superior, at these meetings:

> Over and above the items on the agenda, the material.... that constituted the principal purpose of the conference, he had the opportunity of speaking privately with each one individually and thereby getting first hand knowledge of their inclinations; he also had a chance to encourage and advise them.[128]

Don Bosco's teaching methods attracted the attention of secular bodies, as well as other religious Orders. From time to time the Christian Brothers would come to Bosco's evening classes to observe his methods, what intrigued them being Bosco's way of handling large numbers of boys at the one time.[129] In 1847, a municipal committee with Joseph Dupre as Chairman, officially inquired into the pedagogical methods employed by Don Bosco in his evening schools:

> Since everyone in Turin was talking about Don Bosco's school as a great novelty, and since many professors and eminent people frequently dropped in, word reached City Hall...A committee was formed of (Joseph) Cotta and Mr. Capello.... under the Chairmanship of Commendator Joseph Dupre, to find out whether the rumoured results were really as good as people said they were, or whether they were much exaggerated. The committee members themselves tested the boys' reading knowledge, their enunciation, their knowledge of arithmetic and the metric system, public-speaking, and their knowledge of other subjects. They were quite at a loss to explain how boys who had been completely unschooled until the age of sixteen or eighteen, could have made such progress in so few

months. The committee also noticed that a large number of young adults were gathered at the school to get an education, instead of roaming the streets, and by the time the members of the committee left, they were full of admiration and enthusiasm. The municipal authorities were so satisfied by the committee's favourable report that they awarded a yearly subsidy of 300 lire to Don Bosco's schools, which he immediately spent for his boys....[130]

Chevalier Mark Gonella, Director of La Mendicita Instruita School was also impressed by Bosco's methods, and had his School Board of Trustees grant the Oratory 1,000 lire in recognition of Bosco's work. In 1848, Gonella used Bosco's methods in his own institute, while in the same year, and in the light of Dupre's report of 1847, the municipal schools of Turin adopted Bosconian pedagogical methods, generally.[131]

Canon Ballesio observed that Bosco, in 1863, was "up-to-date in everything: music, arithmetic, grammar, Italian and Latin poetry, ecclesiastical and civil history, and moral and dogmatic theology.... Even in those subjects which seemed outside his field, he was able to hold his own, thanks to his many talents and singular insight."[132] This quality of growth, marked by an eclectic adaptability and willingness to change with changes, has become an accepted part of Salesians' apprehension of their founder's theories. Angelo Franco for instance, a Salesian pedagogist, declared that Bosco's educational program was "full and up-to-date"[133] and that Bosco had never hesitated to make use of every modern method to further his educative mission.[134] Paul Albera[135] understood the Bosconian educational method as being based on "The spirit of Don Bosco.... a living and pulsating spirit" and added, "we cannot remain indifferent to the new tendencies of our age and keep aloof from them. Our spirit must make itself felt; while holding firmly to our traditions we must align ourselves with the best forces of the age...."[136] According to Auffray, too, a living spirit alert to change kept the Salesian movement alive. For instance, it survived the crises of the 1840's because Bosco could "adapt himself marvellously to the demands of contemporary tendencies."[137]

His attitude towards the teaching of less gifted children also showed how advanced he was for his educational times. He anticipated the modern concept of individual differences, in relation to intelligence, as early as 1875:

> As a general rule teachers tend to prefer pupils who distinguish themselves by careful work and intelligence. They are apt to direct their teaching exclusively to them. They are fully satisfied to have the best pupils in their class understand, and they keep up this manner of teaching until the end of the year. On the other hand, boys who are slow or behind in their studies irritate these teachers, who end up neglecting them to their own devices.
>
> Now I see things differently. I feel that it is every teacher's duty to give his attention to the more backward pupils of his class, he should question them more frequently than the others; for their benefit he should explain things at greater length; he should repeat things over and over again until they have understood; and he should adapt the lessons and the homework to their ability. If he follows any other method he will not be teaching the class but only a few choice pupils.
>
> One can easily keep the brighter pupils busy by assigning extra homework and lessons, rewarding them with marks for diligence. Rather than neglect slower students, less important matter may be omitted, and more important topics be adapted especially for them.[138]

Adaptable in times of change, Bosconian methods were tailored to meet the needs of the boys. Bosco accepted worthy ideas of his day and used them to suit his purposes, in the adaptation of which was seen the stamp of Don Bosco's particular personality, so that his Salesians followed him and his ideas in a spirit of adventure. He was, Henri Gheon asserted, a century before his time.[139]

Notes to Part I of Chapter 3

1   "Love and do what you wish."

2   Lemoyne, *op. cit.*, *B.M.* Vol. I, p.254.

3   *ibid.*, Vol. I, p.279.

4   *ibid.*, Vol. I, p.297.

5   *ibid.*, Vol. I, p.382.   Don Bosco wrote down nine resolutions in all, according to Lemoyne.

6   *ibid.*, Vol. III, p.97.   "Don Bosco used to say: 'Boys value things according to the way they have been taught.   It isn't the value of the gift that matters, but the spirit with which it is given and its timing.   This is what they like.' "

7   *ibid.*, Vol. II, p.172.

8   Ronald A. Knox, (Trans.) Matthew 10, 16, p.9.

9   Lemoyne, *op. cit.*, *B.M.*, Vol. II, pp.409-410.   St Francis de Sales' motto read thus: "Da mihi animas caetera tolle."

10   *ibid.*, Vol. III, pp.144-145.   The expression "God sees you" was a favourite of Margaret Bosco, the pedagogist's mother.

11   *ibid.*, Vol. IV, p.304.

12   *ibid.*, Vol. V, p.515.

13   St Philip Neri, 1515-1595, sometimes called 'The Apostle of Rome', due to his efforts to counter the corrupt church in Rome at that time.   He gathered followers around him and urged them to perform good works.   It was one of Neri's customs to give advice, suited to the needs of the person, when so requested.   Don Bosco had a particular interest in the life of this saint, and often quoted his sayings.

14   Lemoyne, *op. cit.*, *B.M.* Vol. VII, p.100.

15   *ibid.*, Vol. VI, p.223.

16   *ibid.*, Vol. VI, p.225.

17   *ibid.*, Vol. VI, p.226.

18   *ibid.*, Vol. VI, p.227.

19   *ibid.*, Vol. VI, p.227.

20   *ibid.*, Vol. VI, p.229.

21   *ibid.*, Vol. VI, p.229.

22   *ibid.*, Vol. VI, p.161.

23   St Vincent de Paul, 1580-1660, whose charitable works among the peasants, the underprivileged, in France, are legion.   Pope Leo XIII proclaimed Vincent de Paul patron of all charitable societies, outstanding among which is that society which bears his name, founded by the academic Frederic Ozanam, in Paris, 1833.

24   Lemoyne, *op. cit.*, *B.M.* Vol. VI, p.452.

25   *ibid.*, Vol. VI, p.230.

Notes to Part II of Chapter 3

1   Ceria, *op. cit.*, *B.M.* Vol. XVI, p.209.

2   *ibid.*, *B.M.* Vol. XVIII, p.126-127.

3   Peter Ricaldone. *Festive Oratory, Catechism and Religious Formation.* St Joseph's Technical School, Madras, India, 1939. p.168.

4   Lemoyne, *op. cit.*, *B.M.* Vol. I, p.295.

5   *ibid.*, Vol. I, p.295.

6   *ibid.*, Vol. II, p.213.

7   *ibid.*, Vol. VII, p.399.

8   Charles Dickens, 1812-1870, English writer whose largely autobiographical novel *David Copperfield*, had the hero of the book, David, subjected to harsh measures by an educator named Creakle.   In another work, *Nicholas Nickleby*, Dickens satirizes the English educational scene in the guise of Wackford Squeers, a teacher who delighted in the maltreatment of his charges.

9   Thomas Hughes, 1822-1896, English novelist whose chief work *Tom Brown's Schooldays* depicted cruelties exhibited by both teachers and pupils at an English public school.   The hero of the story, schoolboy Tom, was often a most unhappy person due to the repressive measures meted out to him by so-called educators.

10   F.A. Forbes. *Saint John Bosco.*   Salesian Press, Tampa, Florida. 1941, pp.68-69.

11   Ricaldone, *op. cit.*, pp.263-283.

12   Auffray, *op. cit.*, p.261.

13   Ricaldone, *op. cit.*, pp.237-263.

14   *ibid.*, p.258.

15   Lemoyne, *op. cit.*, Vol. III, p.39.

16   Ceria, *op. cit.*, *B.M.* Vol. XI, p.7.

17   Fr Peter Braido, Salesian writer on Don Bosco.   His work on Bosco's Preventive System: *Il Sistema Preventivo di Don Bosco*, published in 1964, is considered by Salesians one of the best expositions on this aspect of Bosco's pedagogy.

18   Peter Braido. *Il Sistema Preventivo di Don Bosco.*   See Parte Prima: Esplorazioni Introduttive: Il tempo, l'opera, la personalita di Don Bosco, pp.19-118.

19   *ibid.*, pp.121-229.

20   Ricaldone, *op. cit.*, pp.96-97.

21 Gheon, *op. cit.*, p.194.

22 Lemoyne, *op. cit.*, Vol. V, p.357.

23 *ibid.*, p.360.

24 *ibid.*, Vol. VI, p.184. Bosco was openly criticized for making Holy Communion available to boys on such a regular basis. Contemporary opinion among the clergy was for fewer communions. They regarded Bosco's move with suspicion: he made the Eucharist too easy for the boys they argued. It is noted that daily communion is now the practice in all Catholic boarding schools throughout the world.

25 Ceria, *op. cit.*, *B.M.*, Vol. XI, pp.44-59. In 1875 Don Bosco was again criticized by fellow clerics for introducing a "crash-course" in theology for late vocations. He recognized that there were maturer people who, having seen and experienced life, desired to enter the priesthood and meet the pressing needs both at home and on the mission fields. His course was called the "Sons of Mary" or "School of Fire" project. Bosco set up an accelerated course in which only essential subjects were taught. The curriculum was adapted to their needs, thus older students, who were anxious to speed up things, graduated much to their personal satisfaction, in quicker time than the younger seminarians.

26 Ceria, *ibid.*, Vol. XVIII, pp.192-193.

27 Ricaldone, *op. cit.*, p.155. Reflecting on Bosco's teaching methods writes: "It has so often been said that, in the work of education, it is example that matters."

28 Lemoyne, *op. cit.*, Vol. v, pp.190-191.

29 Forbes, *op. cit.*, pp.66-68.

30 Lemoyne, *op. cit.*, Vol. IV, p.237.

31 Pietro Stella. *Don Bosco Nella Storia Religiosita Cattolica. Vita E Opere*, Vol. I, p.18.

32 Lemoyne, *op. cit.*, p.377. Further accounts on Bosco's versatility in performing different tasks simultaneously, pp.376-377.

33 *ibid.*, Vol. VI, p.189.

34 *ibid.*, p.191.

35 *Giornale della Societa d'istruzione e d'Educazione*, Vol. I, Nos. XIII, XIV, July, 1849.

36 Lemoyne, *op. cit.*, Vol. III, p.381.

37 Ricaldone, *op. cit.*, p.113.

38 Gheon, *op. cit.*, p.198.

39 *Il Giovane Provveduto.* Lemoyne, Vol. III, pp.6-7, noted: "There were many devotional books at the time, but they were for the most part outdated or not particularly adapted to the needs of young people. With this in mind, he wrote *The Companion of Youth*. . . . As a result, to date (1903), this prayerbook had passed by far the six million mark. We can say that *The Companion of Youth* has been well received in academic and trade schools and among the faithful. . . ."

40 Lemoyne, *op. cit.*, p.434.

41 The artisans were those students who boarded in Salesian hospices and were taught trades by professional educators either in Turin or at one of Don Bosco's Oratories. He left specific directions to his Salesians on the educational welfare of the artisans whom he regarded as very important members of his educational family.

42 Ceria, *op. cit.*, *B.M.* Vol. XVIII, pp.700-702.

43 *ibid.*, Vol. XI, p.200.

44 *ibid.*, Vol. XI, pp.270-271.

45 Lemoyne, *op. cit.*, Vol. VI, p.130.

46 *ibid.*, Vol. III, pp.117-118.

47 *ibid.*, Vol. IV, p.9.

48 *ibid.*, Vol. II, pp.337-339.

49 *ibid.*, Vol. II, pp.340-341.

50 *ibid.*, Vol. V, pp.9-10.

51 *ibid.*, Vol. VI, p.451.

52 *ibid.*, Vol. VI, pp.338-339.

53 *ibid.*, Vol. III, pp.306-310.

54 Ceria, *op. cit.*, Vol. XI, p.189.

55 *ibid.*, Vol. XI, pp.429-430.

56 Lemoyne, *op. cit.*, Vol. VI, pp.218-221.

57 *ibid.*, Vol. VI, p.427.

58 *ibid.*, Vol. IV, p.194.

59 *ibid.*, Vol. IV, pp.283-284.

60 *ibid.*, p.284.

61 *ibid.*, p.284.

62 *ibid.*, Vol. III, p.81.

63 *ibid.*, p.16.

64 *ibid.*, p.16.

65 *ibid.*, p.106.

66 *ibid.*, Vol. IV, p.445.

67 *ibid.*, Vol. III, p.412.

68 *ibid.*, Vol. V, p.237.

69 This was one of the many clubs, which Bosco had organized, that were available for boys at the Oratory. The clubs were important to Bosco's pedagogy because they gave the boys opportunities for self-expression, leadership, and developed their sense of responsibility.

70 Lemoyne, *op. cit.*, Vol. V, p.239.

71 A record of this remarkable outing can be found in the *Bollettino Ufficiale della Direzione Generale delle Carceri*, Nos. 1-2, 1888, p.85.

72 Lemoyne, *op. cit.*, Vol. V, p.145.

73 Salesians were given an opportunity to demonstrate their pedagogical methods in connection with gaols only comparatively speaking, recently. The following is taken from John Colussi's unpublished thesis, entitled *Don Bosco and His Preventive Method of Education*, University of San Francisco, 1969, pp.32-34:

"Arese is a small town in the vicinity of Milan, Italy. Since 1906 the Italian Government was maintaining a borstal for 200 teenagers, from all parts, of Italy, ages 12-18. High walls, grated cells, barred doors and confinement cells were all part of the structure and the system.

"It was offered to the Salesians in 1954, in the face of a dismal failure, at the suggestion of the then Archbishop of Milan, Cardinal John Baptist Montini, later Pope Paul VI.

"The new staff's first act was to publicly hand over the key to the confinement cells to one of the boys. The yell of wild joy with which they disposed of it was comparable only to the avalanche of filthy language by which it was followed.

"Soon, under orders of the 'new-comers', latches were torn off, cells got a scrub, partitioning walls tumbled down, food improved, sport was introduced. The new 'jailers' quite unbelievably—mixed with the 'jailed', appeared friendly, agreed with their complaints....

"This was too good to be true; suspicion haunted the youngsters for several weeks. They wanted to discover why these people went out of their way to be 'nice' to them; surely there was a catch in it! What money, for instance, were they paid?

"Slowly, very slowly, things took shape in their minds. The new educators were not paid, they did it out of genuine interest in the inmates. Some of the youngsters began making friends with one or other of the "cassocked supervisors."

"Not all of them could resist the temptation of freedom. The boys were all court cases, with sentences ranging from a few months to several years. The first decade of the new administration registered ten runaways. . . .

"The life of Don Bosco recounts a peculiar betting game among his pupils: who was his closest friend? Each claimed the honour for himself. When this type of relationship is established, the role of the supervisor evolves from that of supervisor to that of educator.

"The institution never had more than 28 Salesians at one time for the 200 boys. The director, however, advocates a ratio of one educator to three or four subjects, and an excellent guidance and counselling centre, coupled with good psychological treatment.

"The curriculum included sport, theatricals, concerts, excursions, and visits from high national and foreign officials.

"Here also, just as in Don Bosco's own school (in Valdocco) the school spirit is the 'family spirit'."

74 Ceria, *op. cit.*, Vol. XVI, pp.167-168.

75 Lemoyne, *op. cit.*, Vol. I, pp.334-336.

76 *ibid.*, pp.335-336.

77 *ibid.*, Vol. III, pp.45-52.

78 *ibid.*, Vol. II, p.199.

79 *ibid.*, pp.432-433.

80 *ibid.*, Vol. IV, pp.23-24. When Marquis Gustavo Cavour would wish to see Don Bosco during Catechism instruction time, he would bypass the classrooms, and automatically set out for the fields surrounding the Oratory where he knew Bosco would be sitting with his boys.

81 *ibid.*, p.23.

82 *ibid.*, Vol. VI, pp.108-117.

83 *ibid.*, p.113.

84 *ibid.*, Vol. II, p.217.

85 *ibid.*, B.M. Vol. IX, p.426.

86 Ceria, *op. cit.*, B.M. Vol. XI, p.18.

87 Lemoyne, *op. cit.*, Vol. IV, p.443.

88 *ibid.*, Vol. IV, p.204.

89 This was made possible through Bosco's foresight. In 1849, in order to encourage the staging of plays, recitations, vocal and instrumental music, he converted a shed, which he had acquired from a Mr Pinardi, into a large hall with a stage. See Lemoyne, *op. cit.*, Vol. III, p.365.

90 Lemoyne, *op. cit.*, Vol. VI, p.129.

91 *ibid.*, Vol. III, p.102.

92 *ibid.*, p.102.

93 *ibid.*, p.102.

94 *ibid.*, p.103.

95 *ibid.*, p.101.

96 Morand Wirth. *Don Bosco et les Salesiens. Cent Cinquante Ans D'Histoire*, Elle Di Ci. Torino—Leumann. 1969, p.96.

97 Lemoyne, *op. cit.*, Vol. V, p.304.

98 Piedmont and Austria were at war.

99 Lemoyne, *op. cit.*, Vol. III, pp.226-227.

100 Wirth, *op. cit.*, p.93.

101 *ibid.*, p.94. Wirth quotes an extract from a letter written by Bosco in Rome, 1884, dealing with the correlation of games and schoolwork: "qu'etant aimes dans les choses qui leur plaisent, ils apprennent grace a la participation (de leurs educateurs) a leurs inclinations d'enfants, a voir l'amour dans les choses qui naturellement leur plaisent peu." (being loved in those things that please them, they will learn (thanks to their teachers) in their innocent way, to see love in those things which naturally please them little).

102 Lemoyne, *op. cit.*, Vol. II, p.312.

103 *ibid.*, p.308.

104 *ibid.*, p.311.

105 The book won the praise of Aporti, authorities, teachers. A newspaper, *Unita Cattolica*, rated it the best textbook and the first of its kind to be published in Piedmont, according to Lemoyne; Vol. II, p.377.

106 The book's full title was: *Il Sistema Decimale Ridotto a Semplicita, preceduto dalle quattro prime operazioni dell'aritmetica, ad uso degli artigiani e della gente di campagna.* per cura del Sacerdote Bosco, Giovanni.

107 Lemoyne, *op. cit.*, Vol. II, p.375.

108 *ibid.*, pp.376-377.

109 *ibid.*, p.377.

110 *ibid.*, p.377.

111 These books were written and published 1845-1850. During these times, Piedmont had undergone political change, due to the widespread revolutions of 1848, which was not sympathetic to Catholic involvement in education. Bosco, by writing these books, strengthened his association with the pro-liberal government, thereby offering some form of security for his educational institutions.

112   These nightly talks were given by Don Bosco to the boys at the Oratory. They began November 24th and concluded December 4th, 1864.

113   Lemoyne, *op. cit.*, Vol. VII, pp.480-487.

114   Anti-clerical factions in Turin were openly enticing youths in the streets of Turin, to abandon Bosco's Oratories, by providing them with food and money.   Also liberal activists were encouraging the Waldensians, a religious sect, to set up youth centres in opposition to Bosco.   The educationist met this challenge head-on by countering with innovative measures.

115   Lemoyne, *op. cit.*, Vol. III, pp.309-311.

116   During March, Constitution Day is celebrated in Turin.   On this festive occasion many young people become involved with the police.

117   Lemoyne, *op. cit.*, Vol. V, p.303.

118   *ibid.*, pp.222-227.

119   *ibid.*, Vol. II, p.433.

120   Forbes, *op. cit.*, pp.69-70.

121   Lemoyne, *op. cit.*, Vol. II, p.274.

122   *ibid.*, pp.334-336.

123   A popular square and market-place in Turin.

124   Lemoyne, *op. cit.*, Vol. III, pp.39-44.

125   *ibid.*, pp.82-84.

126   *ibid.*, p.89.

127   *ibid.*, p.88.

128   Ceria, *op. cit.*, Vol. XI, p.144.

129   Lemoyne, *op. cit.*, Vol. II, p.436.

130   *ibid.*, Vol. III, pp.21-22.

131   *ibid.*, p.22.

132   *ibid.*, Vol. VII, p.274.

133   Franco, *op. cit.*, p.16.

134   *ibid.*, p.175.

135   Fr Paul Albera, 1845-1921, was Rector Major of the Salesian Society from 1910-1921.

136   Franco, *op. cit.*, p.219.

137   Auffray, *op. cit.*, pp.246-247.

138   Ceria, *op. cit.*, Vol. XI, p.200.

139   Gheon, *op. cit.*, p.164.

CHAPTER 4

DON BOSCO'S PREVENTIVE SYSTEM:
REASON, RELIGION, KINDNESS

REASON

Don Bosco believed that if the educand comprehended the reasonableness of what he was doing, or what was being done, he did not need external and repressive measures inflicted on him for the maintenance of discipline. Moreover, this pervading sense of reasonableness of the part of the educator, brought out in the child a desire to be co-operative, a self-discipline from within and not one controlled by external and repressive forces. Bosco's pedagogy was concerned therefore with providing those to be educated with many varied, interesting outlets such as music, games, physical exercises, drama, concerts, excursions, holiday camps, and means for self-expression in lessons. The educand became absorbed in activities which did not allow him time to fall into wasteful habits which were time consuming and led to social inefficiency.

These activities were means to an end: self-discipline. It was through their participation and involvement with their educators in these educational activities, that the desire to please developed in students, because of the close relationship which existed between educand and educator who shared these activities both inside and outside the classroom situation. Because of high motivational levels in the pupils, arising from these desires to please their teachers, and because of the effective supervision which was exercised in terms of co-operation and collaboration by the educator, faults were prevented, teachers became models to be emulated, set examples to follow, and gave asisstance when it was timely.

For Don Bosco, prevention, in education, was better than cure, because the latter often involved repression or the infliction of a penalty for a fault already committed. By providing the pupil with satisfying outlets for his surplus energy, faults and hence repressive measures were minimized, because there was little time to think about them when in the company of an educator who assisted them in their work and at their play.

These practices were not exclusively Bosco's: his two concepts, of prevention, and change within change led him to seek methodologies consistent with his ideas. Consequently, he selected those methods which suited his purpose and times and then added his own particular style to them, adapting them, adding to them, making them his. As early as 1849 he was studying educational methods "used elsewhere".[1] The pedagogist sent Fr. Peter Ponte[2] to look into, among other things, practices of "teaching methods, discipline, and administration"[3] in other areas, and acted on them. Ricaldone stated that Don Bosco decided on those ideas which would be adaptable "to the new needs" and have "such breadth of spirit and power of adaptability, as to be able to respond to successive needs and varying circumstances."[4]

By 1852, Bosco had prepared the first draft of his Regulations[5] of the Oratory of St. Francis de Sales in which some of his educational ideas, on the preventive system, were set down. Bosco's helpers at the Oratory were presented with his booklet entitled: *Il Sistema Preventivo nell' Educazione della Gioventu*[6] (The Preventive System in the Education of the Young) which stressed that educators were to act charitably and reasonably towards their pupils, were to set good example, and teach them about God's love in an atmosphere free from punishments.[7] The reading out of the Regulations was not an educational panacea, and as Don Bosco himself admitted in 1875: "Still, the essence of all Regulations lies in the firmness of the educator."[8]

Bosco saw the "fitness of the educator" in terms of the latter's rationality. Reason was reasonableness, common sense. To be reasonable, one was to avoid complications, artificialities, exaggerations, formalisms, when dealing with those who were to learn. To be reasonable was to be natural: all artificial manifestations of individual or corporate life were to be excluded from school routine. The Salesian school was to be run on family lines: the educator was both father and teacher; the pupils were his sons. And this, in Bosco's view, was both reasonable and desirable. The father-teacher inspired them by his example, encouraged them by his concern for their welfare; they, who were sons, responded to example and love.

This family-type preventive system of education relied heavily on constant supervision. And much depended on the quality of that supervision exercised by the assistants in Bosco's schools. Salesians talked about "assistance" rather than "supervision." The very word "assistance" suggested what was expected of Bosco's educators. It meant that, where possible, boys were never to be left without some sense of the presence and concern of their teachers. More responsible pupils in his Oratories were entrusted with supervisory duties and became junior assistants,[9] to help make this possible.

Lemoyne reported that Bosco "never relaxed his vigilance"[10] when he was with his boys, especially during the formative years at the Oratory from 1847 on.

Angelo Franco noted that Bosco was severe on anyone who left pupils unsupervised, regardless of the reasons offered.[11] In one case, the Salesian who was admonished by the priest-educator for improper supervision was suffering from heat exhaustion and had left the boys for a time. On his return he was reminded by Bosco that his place was with the children and that he could rest at another time.

Don Bosco, himself, would sometimes combine supervision with counselling, on a tour of playground duty, for instance, he sought out those who needed his help and gave them assistance.[12] He was convinced that 'round the clock' supervision was both reasonable and preventive of disquiet or insecurity, telling the catechists: ". . . . never leave the boys to themselves; keep an eye on them, always and everywhere."[13] This 'assistance' was to be relaxed and natural but painstakingly conscientious; in the event of antisocial or unco-operative or disruptive behaviour, there were to be few admonitions; students were simply moved on to some other activity.[14] Bosco advised his assistants: "Supervise your boys constantly and everywhere; make it just about impossible for them to do wrong. Be more alert in the evening after supper, so as to prevent the smallest disorder. . . ."[15]

Often when in the playground during the evening, Bosco subtly enlisted the aid of pupils who were near him to supervise more remote areas of the school while enjoying a game:

On certain evenings Don Bosco would line up in single file the boys who swarmed around him; then, standing at their head, he would bid them play "follow the leader". He would clap his hands, hop on one foot, walk with a stoop or with arms aloft, snap his fingers, or bend his knees. As they tried to keep up with him, some boys would sprawl all over the ground, to the glee of others who were watching. Finally, all would join the line, following Don Bosco around pillars and into hidden corners and dark, deserted areas. Thus singing, laughing, and gesticulating, he made sure that nothing untoward was taking place.[16]

Bosco was so convinced about the efficacy of constant supervision that he enouraged his staff to make daily tours of stairs and corridors, even when they had nothing programmed to do and were not on official duty.[17] The pedagogist was very demanding, asking much of his staff in the supervision of children, since, as far as he was concerned, there was no fine distinction between being on or off duty. It was reasonable that one was always on duty, in a supervisory capacity, when among children.

Lemoyne was of the opinion that Bosco seemed "to have a sixth sense in supervision."[18] In 1863, however, when addressing newcomers to the Oratory, Bosco explained that continuing companionship led to an understanding of students, to a relationship that allowed him to be of assistance to them when they needed it.[19] Rather than make the supervisor appear as an inspectorial figure, Bosco saw him in the roles of helper, companion, adviser.

At the Congregation's General Conference in 1877, Bosco reminded his Salesians that supervision was the responsibility of all and that no one was exempt,[20] and again, in 1885, he told his teaching colleagues that supervision involved friendliness and familiarity between educators and educands. If friendliness was removed, he warned, there would follow a loss of confidence of the pupils in the teachers, and then no joy. Bosco believed that they who wanted to be loved, must be shown through a form of paternal assistance, that they were loved.[21]

Discipline, too, was to be based on reasonableness, and played a vital role in Don Bosco's preventive system. It consisted of obedience to an objective order of rationality which was applicable to all: in practice, obedience to the rules, regulations and traditions which governed the Salesian family. "By discipline," he wrote in 1873, "I understand a way of conducting oneself which is in conformity with the rules and customs of an Institute. Therefore, in order to obtain good results from discipline, it is first of all necessary that all the rules be obeyed by all.... This observance must be found among the members of the Congregation as well as among the boys entrusted to our care."[22]

Hence, in the Salesian Congregation all were equal before those laws which were framed in a setting of justice and charity. Teachers assumed parental roles and made friends of their pupils who in turn saw their educators as friends; friends who were under the same law as they, sharing, according to age and experience, in a fatherly and brotherly authority in an atmosphere of charity. The aim of Bosconian discipline, therefore, was akin to a family discipline based on respect, obedience, confidence, self-surrender, self-dedication, fatherly and brotherly love. Each school became a home: the Rector or Headmaster its father, the staff its brothers, the pupils its children.

This family spirit was to be based on the four principles of: reason, religion, fatherliness and cheerfulness, the single overwhelming factor being that of 'agape' or brotherly love. In this charitable atmosphere Don Bosco, although never relinquishing his punitive authority,[23] seldom had to use it because his boys respected him "with the love of those who know they are loved in return."[24] Chiosso, a boy who frequented Bosco's Oratory in 1847, for instance, declared that the boys' feelings were always on Don Bosco's side because of this: he rarely punished.[25]

In such a family atmosphere, Bosco's discipline was seen as reasonable, purposeful: "In cases of insubordination the policy was to be lenient; punishment was to be replaced with friendly, frequent and effective admonitions."[26] And the methods of correction were said to be effective "because they appealed to the conscience and not to fear of reprimands or punishments."[27]

For those who had little social or religious conscience, such as the tough "Cocca"[28] who frequented the slums of Vanchiglia, Turin, and threatened the security of Bosco's Guardian Angel Oratory there, this policy of the pedagogist made it possible for Bosco to return insolence with kindness, offer them meals, gifts, organise games for them, and by persisting in this way he finally won them over.[29]

"Discipline was no problem" according to Lemoyne, in the Valdocco Oratory of St. Francis de Sales of 1854, "because duties were carried out with love; study and work were enjoyable because they were prompted by a sense of duty and honour."[30] The educands were intent on pleasing their educators by showing them how well they could assume their responsibilities. And this desire to please on their part was due not only to their gratitude for educational chances, but also to the active involvement of their teachers in the objectively placed rules of the establishment. What was carried out by all, staff and pupils alike, was subjected to all. The justice of this principle aimed at prompting a charitable reaction, in relation to school routine, from the Oratory students.

By 1863, Bosco's Oratory methods of discipline were remarked upon, and noted by politicians, noblemen, clergy, and people interested in education from different parts of the Continent. What usually impressed them was the order, discipline, diligence, and cheerfulness of the Oratory boys.[31] That which was seen to be reasonable in behaviour, seemed to have become accepted as reasonable for both teachers and taught in the Salesian community, for Bosco urged his boys to develop a form of self-discipline which the Salesian clerics practised. Through their example the students were being taught that to overcome laziness one had to work, and to overcome themselves they had to relate their work to the welfare of others.[32]

References, academic records, profiles on students were always kept at the Oratory so that ex-students could call in and obtain character references for purposes of employment, thus extending the concept of the caring family beyond schooldays. It was understood, too, that it was reasonable to build a good reputation for such references. Don Bosco, in 1875, for instance, reminded the boys that their progress through the school was carefully recorded, and that references could be important in the everyday world:

Nor should you imagine that the marks given every week lose their value after a number of years. I must tell you something which occurred just a day or so ago, and which happens quite frequently. A gentleman with a handsome beard came to see me. I did not recognise him, but he greeted me by name, and asked, 'Do you no longer remember me? I am So-and-So, who was here at the Oratory a long time ago. I need a character reference.' Now what did I do? I checked the files—we have files going back 10, 15, and 20 years—I write the character reference on the basis of this record; it would be impossible to furnish a reference any other way.

Therefore, remember your records will remain and even many years from now will supply a favourable or unfavourable character reference.[33]

It was reasonable, argued Bosco, that if the disciplinarian was charitable, he could be as firm as he wished.[34] The Salesian educator was to act always in such a way that his demands were tempered with charity and friendliness of manner. In return the boys would comply with what was being asked, because they would recognize the concern their educator had for them. They would know that he cared, and that this care would continue for them beyond the immediate school situation; a caring that was not sentimental, but firm and lasting.

When, in 1879, Don Bosco was asked by Prince Gabrielle, a Roman nobleman who had an interest in St. Michael's hospice, to take over this large but run-down institution, Bosco insisted on three conditions being met, one of which was that his Salesians were to be allowed full liberty in connection with discipline. Upon being questioned on this by Gabrielle, Bosco explained that his methods were different to those used at St.Michael's. He would have no threats or punishments of a repressive nature. He would introduce gentle methods. Reason, love, affection, a special sort of surveillance would be the means used to ensure discipline and morality.[35] The Salesians did not take over St. Michael's, however, because Bosco's methods were not acceptable to Prince Gabrielle and those he represented.

Peter Ricaldone in his work *Fidelity to St. John Bosco*[36] attempted to explain further what Salesian discipline and reasonableness entailed.

It was, he stated, the development of a harmony between authority and freedom, achieved in a concord of educators and educands. Discipline was more reasonably maintained in an atmosphere of companionship and love than in one where repression and fear were dominant. Harmony would develop in a community situation where leaders who set fine examples not only acted, but knew how to act. And discipline was present when each person in the establishment knew his role and acted accordingly. The regulations of the school, therefore, were to be explained and observed by all, regardless of position and status. Orders were to be given clearly and kindly, and were not to be outside of the general framework of the school regulations with which all members were to be conversant. Abusers of the school routine were to be dismissed instantly. A weak Head only increased the indiscipline of the non-observant. Salesian harmony, then, did not permit lawlessness or unreasonable resistance: no one had to remain, none was compelled to stay. Expulsion, though it took place discreetly, nevertheless was accepted as a reasonable action in certain circumstances.

Acceptance of what could be called ground-rules, was essential for teacher and student alike. For instance,.... Don Bosco when asked in 1875: 'Why should we do things?', replied: "Let us not do things because we like doing them, or because we like the person who orders us to do them, or because of the manner in which the order is given. Let us do them, and cheerfully, only because they are commanded...."[37] That the pedagogist asked for a total submission to the laws of the house necessitated an act of the individual will and a negation of the self for a common purpose: the welfare of the school community. This demand, framed in a Christian context, that of the caring family, became reconciled to the Catholic virtue of obedience.

A great deal, nevertheless, was expected of each individual for this concept of obedience to be successfully carried out. A certain amount of strain or tension was to be expected on both sides: educators had to be seen to maintain a harmony among themselves in order to show by good example their own allegiance to the school regulations; the students, in turn, would strive to please their teachers by carrying out their duties without complaint. On the other hand, unquestioning obedience on their part depended, to a large extent, on the reasonableness of the commands or prescriptions given them by the Superiors who could not afford to depart from anything but a rationally balanced approach.

It would appear then that Bosco's educational conception of obedience depended largely on the outstanding personal qualities of each Salesian, particularly the school Head. The system, as such, could not afford one weak leader, too much was at stake: smooth administration and discipline were dependent on outstanding example by those in authority. If this was not forthcoming then student motivation and desires to please their teachers through self-discipline would break down.

Don Bosco was realist enough to see that when his preventive system failed to work in certain cases, he was required to deal with recalcitrants in another way.

He had to come to terms at a point in his pedagogical rationale with the concept of punishments and how they were to be best administered. He was adamant about one thing: corporal punishment was forbidden. By 1852 his thoughts on punishments had crystallized.[38] Striking, humiliating, irritating, were forbidden; so were collective punishments. He found the "cold-shoulder" treatment, and the withdrawing of privileges, effective. He urged his teachers to hear both sides of every case before taking action, then the isolation of the offender, in some cases, was recommended.

To be reasonable in the administering of punishments, the educator should set the mood:

> Do not reprimand or correct when you are angry or upset, lest your pupils attribute it to anger, but wait, even a few days if necessary, until you have calmed down. Likewise, when you must correct, reprimand, or warn a pupil, always try to do it in private and when he is not upset or angry. Wait till he is calm and at ease. Then tell him what you must, but end up with an encouraging word—for example, that from now on you want to be his friend and you will help him all you can.
> And he would add: Be quick to forgive—and do so wholeheart-

edly—whenever a pupil shows he is sorry. In this case forget everything.... When punishment is unavoidable, take your pupil aside and show him his wrong as well as your regret to have to punish him.

Never punish a whole class or dormitory. Try to single out the culprits, and if necessary have them sent away; but never lump together the good and the bad—the latter are always a few—lest all be made to suffer for them. At the same time encourage the guilty ones who show good will and give them a chance to straighten themselves out.[39]

Lemoyne noted that in 1863, Don Bosco when addressing newcomers to the Oratory said: "I tell you quite frankly that I hate punishments. I dislike giving orders and threatening punishments for those who disobey. That is not my way. Even when someone does wrong, I'd rather correct him kindly."[40] But Bosco did add that disorderly and undisciplined pupils would be sent away from the Oratory,[41] which seemed a greater penalty in the long run than that of corporal punishment.

Again, in 1868, Don Bosco alluded to the subject of punishments. He reaffirmed his disciplinary credo: pupils were to be treated kindly when corrected; they were not to be punished in anger, nor were they to be reminded of their misdemeanours once they were corrected. The subject was to be forgotten, the incident closed; all forgiven. Salesian teachers were to edify their charges with exemplary behaviour and teach by good example.[42] Again, the demands upon staff were heavy, yet visitors who came to the Oratory in 1876 could not quite understand how the school ran so smoothly without resorting to the fear of punishment which was common in many other schools of the day. Salesian priests were coming to teach in great enough numbers, not only to maintain, but also to extend the system at this time; on the other hand, other Catholic Orders were not often producing the same atmosphere within their schools, and although it was explained that 'fear of the Lord', not fear of punishment, gave Salesian schools their smooth-running qualities,[43] this could not account for Bosco's success in full; there were many Catholic schools where students tried to satisfy the tenets of their religion. Salesians, however, included the confessional as an added means to an educand's redirected behaviour. Not only could a Salesian educator counsel in the classroom and playground; he could advise in the confessional. A two-pronged corrective correlation was part and parcel of the Salesian priest-educator's method.

In 1883, just five years before his death, Bosco wrote a letter to his school heads on the subject of punishments.[44] Further explanations of his methods suggested: (i) if the pupils were to bend to the educator's will, then the measures adopted were to be those of persuasion and charity and not of coercion; (ii) if human nature had to be constrained by severe methods, his were still to be those based on consoling techniques; (iii) Salesians were not to forget that they were the 'parents' of these youths, hence, when correcting, they were to remain on friendly terms with them; (v) that behind all punishments were principles of reason and justice: never punish until all other means were exhausted; every punishment needed an opportune moment; punishments were not to be administered in anger; when given, the pupil was to be forgiven and left with a sense of hope; that the Rector in order to preserve his fatherly image, and leave the way open for those corrected to seek his advice, was to delegate his authority in relation to punishments.

A. Auffray, in his book *Saint John Bosco*, attempted to sum up Bosco's pedagogy on punishments:

> But in spite of his zealous watchfulness, Don Bosco could not stop some boys going astray. Then, what was to be done in the way of punishment? .... He then required the punishment to be in accordance with the principle of the system. It must take care not to harden the heart of the boy, and thus close it against the positive work of education. In virtue of this principle, punishments, in his Houses, must have the following characteristics: they were to be deferred as much as possible; they were to be neither humiliating nor irritating; they were to be reasonable; they were to be prompted by kindness, with an appeal, as far as possible, to the heart of the child. No public punishments, or hardly any; no irritating corporal punishments; even expulsions, made inevitable by scandals or obstinate disobedience, were carried out with consideration; no punishments for slight and thoughtless offences; no general punishments when the culprit could not be traced; no uniform rule applying a fixed scale without regard for the degree of the offender's culpability; no chastisements to be inflicted while

in anger. But an abundant use of the sort of punishments a mother can use so adroitly: an expression of disapproval, a cold or indifferent remark, and rebukes winning the rational acceptance of the erring one. He often used to say that a punishment is beneficial as soon as its reasonableness is perceived by the child.[45]

Don Bosco's last and most reluctantly enforced disciplinary measure to ensure the survival of the Oratories, expulsion, was used only in very compelling and extraordinary circumstances,[46] nevertheless, he firmly believed that the few who would not comply with school rules had to be stood down. Although a severe punishment, it was a reasonable and charitable one in Bosco's view, because the well-being of the majority had to be considered above that of the few who chose to ignore the welfare of their fellow students. The educand was not simply dismissed without due regard to his own feelings. The priest-educator tried to ensure that the expelled pupil understood why it was better for him to withdraw and made sure that the reputation and character of the expelled was protected. In many cases, employment was found for him.

To Don Bosco there were distinctions between wants and needs; the one could be done without, the other was absolutely necessary. Material goods for example, not strictly necessary, he would rather go without.[47] Lemoyne noted: "Whoever lived at his side for a long time can bear out that he was utterly detached from comforts and riches. Huge sums of money were entrusted to him.... but he always used them exclusively for the benefit of others; nothing ever for himself. His ideal was the poverty of.... Christ."[48] To this end, though his clothes were clean, they were old, and his room furnished with the barest necessities.[49] Personal testimonies of Joseph Brosio, John Cagliero, and Hyacinth Ballesio, all of whom had witnessed the pedagogist at work among his pupils, support this. Brosio remembered for example, in 1857, when Bosco used to say: "Poverty, yes! Dirt, never!"[50] Bishop Cagliero, too, remembered Don Bosco, in front of his boys: in odd white trousers and wearing wooden clogs; and the sympathetic looks on the boys' faces "because they knew that he was poor for their sake."[51] Bosco's socks were all darns, his old factory-reject military greatcoat several sizes too big for him. A military horse-blanket covered his bed.[52] Canon Ballesio testified to the poverty of Bosco's fellow Salesians, too, who worked long hours at the Oratory and showed in their daily routine a self-denial which impressed their onlookers.[53]

It was because of his love of poverty that Don Bosco preferred teaching the underprivileged, the poor, the needy. Bosco believed that it was reasonable that his fellow Salesians had to be poor themselves in order to establish a practical solidarity with them. In modern times, the Salesians are still concerned about poverty and their relationship to it. Some Salesians feel that the forces of materialism are infiltrating the spirit of the Order and that steps should be taken to rectify this. For example, at the 1965 XIX General Chapter of the Salesian Society held in Rome, the Chapter Fathers wrote:

> Our particular mission implies that we should have whatever is necessary and useful for the development of the work of education. Nevertheless "besides the poverty of the individual members, we must not overlook the collective poverty of the institute as a whole: the family as such must bear its witness to poverty. In their buildings and activities religious institutes must avoid all that is showy or affected or that savours in any way of luxury. Let them take into account the social condition of the poor who live in the area."[54]

Again, the Superior Council of the Salesian Society of 1965 decided: "In the equipment of our own living quarters we should also observe the criteria of poverty. The higher the level that we achieve in those parts of the house which are devoted to the education of the boys, according to the needs of the country, so much the greater should be our own dedications to poverty in our personal lives."[55]

Throughout his educational career Don Bosco was mindful, too, of the crises which boys face, particularly in their teens, regardless of class or economic background in relation to sex. The pedagogist was very much aware of the situation of his Salesians among young men and boys, many of whom boarded at the Oratory. Clear unequivocal prescriptions were necessary to deal with this situation, for Bosco wanted to acknowledge that there was no greater problem to prevent, than sexual indiscretions among young men. It was reasonable that rules should be provided to control the situation.

In 1861, Lemoyne noted that Joachim Berto, an observer of Bosconian pedagogy, claimed that the secret to Don Bosco's own sexual balance was "....a constant intellectual activity, an excessive load of work both day and night, and an imperturbable calm...."[56] Don Bosco himself believed that a great deal of the answer lay in the creation of a healthy environment: "It is necessary to have resource to all means to obtain, to foster, to propagate, and to ensure morality."[57] The morality to which he referred contained the broad, Catholic teachings on the roles of sex, personal relationships and family life—in human development and expression. Within the boarding school situation, and within the less demanding day-school, or evening class situation, the first step in the creation of a healthy environment was in the personal example set by the Salesians who had to be seen by their pupils to be above reproach in their dealings with their fellows. Don Bosco made it clear to his followers that their duty was to foster and preserve innocence among the youths entrusted to their care.[58] What was required of Salesian educators was detachment, disinterestedness, amiability, and charity. He instructed his educators to avoid physical contacts: fondling, holding of hands, putting hands around the neck; he discouraged suggestive looks, handshakes, and gifts to students.[59] Only the Head was allowed to appear less detached in order to instil confidence in any pupil who needed encouragement in his studies.[60] Thus, though Salesians were to work in an atmosphere of love and trust, Bosco forbade particular friendships, discouraged Salesians meeting anyone in secluded places, in writing sentimental letters, and offering gifts in a private capacity.[61]

The second step towards creating a Salesian moral environment was that the educator maintain a thorough and untiring assistance or supervision so that moral lapses would be prevented.[62] The elimination of the occasions for sexual improprieties was the ideal. What really happened was that these offences were kept to a minimum, and, when they were discovered, the offender was usually persuaded to leave the Oratory, but not before employment was found for him in Turin. The boys were frequently reminded by Bosco what the penalties were in these matters and that he would act on them when the circumstances demanded such extreme measures.[63]   Consequently, there was little surprise among the boys when one of their number suddenly left the Oratory and was found employment in town.

The environment alone could not guarantee a sexual morality acceptable to the Salesians.   Don Bosco placed great importance on the role of the individual's will and its application to Catholic confession and communion in confronting the vicissitudes of sexual drives.   Precaution, and even flight, through the preventive system, were aids to Catholic morality, but the main issues had to be confronted, argued Bosco, and the ascendancy was essentially that of the intellectual assent of the will over emotional desires which could rise without warning.

Aware of this, through his own personal experiences, and those of his pupils, Bosco devised ways and means which helped the individual to face up to these problems.[64]

The most direct method in maintaining purity was in the practice of temperance in eating and drinking;[65] in prompt rising in the morning,[66] and in not going to bed after dinner.[67]   Another form of temperance was that of the practice of humility: the willing of the intellect to minimise the self.[68]   These acts were based on the theological concept of mortification, which was in turn based on the premise that if spiritual life proceeded from material death, then it was from the control of the superior faculty of the will over the less spiritual instincts, that harmony, equilibrium, and joy sprang forth.[69]

Don Bosco also advocated that his boys busy themselves in their studies and duties; he recognised the correlation between idleness and impurity.[70]   He advised them to shun improper conversations, vulgar companions,[71] and indecent literature.[72]   He was always reminding his pupils to be decorous in their behaviour; the dignity of the human person[73] was constantly raised in discussions he had with them.   Counselling in these matters was two-fold: each boy had recourse to advice through his classroom teachers, and if necessary, through his father confessor.

The positive aspect of purity was underlined by Bosco who referred to it as the beauty of virtue rather than as the negative ugliness of vice.[74] Something beautiful was more attractive and therefore more reasonable for the boys to follow than that which was ugly. The pedagogist was not afraid to ask his boys to attempt the heights of virtuous idealism even though he recognised that the acceptance of sexual purity was not easy. He placed great emphasis on frequent confession,[75] communion,[76] and prayer[77] which he believed were efficacious means to support their ideals of innocence and purity.

In addition, Don Bosco put great trust in personal cleanliness, modesty, and good manners to help the individual maintain a dignity proper to his Christian beliefs in the sanctity of the human body. There were specific directions on modesty and cleanliness in the Constitutions and Regulations of the Society of St. Francis of Sales.[78]

Finally, in relation to the subject of purity, Bosco believed that information on these matters was preferable to silence. By the time his students were ready to leave his schools, they were cognizant of the realities and dangers, as well as the legitimate pleasures of the outside world.[79] Although he wished them to remain innocent, it was considered reasonable that they were not allowed to remain ignorant.

The social value of good manners was stressed in the preventive system of Don Bosco. It was considered reasonable that training in decorum and modesty through the learning and practice of a socially acceptable deportment would assist his pupils in furthering their own careers, in supporting their families and in becoming worthy citizens of the state. Furthermore, Don Bosco believed that lack of manners, and a coarse rough behaviour were inhibitory factors to Christian charity. He believed that it was the duty of every Christian citizen to be polite. Hence, an Oratory education was incomplete without the attainment of social graces.

The Prefect[80] at the Oratory was expected, among other things, to see to it that the boys learned acceptable canons of good behaviour in church, classroom, study-hall, workshop, and auditorium. In addition, he was expected to teach them how to behave towards their teachers and their friends; how to conduct themselves within the school and in the town,[81] where the behavioural patterns of Don Bosco's poor boys were often open to public concern.

At least once a week, from 1859 on, classes were held in deportment and good manners at the Oratory.[82] During these lessons Bosco gave his pupils, who had often had little experience in normal exchanges, advice on how to behave in various social situations. He would often draw on recent happenings in the school to illustrate his talks, or use social dramas and play-acting to help. In 1861, for example, he wrote and produced a three act comedy which was aimed at correcting common breaches of acceptable behaviour.[83] The reasonableness of the social graces was conveyed to the audience through the popular medium of humour: while laughing they were also learning how to behave.

Don Bosco believed whole-heartedly in the dignity of work, as well as the dignity of courtesy and concern for others. From his earliest years he had been taught by his mother to look upon work "as a welcome part"[84] of his life, and as early as 1841, prior to his ordination, he wrote down in his notebook: "Work is a powerful weapon against the enemies of the soul...."[85] He believed that one's work should be offered up as a sacrifice to God. It was reasonable then, in a Catholic context, that whatever the task, whether pleasant or duty-bound, important or menial, that it should be done in a spirit of love and to the best of one's ability. All work done with the right intention had a value in itself and gave to the doer a dignity and grace which added substance to his Christian character.

The preventive system, then, relied heavily on a solid program of work from both educator and educand. Bosco's Salesians set the rhythm for the working pattern in their commitments to round-the-clock supervision. This in itself was an exhausting schedule.[86] The Oratory boys were expected, too, to use their time wisely. It was their Christian duty, argued Bosco, that time, which was precious, was not eroded by idleness. Piero Bargellini[87] claimed that:

> Don Bosco was among the first educators to recognize the importance of work. Daily work, regularly and conscientiously performed was a sure stepping-stone to sanctity. The schools which he opened for the teaching of arts and trades to poor boys had a two-fold aim. They were indeed to help boys to equip themselves to take employment and to earn a living. But that was not all. The boys were taught to see how God

could be served, and their own lives sanctified, in the daily round. Generations of lads in the Salesian schools of arts and trades, and in other types as well, have learned, thanks to Don Bosco and his sons, the love of work conscientiously done and its value for heaven.[88]

In this context, work done with the right intention, for the welfare of others, was to God's glory. Hence it was well motivated, and conscientiously done. This constituted good example, the attainment of some end which imparted to each pupil a feeling of confidence in himself and others, giving him a sense of security and wellbeing. If confidence lagged and work slackened, the reason was held to be that the teachers themselves had failed to give constant and consistent good example. In 1885, for instance, the Salesians in Argentina were reported to have had disciplinary problems in one of their schools. Bosco, on hearing this disquietening news, wrote a letter urging them to: lovingly give good example, and then wisely proffer advice. If this were done, a feeling of confidence, a sense of liberty would be restored and school discipline improve,[89] allowing the work of education to continue. It was Auffray who noted that one of Bosco's constant sayings was: "Without affection, there is no confidence, and without confidence, no education."[90]

In each Oratory the Rector or Head was looked on as a "father figure". It was thought reasonable, therefore, that around the Rector should be grouped Sodalities or "families" of clubs comprising groups of pupils who actively and freely worked and associated in helping run the Oratory. These Sodalities were outcomes of two essential elements found in every Salesian school: reasonable and well-ordered freedom, and apostolic and religious activism. The Sodalities became hard-working and indispensable factors in the preventive system of Don Bosco, each member contributing, as he could, to the group.

In each Salesian School, although membership was on a free participatory basis, each person, once a member of the Sodality, was expected to fulfil his particular duties of Christian charity. All organizational work and activities were initiated by the boys who were under the guidance of a catechist or spiritual director. The aim of each club or Sodality was to stress the primacy of charity in

the education of youth and the fundamental function of the apostolate in the building up of energetic and integrated Christian characters. Don Bosco saw educational value in these Sodalities as they
gave expression to the individual's initiative and involved him in
the community welfare.

As early as 1847 Don Bosco opened his first club, the Sodality
of St. Aloysius,[91] which was begun "to arouse their enthusiasm"[92]
and engender a collective confidence of the Oratory boys in themselves and in their faith. Extending this idea to adults, in 1850,
Don Bosco formed a Mutual Aid Society which was a union of Catholic artisans who pledged themselves to gain equality of rights, improved
living conditions, fair labour and work contracts, and insurance against
unjust employer demands.[93]

The Immaculate Conception Sodality was founded in 1856,[94]
the Blessed Sacrament Sodality a year later, in 1867.[95] In the same
year, an Altar Boys Sodality was formed.[96] By 1875 there were six
clubs in each of the Oratories.[97] These Sodalities used the preventive system in that each Sodality member assigned himself to a new-
comer or "difficult" boy and then helped him in his work and problems. The Sodalities were of educational value because they gave
members opportunities to express themselves and initiate movements
which helped them to become confident, independent, and socially
mature. Sodalities also promoted lines of communication between
staff and students, encouraged self-discipline, and gave hours of
enjoyment to members who were co-operating in works of charity
and in helping to foster a school spirit.

Modern Salesian, Carlo Fiore, commented on these groups in
the mid 1960's:

> From the free and spontaneous environment in which the
> Sodalities live, results a greater personal compliance with
> the educative work of the superiors. The contrast between
> authority and freedom diminishes greatly. The members
> are invited to intimate collaboration with their superiors,
> while the separation of the student body into smaller educative
> and homogeneous groups avoids the pitfalls of an always
> problematic mass education. The boy discovers a sense of
> freedom and personal responsibility.[98]

While it was considered reasonable that the Sodalities on a weekly basis were to encourage students in the duties of charitable works for the welfare of others, Don Bosco, from 1847 on,[99] was keen to have as a follow-up procedure, an annual retreat in which most of the boys participated. By 1849 he had organised yearly retreats for the artisans.[100] This event was applauded by parents and by employers who allowed their apprentices time off to attend Bosco's annual spiritual holiday camp. The pedagogist was of the opinion, too, that annual retreats were helpful to those recalcitrant students who would not co-operate with their superiors or fellow students[101] in the ordinary day-to-day situations.

Finally, it was believed reasonable that part of Don Bosco's preventive system of education should be based on 'the Recreation'. Games had played a major part in the initial popularity of his Oratories, and their subsequent growth, from 1841 on.[102]

The Recreation figured largely in the daily program. Don Bosco was well aware of the attraction that organised games had for youth: the games being tailored to the needs of the moment and the spirit of the times.[103] During the Recreation, Bosco and his Salesians would actively participate.[104] In this manner they could get to know their students in a far more relaxed environment, and they could induce the youngsters to transfer the happiness of the playground scene to that of the classroom, without developing from games to competition.

Since it was during the Recreation that the educational work was to begin, Bosco insisted on the games being a joyous experience for the youngsters.[105] The Recreation was to become an educative means to relaxation, exuberance, freedom, physical fitness, confidence, control and self-expression.[106]

To Peter Ricaldone, a former Rector Major of the Salesian Congregation, for example, games meant spontaneous and natural lateral communication:

> Don Bosco's example has created a tradition which is one of the most admired and characteristic features of our Society: the Salesian who plays games. On how many occasions have relatives of the boys and other visitors stood in amazement,

enraptured and spellbound at the sight of Masters and Assistants running about in the playground, nimble and breathless, making themselves boys with boys and uniting their pupils and themselves in the enjoyment of one common pleasure, in a happy family spirit, which could not fail to impress everyone by its simplicity, charm and eminently educational influence. This is the same spirit that our Holy Founder himself created and wished to be perpetuated in our traditions. Under those conditions, especially, the Salesian's power over the boys in his charge is supreme; following in Don Bosco's footsteps, he is not slow to seize an opportunity of giving a word of advice which, precisely because it is unexpected and above suspicion, goes home, breaks down barriers, and obtains unexpected results.[107]

In conclusion, the success of the preventive system was to be dependent, to a large degree, on what Bosco held to be the "reasonableness' of its methods in relation to its regulations, supervision, discipline, punishments, including expulsion; and in Salesian attitudes to obedience, purity, love of poverty, and the dignity of work. Finally, in its instilling of a pedagogy of confidence through the workings of its Sodalities, retreats, and recreations, the preventive system would encompass every-day life.

Notes to Chapter 4

1 Lemoyne, *op. cit.*, *B.M.* Vol. III, p.403.

2 Father Peter Ponte, in 1849, was the Director of the St Aloysius Oratory, Turin. This was the second Oratory founded by Bosco to educate poor and abandoned youth. Fr Ponte was sent to Milan, Brescia, and other cities to study Regulations pertaining to successful boarding schools in those areas. Ponte reported back to Bosco, armed with "useful notes and observations." See Lemoyne, *ibid.*, p.404.

3 *ibid.*, p.404.

4 Peter Ricaldone. *Festive Oratory: Catechism and Religious Formation.* St Joseph's Technical School, Madras. India, 1939, p.53.

5 The Regulations, completed in 1854, were later read out to full school assemblies (staff included) so that both parties were informed of what

was expected of them. This Bosconian method of communication began each school year on a note of collective responsibility and co-operation. It was efficacious for the students to know that teachers had duties to perform, too. See Lemoyne, *op. cit.*, Vol. VII, p.313.

6 *Constitutions and Regulations of the Society of St Francis of Sales.* St Joseph's Technical School, Madras, 1967, pp.195-211. This version which appeared in 1874 was very similar to the original booklet issued in 1852.

THE PREVENTIVE SYSTEM IN THE EDUCATION OF THE YOUNG

On several occasions I have been asked to express verbally or in writing some thoughts about the so-called preventive system, which is in general use in our houses. Through lack of time I have so far been unable to meet these wishes; but as I now intend to print the rules of the houses, which until now have nearly always been used traditionally, I think it opportune to give a brief sketch, which may perhaps serve as an outline to a small book which I am preparing and hope to finish, if God gives me life enough, my sole purpose being to help in the difficult art of the education of the young. Wherefore I shall explain: in what the preventive system consists; why it ought to be preferred; and its practical application and its advantages.

I

IN WHAT THE PREVENTIVE SYSTEM CONSISTS AND WHY IT SHOULD BE PREFERRED

There are two systems which have been in use through all ages in the education of youth: the *preventive* and the *repressive*. The *repressive system* consists in making the law known to the subjects, and afterwards watching to discover the transgressors of these laws, and inflicting, when necessary, the punishment deserved. According to this system, the words and looks of the superior must always be severe and even threatening, and he must avoid all familiarity with his dependents.

In order to give weight to his authority the Rector must rarely be found among his subjects, and as a rule only when it is a question of punishing or menacing. This system is easy, less troublesome, and especially suitable in the army and in general among adults and the judicious, who ought of themselves to know and remember what the law and its regulations demand.

Quite different from this and I might even say opposed to it, is the *preventive system*. It consists in making the laws and regulations of an institute known, and then watching carefully so that the pupils may at all times be under the vigilant eye of the Rector or the assistants, who like loving fathers can converse with them, take the lead in every movement and in a kindly way give advice and correction; in other words, this system places the pupils in the impossibility of committing faults.

— 111 —

This system is based entirely on reason and religion, and above all on kindness; therefore it excludes all violent punishment, and tries to do without even the slightest chastisement. This system seems preferable for the following reasons:

1. Being forewarned the pupil does not lose courage on account of the faults he has committed, as is the case when they are brought to the notice of the superior. Nor does he resent the correction he receives or the punishment threatened or inflicted, because it is always accompanied by a friendly preventive warning, which appeals to his reason, and generally enlists his accord, so that he sees the necessity of the chastisement and almost desires it.

2. The primary reason for this system is the thoughtlessness of the young, who in one moment forget the rules of discipline and the penalties for their infringement. Consequently, a child often becomes culpable and deserving of punishment, which he had not even thought about, and which he had quite forgotten when heedlessly committing the fault he would certainly have avoided, had a friendly voice warned him.

3. The *repressive system* may stop a disorder, but can hardly make the offenders better. Experience teaches that the young do not easily forget the punishments they have received, and for the most part foster bitter feelings. along with the desire to throw off the yoke and even to seek revenge. They may sometimes appear to be quite unaffected but anyone that follows them as they grow up knows that the reminiscences of youth are terrible, and some have even been known in later years to have had recourse to brutal vengeance for chastisements they had justly deserved during the course of their education. In the *preventive system*, on the contrary, the pupil becomes a friend, and the assistant, a benefactor who advises him, has his good at heart, and wishes to spare him vexation, punishment, and perhaps dishonour.

4. By the *preventive system* pupils acquire a better understanding, so that an educator can always speak to them in the language of the heart, not only during the time of their education but even afterwards. Having once succeeded in gaining the confidence of his pupils he can subsequently exercise a great influence over them, and counsel them, advise and even correct them, whatever position they may occupy in the world later on.

For these and many other reasons it seems that the *preventive system* should be preferred to the *repressive*.

II

APPLICATION OF THE PREVENTIVE SYSTEM

The practice of this system is wholly based on the words of St. Paul who says: Caritas patients est, benigna est. Omnia suffert, omnia sperat, omnia sustinet."Love is patient and kind.... Love bears all things.... hopes all things endures all things." Hence only a Christian can apply the *preventive system* with success. Reason and religion are the means an educator must constantly apply; he must teach them and himself practise them, if he wishes to be obeyed and to attain his end.

It follows that the Rector must devote himself entirely to the boys; he should therefore, never accept engagements which might keep him from his duties, and he should always be with his pupils whenever they are not engaged in some occupation, unless they are already being properly supervised by others.

Teachers, craftmasters and assistants must be of acknowledged morality. They should strive to avoid as they would the plague every kind of affection or sentimental friendship for their pupils, and they should also remember that the wrong-doing of one is alone sufficient to compromise an educational institute. Care should be taken that the pupils are never alone, as far as possible the assistants ought to precede the boys to the place where they assemble; they should remain with them until others come to take their place, and never leave the pupils unoccupied.

Let the boys have full liberty to jump, run and make as much noise as they please. Gymnastics, music, theatricals and outings are most efficacious means of obtaining discipline and of benefiting spiritual and bodily health. Let care be taken however that the games, the persons playing them as well as the conversation are not reprehensible. "Do anything you like," the great friend of youth, St. Philip, used to say, "as long as you do not sin."

Frequent confession and communion and daily Mass are the pillars which must support the edifice of education, from which we propose to banish the use of threats and the cane. Never force the boys to frequent the sacraments, but encourage them to do so, and give them every opportunity. On occasions of retreats, triduums, novenas, sermons and catechism classes let the beauty, grandeur and holiness of the Catholic religion be dwelt on, for in the sacraments it offers to all of us a very easy and useful means to attain our salvation and peace of heart. In this way children take readily to these practices of piety and will adopt them willingly with joy and benefit.

Let the greatest vigilance be exercised so as to prevent bad books, bad companions or persons who indulge in improper conversations from entering the college. A good door-keeper is a treasure for a house of education.

Every evening after night prayers before the boys go to rest, the Rector or someone in his stead shall address them briefly, giving them advice or counsel concerning what is to be done or what is to be avoided. Let him try to draw some moral reflection from events that have happened during the day in the house or outside; but his words should never take more than two or three minutes. This is the key to good behaviour, to the smooth running of the school and to success in education.

Avoid as a plague the opinion that the first communion should be deferred to a late age, when generally the Devil has already gained possession of a boy's heart, with incalculable prejudice to his innocence. According to the discipline of the early Church, it was the custom to give little children the consecrated hosts that remained over after the Easter communion. This serves to show us how much the Church desires children to be admitted to holy communion at an early age. When a child can distinguish between Bread and bread, and shows sufficient knowledge, give no further thought to his age, but let the heavenly King come and reign in that happy soul.

Catechisms invariably recommend frequent communion. St. Philip Neri counselled weekly and even more frequent communion. The Council of Trent clearly states that it greatly desires that every faithful Christian should receive holy communion whenever he hears Mass, and that this communion should not only be spiritual but also sacramental, so that greater fruit may be reaped from this august and divine sacrifice (Conc. Trid., Sess. XXII, Chap. VI).

III
ADVANTAGES OF THE PREVENTIVE SYSTEM

Some may say that this system is difficult in practice. I reply that for the pupils it is easier, satisfactory and more advantageous. To the teacher it certainly does present some difficulties, which however can be diminished if he applies himself to his task with zeal. An educator is one who is consecrated to the welfare of his pupils, and therefore he should be ready to face every difficulty and fatigue in order to attain his object, which is the civic, moral and intellectual education of his pupils.

In addition to the advantages already mentioned, the following may be added:

1. The pupil will always be respectful towards his educators, and will ever remember their care with pleasure. He will look upon them as fathers and brothers. Wherever they may go, Salesian pupils are generally the consolation of their families, useful citizens and good Christians.

2. Whatever may be the character, disposition and moral state of a boy at the time of his admittance, parents can rest assured that their son will not become worse; indeed, it can be held as certain that he will always make some improvement. In fact, certain boys who for a long time had been the scourge of their parents, and had even been refused admittance to houses of correction, have changed their ways and habits when trained according to these principles, and begun to live upright lives, and are now filling honourable positions in society, and are the support of their families and a credit to the country they live in.

3. If it should happen that any boys who have already contracted bad habits enter the institute, they could not have a bad influence on their companions, nor would the good boys suffer any harm from association with them,

since there is neither time, place nor opportunity, because the assistant, whom we suppose to be present, would speedily intervene.

IV
A WORD ON PUNISHMENTS

What rules should be followed in inflicting punishments? First of all never have recourse to punishments if possible, but whenever necessity demands stern measures, let the following be borne in mind:

1. An educator should seek to win the love of his pupils if he wishes to inspire fear in them. When he succeeds in doing this, the withholding of some token of kindness is a punishment which stimulates emulation, gives courage and never degrades.

2. With the young, punishment is whatever is meant as a punishment. It has been noticed that in the case of some boys a reproachful look is more effective than a slap in the face would be. Praise of work well done, and blame in the case of carelessness are already a great reward or punishment.

3 Except in very rare cases, corrections and punishments should never be given publicly, but always privately and in the absence of companions; and the greatest prudence and patience should be used to bring the pupil to see his fault, with the aid of reason and religion.

4. To strike a boy in any way, to make him kneel in a painful position, to pull his ears, and other similar punishments, must be absolutely avoided, because the law forbids them, and because they greatly irritate the boys and degrade the educator.

5. The Rector shall make sure that the disciplinary measures, including rules and punishments, are known to the pupils, so that no one can make the excuse that he did not know what was commanded or forbidden.

If this system is carried out in our houses, I believe that we shall be able to obtain good results, without having recourse to the use of the cane and other corporal punishments. Though I have been dealing with boys for forty years, I do not recall having used punishments of any kind; and yet by the help of God I have always obtained not only what duty required, but also what was simply a wish on my part, and that from the very boys in regard to whom all hope of success seemed lost.

V
OTHER THINGS RECOMMENDED

All those who hold office or have the care of the boys whom divine providence has entrusted to us, also have the duty of giving advice and counsel to any boy of the house every time there is reason to do so, and especially when it is a question of preventing an offence against God.

Let every Salesian strive to make himself loved, if he wishes to be feared. He will attain this great end if he makes it clear by his words, and still more by his deeds, that his care and solicitude are directed solely towards the spiritual and temporal welfare of his pupils.

The assistant should be a man of few words but many deeds, and he should give his pupils every opportunity of expressing their thoughts freely. Attention however should be paid to rectifying and correcting expressions, words and actions which are not in accordance with a good Christian education.

Boys are wont to show one of the following characters: good, ordinary, wayward or bad. It is our bounden duty to study how to keep lads of these different characters together, so as to do good to all of them, without allowing some to do harm to others.

In the case of those who are naturally of good disposition, a general supervision is sufficient, after the rules of discipline have been explained and their observance recommended to them.

Most boys belong to the number of those who possess an ordinary disposition, and are somewhat inclined to fickleness and indifference. Such boys have need of short but frequent exhortations and advice. It is necessary to encourage them to work, even by means of small rewards, and by showing them that we have great confidence in them, without however neglecting our watchfulness.

But all our efforts and solicitude must be especially directed towards those in the remaining categories: the wayward and the bad. The number of such boys average one in fifteen. Every superior should try to understand them, and obtain information regarding their past life. He should show himself to be their friend, allow them to speak freely, but limit himself to just a few words consisting mainly of short examples, maxims, episodes and the like. These boys should always be kept under observation, but without giving them to understand that no confidence is placed in them.

Masters and assistants, whenever they go amongst their pupils, should at once look around for these boys, and on noticing that any one of them is missing, they should immediately send for him, on pretext of having something to say to him.

Whenever blame advice or correction has to be given to this class of boy, it should never be done in the presence of companions. But use can be made of facts and episodes that have befallen others, in order to point out the praise or blame that is likely to come to those of whom we now speak.

The foregoing articles serve as an introduction to our regulations. But we all need patience, diligence and prayer, without which no regulations would be of any avail.

Fr. John Bosco.

7 *Ibid.*, Vol. IV, pp. 377-378.

8 Ceria, *op.cit.*, B.M., Vol. XI p. 137.

9 Lemoyne, *op.cit.*, Vol. III, pp. 70-71.

10 *ibid.*, p. 80.

11 Franco, *op.cit.* p. 153.

12 Lemoyne *op.cit.* Vol. III p. 241.

13 *ibid.*, Vol. IV p. 264.

14 *ibid.*, Vol VI pp. 37-38.

15 *ibid.*, p. 216.

16 *ibid.*, p. 244.

17 *ibid.*, p. 452.

18 *ibid.*, Vol. VII p. 37.

19 *ibid.*, p. 302.

20 Ceria, *op.cit.*, M.B., Vol. XIII p. 716.

21 *ibid.*, Vol. XVII, p. 110.

22 Angelo Amadei. *Memorie Biografiche* Vol. X. pp. 1101-1102.

23 Bosco's mother's influence can be seen here. Apparently she did not have to resort to corporal punishment to discipline her children because there stood in the corner of the room a cane which was never used. The point was made: although she did not use that cane, she did not relinquish her right to use it. See Lemoyne *op.cit.*, Vol. I, p. 44.

24 *ibid.*, Vol. II, p. 306.

25 *ibid.*, Vol. III, p. 77.

26 *ibid.*, p. 66.

27 *ibid.*, p. 262.

28 The "cocca" (gang) which frequented this area of Vanchiglia was feared by the police. Very few citizens took it upon themselves to be in this vicinity after dark as their safety was jeopardised by this group of delinquents.

29 Lemoyne, *op.cit.*, Vol. II, pp. 394-395.

30 *ibid.*, Vol. V, p. 125.

31 *ibid.*, Vol. VII pp. 337-338.

32 *ibid.*, Vol. VII, p. 412.

33 Ceria, *op.cit.*, B.M., Vol. XI, pp. 430-431.

34 *ibid.*, M.B., Vol. XIII, p. 14.

35   *ibid.*, Vol. XIV, p. 321.

36   Ricaldone, Peter. *Fidelity to Saint John Bosco.* St. Joseph's Technical School. Madras, India. (no date), pp. 215-263.

37   Ceria, *op.cit.*, Vol. XI, p. 333.

38   Lemoyne, *op.cit.*, Vol. IV, pp. 380-390.

39   *ibid.*, Vol. VI, pp. 216-217.

40   *ibid.*, Vol. VII, pp. 302-303.

41   *ibid.*, p. 303.

42   *ibid.*, *M.B.*, Vol. IX, p. 357.

43   Ceria, *op.cit.*, Vol. XI, p. 203.

44   *ibid.*, Vol. XVI, pp. 439-447.

45   Auffray, *op.cit.*, pp. 248-249.

46   Lemoyne, *op.cit.*, Vol. IV, p. 397.

47   Don Bosco was offered a free railway pass by the Turin Government in recognition of his educational work.   He accepted the pass only on condition that he was able to travel third class as he regarded first class as an unnecssary luxury.

48   Lemoyne, *op.cit.*, Vol. I, p. 297.

49   *ibid.*, Vol. III, p. 19.

50   *ibid.*, Vol. V, p. 443.

51   *ibid.*, p. 448.

52   *ibid.*, pp. 449-450.

53   *ibid.*, p. 451.

54   *XIX General Chapter of the Salesian Society.* Progress Press Co., Ltd., Valetta, Rome, 1965, p. 82.

55   *ibid.*, p. 339.

56   Lemoyne, *op.cit.*, Vol. VII, p. 54.

57   Ceria, *op.cit.*, *M.B.*, Vol. XI, pp. 353-354.

58   Amadei, *op.cit.*, *M.B.*, Vol. X, pp. 1104-1105. See also Ceria, *op.cit.*, *M.B.*, Vol. XIII, p. 247.   See also *XIX General Chapter of the Salesian Society*, *op.cit.*, pp. 83-85.

59   Lemoyne, *op.cit.*, *M.B.*, Vol. IX, p. 403, p. 707.   See also Ceria, *op.cit.*, *M.B.*, Vol. XI, p. 356.

60   Ceria, *op.cit.*, *M.B.*, Vol. XVI, pp. 416-417.

61   *ibid.*, *M.B.*, Vol. XI, p. 583; Vol. XII, p. 22; Vol. XIII, pp. 84-86.

62 *ibid.*, Vol. XIII, p. 86, p. 248.

63 *ibid.*, *M.B.*, Vol. XI, pp. 246-247. See also Amadei, *op.cit.*, *M.B.*, Vol. X, p. 1035.

64 *ibid.*, *M.B.*, Vol. XI, p. 242.

65 *ibid.*, *M.B.*, Vol. XII, pp. 20-21.

66 *ibid.*, *M.B.*, p. 20.

67 *ibid.*, *M.B.*, Vol. XIII, p. 279; pp. 432-433.

68 Lemoyne, *op.cit.*, *M.B.*, Vol. IX, p. 436.

69 Ceria, *op. cit.*, *M.B.*, Vol. XII, pp. 143-146.

70 Lemoyne, *op.cit.*, *M.B.*, Vol. VIII, p. 896. See also Ceria, *op.cit.*, *M.B.*, Vol. XII, p. 16; Lemoyne, *op.cit.*, *M.B.*, Vol. IX, pp. 458-459.

71 Amadei, *op.cit.*, *M.B.*, Vol. X, p. 1038, p. 740, p. 742. See also Lemoyne, *op.cit.*, *M.B.*, Vol. IX, p. 622; Ceria, *op.cit.*, *M.B.*, Vol. XI, p. 308.

72 Ceria, *op.cit.*, *M.B.*, Vol. XVII, pp. 196-197.

73 Lemoyne, *op.cit.*, *M.B.*, Vol. VII, pp. 721-722. See also Vol. VI, pp. 703-704.

74 *ibid.*, *M.B.*, Vol. V, pp. 157-158. See also Vol. IX, p. 387.

75 *ibid.*, M.B., Vol. VII, p. 84.

76 Ceria, *op.cit.*, *M.B.*, Vol. XIII, pp. 270-271, p. 273.

77 Lemoyne, *op.cit.*, *M.B.*, Vol. VII, p. 825. See also Ceria, *op.cit.*, *M.B.*, Vol. XI, pp. 241-242; Vol. XIII, p. 507. Lemoyne, *op.cit.*, *M.B.*, Vol. VII, pp. 83-84, pp. 958-959; Vol IX, p. 436.

78 *Constitutions and Regulations of the Society of St. Francis of Sales*, *op.cit.*, on modesty: Art. 153, p. 117; on cleanliness: Art. 137-145, pp. 219-220.

79 Lemoyne, *op.cit.*, *M.B.*, Vol. VII, p. 192.

80 A Prefect is a Vice-Rector, or Deputy Head, and is responsible for the administration in Salesian schools.

81 *Regulations for the pupils.* Chapters IV, VI, VII, VIII, IX, XII, XIII, XV.

82 Lemoyne, *op.cit.*, *M.B.*, Vol. VI, pp. 108-118.

83 *ibid.*, p. 117.

84 *ibid.*, Vol. I., p. 67.

85 *ibid.*, p. 383. Bosco wrote down nine resolutions at this time. Number seven was about the efficacy of work as a means to combat temptation.

86 A criticism of Salesian assistance is warranted here. There is need for some revision of the idea that a Salesian educator is always on duty. From

personal observation, many of these dedicated educators are prone to fatigue due to lack of rest. Some experience retroactive inhibition due to excessive supervision chores. They should have the pleasure of looking forward to at least one full rest day per week.

87　Author of article on *Saint Dominic Savio* in *Don Bosco in the World*, pp. 96-97. Bargellini makes a comparison between Rousseau's Emile and Bosco's Savio. Whereas the former pedagogist's masterpiece is a fictitious paper character, the latter's is a real person and example of Salesian education.

88　*Don Bosco in the World*, op.cit., p. 96.

89　Ceria, *op.cit.*, *M.B.*, Vol. XVII, p. 628.

90　Auffray, *op.cit.*, p. 255.

91　The pledge card which each prospective member of this Sodality signed, partly read as follows:

I, ... pledge to do all I can to imitate St. Aloysius Gonzaga. Therefore, I resolve to flee from bad companions, to avoid bad talk, and to encourage others to virtue by my word and example both in church and elsewhere. I also pledge to observe all the other Sodality rules....

See Lemoyne, *op.cit.*, Vol. III, p. 150.

92　*ibid.*, Vol. III, p. 147.

93　*ibid.*, Vol. IV, pp. 53-56.

94　*ibid.*, Vol. V, pp. 312-321.

95　*ibid.*, p. 499.

96　*ibid.*, pp. 517-519.

97　*ibid.*, Vol. XI, pp. 206-207.

98　*Don Bosco in the World*, *op.cit.*, p. 137. The number of Salesian Sodalities in existence, in 1965, was 2295 spread over 65 countries with an enrolment of 100,000 members.

99　Lemoyne, *op.cit.*, Vol. III, pp. 151-153.

100　*ibid.*, pp. 424-426.

101　Ceria, *op.cit.*, *M.B.*, Vol. XIII, p. 398.

102　Lemoyne, *op.cit.*, Vol. II, pp. 336-338.

103　*ibid.*, Vol. III, p. 226.

104　*ibid.*, p. 85. See also Ceria, *op.cit.*, *M.B.*, Vol. XIV, p. 839.

105　Wirth, *op.cit.*, p. 91.

106　*ibid.*, pp. 93-94.

107　Ricaldone, *op.cit.*, pp. 379-380.

CHAPTER 5

DON BOSCO'S PREVENTIVE SYSTEM: REASON, RELIGION, KINDNESS

RELIGION

The preventive system was, of course, not only based on reason, but also on the precepts of the Catholic religion which, Don Bosco believed, offered students steady guidelines of behaviour to follow while giving them, through prayer, confession and communion, the means of grace to atone for failures and disappointments, and the strength to continue with renewed commitment and confidence.

In this context of the Catholic religion, Bosco's pedagogy included a training, largely through Salesian example, in an awareness, understanding, and practice of the Christian ideals of love, humility, piety and prayer together with encouragement in the use of the available means to grace: confession, communion, penance, and mortification.

The New Catholic Dictionary[1] defines Mortification as "....a practice of Christian asceticism. The purpose of which is twofold: negatively, to cause death to sin, to overcome the desires of the flesh, to conquer evil habits; positively, through penances, hardships, austerities and continued good actions, so to strengthen the will that a man may pursue a desired object despite difficulties. A natural form of mortification is used by anyone who labours long hours to be successful; supernatural mortification aims at progress in virtue and the possession of God and depends on sanctifying grace...."

Thus, students' aims and teachers' objectives operated within a framework of existing Catholic doctrine and attitudes, Bosco's pedagogy being imbued with teachers on the impermanence of life and the transient nature of things, the fear of the Lord, and the religious sense of duty.

Concerned with the practices of piety and prayer, as an integral part of those religious beliefs which activated both Bosco the man, and Bosconian pedagogy, Salesian students were encouraged to understand piety in terms of self-reflection and action: "They must, in general, meditate upon whatever is calculated to inspire them with a growing horror for sin, upon the causes of their own faults, upon mortification that removes such causes, upon the principal duties of their state, upon fidelity to grace and its abuse, upon Jesus Christ, a model for penitent sinners."[2] Piety entailed the active, as well as the reflective; lessening of evil by the growth of goodness, without, however, turning the path of virtue into a process of "self-aggrandizement."[3] Bosco's "pratiche di pieta" were to be works of charity undertaken by the pupils, who, at the same time, were expected to understand the religious implications of what they were doing in the community of the school, and later in the larger community of life.

He encouraged the boys to be on their guard against routine-like, mechanistic piety. He believed that the way to educate to a spirit of piety was to establish in the pupils firm convictions about their religion, thus placing great importance on religious instruction: "He considered catechetical instruction as the basis of the moral education of his boys."[4] But piety based on religious conviction was to be practised in an atmosphere of freedom which was to permeate every Salesian school.[5] There was "no moral pressure to frequent the sacraments."[6]

Bosco measured their piety in terms of religious duties well done; spiritual chores uncomplainingly carried out. It was not sufficient to be well instructed in what constituted Christian piety: understanding had to be expressed in practices of piety, learning by doing. The boys at the Oratory went to daily Mass, recited their prayers,[7] engaged in spiritual reading, listened to brief homilies, were reverent in church. Visitors to the Oratories were usually impressed by the family spirit and piety exhibited there by Bosco's pupils.[8]

Eucharistic piety was encouraged by Don Bosco. He believed that the pedagogy of the sacraments instilled in each individual the need of right intention and effort, which consisted in his approaching the sacraments emptied of vanity and affectation. All this was exacting: it demanded personal sacrifice, effort, and co-operation from the boys who were asked virtually to lose themselves in times given over to reflection, meditation, and participation at Mass, yet, the General

Chapter of the Salesian Society in 1965, clearly reinforced this for modern students:

> The General Chapter:
> Solemnly confirms that the Salesian tradition concerning daily Mass retains all its force. Calls upon all the confreres to re-affirm their faith in these principles in the full awareness of the gravity of this matter which touches upon the fruitfulness of their work as educators. Let all recall that training the boys in piety is the task of the entire community and let all be united in an energetic effort to form in the boys the spirit of faith and a sense of the liturgy. Thus the boys will assist at Mass in a way that corresponds with the mind of Don Bosco and with the will of the Church today.[9]

It was as early as 1846, when Don Bosco had only the use of a field in which to conduct his Oratory, that the boys under his guidance practised an open-type of piety which attracted the attention of curious onlookers who speculated on what the priest-educator was trying to do.[10] By 1847 there were many people who openly criticised Bosco's Oratory practices of piety. They considered that the pedagogist's demands in this regard were excessive and they feared that the boys would come to dislike their devotional programs. Don Bosco's reply was to remind them that the word "oratory" implied that prayer and piety were complementary conditions of Christian behaviour.

With the establishment of various clubs or sodalities within the Oratories, the practices of piety were identified with an environment other than that of the Church. Piety was seen in these clubs in a family-like unstructured group situation, where supervision was relaxed and individual initiative and freedom were allowed expression.[11] Practices of piety were as a part of an existential experience rather than as something reserved for a specifically religious occasion. A sort of transcendental Christian existentialism was seen as essential to life, religious practices as something for living. Within the sodalities these became natural expressions of Christian existence.

Ceria wrote: "An outstanding mark of 1875 was the growth of the sodalities; they encouraged piety and helped discipline.... Quite unwittingly the members derived two important advantages from these various sodalities. One was intimate relationship with their Superiors. A second advantage was growth in virtue since it was customary for a boy, as he grew older, to be promoted to a higher sodality without losing his membership in the lower one."[12] This emphasis on moral education, the establishment of youth clubs, and practical expressions of 'good works', all carefully reinforced the educational influence of dedicated religious teachers:

> That was the end he had in view: to establish perseverance in right living, based upon sound devotion, when the lad came across temptations to evil at every turn in his after career.
> But on this ground as upon all the rest, he wanted reason and faith to direct and control the way. There must be piety, of course, but it must be sustained by a body of religious truths, which could alone suffice.... to prevent utter shipwreck....
> He tried in every possible way to permeate his boys with it. The lessons were short, but lively, vivid and practical—catechisms, well prepared but followed with attention, five-minute sermons after evening prayers, leaving in the heart a serious thought to sleep over—terse readings after Mass or before Benediction—religious or moral hints, naturally summing up whatever was met with, either in school or playtime, a passage of Virgil or a good story told during recreation—a frequent reminder of fundamental truths, not dragged in tiresomely, but aptly suggested by the ingenuity or readiness of the teacher....
> Such piety did its best, and almost always successfully, to make religion attractive, and not irksome or boring....[13]

Salesian objectives were supported by more, however, than youth clubs and doctrinal clarity. Within the Christian context, Don Bosco regarded the confessional as a means to pedagogical action. The educational value of confession had, for him, two important aspects: one, it was in itself a sacrament, and hence a means to grace; two, it provided spiritual and practical direction. As a sacrament, Bosco believed that the confessional had therapeutic value because of its psychological functions: the boy who was absolved was more relaxed, secure, and ready to get on with the business of learning, since confession accounted for an elimination of moral and psychological obstacles inherent in the penitent. If these inhibitors to Christian grace were not removed, then educational construction was difficult.[14]

If confession were seen as a form of spiritual and practical direction, then it created a bond or relationship between the penitent and the confessor. It was important then that the pupil being confessed had a particular confessor who was not simply a distributor of absolutions, but who was required to be an educator as well, a person of keen psychological insight, patience, charity and kindness[15] who could give sound advice. He could be called upon in many situations and places, not just inside the church. Not every priest could, however, emulate Don Bosco, who was a very popular confessor,[16] hearing confessions in streets, on board coaches and in coach sheds, hotels, houses, open fields, as well as in the confessional.[17] He was, however, an adviser to confessors[18] and gave talks to fellow-priests on the subject.[19] Confession was essential to Don Bosco: himself going every week to confession to Father Cafasso, "not privately, but, as he did throughout his life, publicly in church, in view of all the people,"[20] manifestly living the Christian life he shared with his students. He made it clear he was one of them. Bosco was particularly adept in hearing youngsters' confessions[21] and those of sceptical educated persons who were reluctant to be confessed.[22] His methods were quick, not burdensome.[23] Perhaps, however, the most controversial contribution the pedagogist made about confession was the freedom he was to associate with it:

> There was to be the greatest possible freedom in frequenting the sacraments. There was no obligation to secure a confession certificate. No boy could be reprimanded for staying away from confession.... Nor would Don Bosco hear of any fixed arrangement for confession: the boys were to be heard as they came, so that anyone wanting to withdraw could do so unnoticed. The same rule applied to Holy Communion. When on solemn feast days the boys were treated to a breakfast, everybody was welcome whether he had gone to Communion or not.[24]

Similarly, parents, many of whom had been negligent of the boys, were made to feel free to re-establish relationships with their sons. In 1850, for example, the wayward fathers of some of the Oratory boys were invited to attend their sons' first holy communion. In the course of proceedings, many of the fathers were re-united with their sons, and some pledged to begin family life afresh after they had talked over their problems with Bosco who surprised them with his understanding of the problems of life.[25]   Thus, through social and religious communication, through the particular sacraments of confession and communion, Bosco and his Salesians influenced many people, not only his students.   Often preventing further unhappiness by offering spiritual and psychological advice, Salesians also aimed at giving positive directions to follow.

The exercising of self-control, another aspect of piety, was considered by Don Bosco to have a valid place in his pedagogy.   He took pains to stress the positive side of this practice.   He particularly discouraged practices of self-discipline which were detrimental to health, and encouraged instead, reasonable commitments to religious obedience, the fulfilment of one's duty, and bearing cheerfully with the vicissitudes of life.   In training the will Bosco saw the means to humility, a virtue which he held to be of primary importance in equipping youth to face reality.

Throughout his own life, Don Bosco practised "mortificazione".[26] Although, for instance, he contracted petechial typhoid when visiting the victims of the 1845 epidemic in Turin, he gave no indication, to his friends, of the pain he subsequently suffered.   His body, after death, bore the signs of acute herpes, according to Father Sala who tended him.[27]   No one knew that he had even contracted the disease. Although his constant cheerfulness gave impression of continued good health, in fact he suffered from frequent migraine headaches, inflammation of the eyes, toothaches, varicose veins, and persistent insomnia.[28] Strict with himself in this respect he was understanding with his students;[29] but being cheerful despite set-backs was a practical form of mortification he asked of them.   Practices of mortification were considered to be instrumental in training the individual in self-control, and self-discipline, in order that he might function more freely in the Catholic sense of abandonment of the self to God.   For the "Fear of the Lord" was regarded by Don Bosco as the beginning of wisdom for youth, and the basis of his educational system.   Theologically, the "fear" envisaged was not the servile sort, but one based on love and reverence for God who is omnipotent and judge.   Students with filial reverence and respect for the grandeur of God, for instance, would shun sin for fear of offending Him and would accept practical everyday forms of mortification for a purpose.

Allied to Bosco's "Fear of the Lord" was his pedagogy of the "Last Things": both demanded a life of grace, a horror of sin, and the possession of a clear conscience. At every opportunity Bosco taught his pupils "the importance of keeping one's conscience free from sin",[30] again, for a definite purpose. The pedagogy of the "Last Things" was aimed at detaching the pupils from what was transient and apparent only and fixing their attention on those things which, in a Catholic context, were essential and eternal. There was to be nothing morbid about the teaching of the "Last Things" which were to become part and parcel of every real situation that confronted the pupils and not merely the object of a theoretical acceptance.

Bosconian pedagogy, at this point, was permeated by an awareness of the distinction between what was illusory and what was lasting. It followed that to embrace those things which were illusory was to waste time. If, in the final analysis, the prime aim of man was to know, love and serve God,[31] then the eternal truths of Christianity were the things to be accentuated. To know about the end, and what the means to that end were, was the inherent right of every individual. Bosco, throughout his career, therefore, spoke to his pupils on the end of Man: on sin, death, judgement, hell, heaven.[32] In this sense, Don Bosco's pedagogy had a clear conception of the end-in-view; his educational program, based on the educand's co-operation, actuated in an atmosphere of trust, friendliness, and confidence which placed an optimistic construction upon that end: the salvation of one's soul. Present-day Salesian educator, Pietro Braido,[33] claims that educators such as Pestalozzi, Froebel, and Dewey, lacked Bosco's conception of what constituted the end of education—they mainly concentrated on the means—whereas Bosco's pedagogy was a Christian teleological conception of means to that end.[34]

Once every month, in Salesian schools today, there is held a religious service, first instituted by Don Bosco, which is called The Exercise for a Happy Death. It is a short, frank acceptance of the fact that our lives are brittle, that death comes unexpectedly, and that the Christian must strive every day to be in a state of grace so as to face the possibility of a sudden death. The educational merit of this idea, it is argued, is the individual's acceptance of death as a normal and natural subsequent to life, and the responsibility that each person has in facing up to living every day in a state of grace.

Associated with this was an emphasis by the Salesians on the need for self-effacement or humility. Humility is a moral virtue which allows a person to acknowledge his own shortcomings, defects, weaknesses, presumptions, self-aggrandizement, domination over others, because of his relationship to God and subjection to His laws. It is a willed act of submission to others for God's sake and is a necessary condition for personal salvation,[35] being an opposite to pride. To his contemporaries Bosco himself was seen as a man who did not parade his wide knowledge of languages, who humbled himself by submitting for criticism drafts of his writings to young clerics; who was not upset by admonitions he received over the years about his ideas. It was said that he shunned honours, declined high church positions, was at ease with both rich and poor. It was as if he had a sincere conviction of his own nothingness.[36] Lemoyne recalled: "Everyone admired his honest simplicity and humility."[37]

The talks and examples given by Don Bosco and other Salesians in humility, were noted by many of the pupils at the Oratory. They were taught that pride led to self-love, conceit, and selfishness, whereas humility was reflected in a genuine awareness and interest in the welfare of others. Paradoxically, in losing themselves they discovered others. Hence a learning process went on in an atmosphere of respect for the other person who, in return, had something to offer. It was learning by caring.

A religious sense of duty would then come to develop in student and teacher alike. If the fulfilment of duty was time-consuming then it was important that the time used was well spent. In moments of time, Bosco argued, the individual acquired knowledge, performed acts of charity, or prayed. These acts were functions to be understood in the light of eternity. Bosco had written on a wall in his room: "Every moment of time is a treasure." Duty, for him, whether study or work, was something sacred; a series of ends leading to the ultimate end: eternity.

He taught that man was born to work. Such work included those duties necessary for the enrichment of the spiritual life, obliga-

tions to study, and manual labour.   Work done with the right intention and offered up to God gained merit towards one's salvation.
Those who did not work, who became idlers, would suffer remorse
at the end of their lives because of their awareness of the valuable
time they had forfeited.   Therefore, because work was sacred, students had an obligation to devote themselves to it.   Nothing should
be lost; all would be accounted for; Don Bosco's many talks on duty
and laziness have been recorded.[38]   Duty, well-performed, was seen
as a service and obedience to God.   Work not done to the best of
one's ability was offensive to God and was, therefore, in a religious
sense, an act of disobedience.   Studies and duties well done, besides
pleasing to God, had merits for the doer: a source of spiritual and
mental well-being and joy.[39]

Bosco's "pedagogy of duty" was bound up in his ethico-religious
conception of life.   Being, for Don Bosco, was not simply a gift from
God, but a talent or potential which had to be developed or actualized.
This actualization of one's talents entailed a moral responsibility on
both the student's and educator's parts.   The educator saw to it
that the environment of his student was well-planned and reflecting
an ethic which was in conformity to Christian ideals.   The means
to this development were those of reason and religion which were to
inculcate in each person a sense of duty to God and to Man.   For
Don Bosco each life was in itself a mission, the end of which was the
salvation of that soul.

An example of Bosco's "duty" at work occurred in 1854.   Turin
was in a state of emergency due to a cholera outbreak which claimed
thousands of lives.   At the height of this epidemic, Bosco and older
Oratory boys volunteered their services to help combat the contagion.
His invitation was gladly accepted and the boys spent weeks caring
for the sick and infirm.   The boys, numbering over forty, were divided
into groups responsible for medical first-aid, the care of the sick in
private homes, searching for victims, and for emergency purposes.
Their religious sense of duty, instilled in them at the Oratory through
Bosconian word and example, was borne out by what they did in
1854:

He explained what a great act of charity it would be for anyone to devote himself to nursing the sick.... His invitation did not fall on deaf ears.... Fourteen volunteered at once, a few days later another thirty enlisted in the cause....

It must be remembered that in those days fear had so gripped the populace that many, including doctors, were fleeing the city; even relatives were abandoning their own kin. In view of this and the instinctive repugnance felt by the young for sickness and death, one cannot help admiring this unselfish gesture of Don Bosco's boys....

As soon as the word spread that the Oratory boys had volunteered to nurse the sick and were doing an extraordinary job, there was such a great demand for their services that within a week scheduling became impossible....[40]

Every act of duty was to be expressed in a spirit of Christian love. It was Bosco's love for his fellowmen that instigated his educational work.[41] And in educating the young it was essential to win their love first; then their educational development would be successful because of the educands' reluctance to displease a teacher who loved them.[42]

Because the pupils in the Oratories felt loved,[43] they loved their teachers in return.[44] In this atmosphere the Oratory was like a home to the insecure, the sick, the homeless, the lonely, and even those who were opposed to Bosco's beliefs.[45]

Love was the basis of his system "for he was firmly convinced that to educate boys one must find the way to their hearts.[46]

Auffray, a twentieth century Salesian, has written:

First, there must be no barriers between pupil and master, no keeping at a distance, no outbursts of anger, no blows, no public humiliation. But there must be mutual sympathy in both hearts, a family spirit, watchful and active kindliness, lenient towards weakness or ignorance, mercy which can shut its eyes and not punish on all occasions, but pardon easily— that constant care for the boy which makes one take an interest in his health, his parents, his needs, his troubles, his progress and his joys—protective vigilance, that shields him from the stone of scandal as well as from the roughness of the weather— real and expressed affection—constant, but maternal, supervision—readiness to think out whatever may enliven, inform or expand a boy's life—gentleness that never raises its voice, and has an ever ready smile amidst the worst mischances, which can punish with a look of sadness, a mouth that says nothing, a face that turns away—confidence shown in a host of ways, and infallibly attracting confidence in return—condescension, which opens the door wide to the little boy of ten as if he were a grown man—healthy familiarity, which joins in the boy's games and childish amusements: all these things, and how many others besides, are contained in that too often misused but divine word: love.

The great educator has resumed all this procedure in two famous words. To himself he said: "Make thyself loved if thou wouldst be obeyed." To his sons, he said: "Be not superiors, but fathers."[47]

Notes to Chapter 5

1   *The New Catholic Dictionary.* (Ed. Pallen and Wynne), p. 652.

2   A. Tanquerey. *The Spiritual Life. A Treatise on Ascetical and Mystical Theology,* p. 326.

3   Gerald Vann. *Morals and Man,* p. 54.

4   Lemoyne, *op.cit., M.B.,* Vol. II, p. 148.

5   *ibid., M.B.,* Vol. VII, p. 677.

6   Ceria, *op.cit., M.B.,* Vol. XI, p. 224.

7   Don Bosco was of the opinion that collective vocal prayer was best for youth: "Boys are so made that, unless they pray aloud and all together, left to themselves, will not pray neither aloud nor mentally." Lemoyne, *op.cit., M.B.,* Vol. VI, pp. 172-173.

8   *ibid., M.B.,* Vol. IV, pp. 287-288.

9   *XIX General Chapter of the Salesian Society, op.cit.,* p. 189.

10   Lemoyne recorded Ascanio Savio's impressions of this form of piety practised by Don Bosco's earlier pupils. See Lemoyne, *op.cit.,* Vol. II, pp. 293-296.

11   *ibid.,* Vol. VI, p. 215.

12   Ceria, *op.cit.,* Vol. XI, pp. 206-207.

13   Auffray, *op.cit.,* p. 256.

14   Ceria, *op.cit., M.B.,* Vol. XII, p. 91.

15 Lemoyne, *op.cit.*, *M.B.*, Vol. VI, pp. 885-886.

16 *ibid.*, Vol. II, p. 113.

17 *ibid.*, Vol. III, pp. 54-63.

18 *ibid.*, Vol. II, p. 116.

19 *ibid.*, pp. 120-121.

20 *ibid.*, p. 125.

21 *ibid.*, Vol. III, pp. 105-109.

22 *ibid.*, Vol. IV, p. 115.

23 *ibid.*, Vol. III, p. 330.

24 *ibid.*, pp. 66-67.

25 *ibid.*, Vol. IV, p. 41.

26 Lemoyne recorded that Bosco, who played the violin, and took part in hunting wild game, denied himself both pursuits so that he could be worthier to carry out his mission in education. Although he no longer played the violin for his own pleasure, he continued teaching violin to those who wanted to learn. See Lemoyne, *op.cit.*, Vol. I, p. 313.

27 *ibid.*, Vol. II, pp. 128-129.

28 *ibid.*, Vol. IV, pp. 143-152.

29 *ibid.*, p. 150.

30 *ibid.*, Vol. II, p. 412.

31 *ibid.*, *M.B.*, Vol. VIII, pp. 114-115.

32 *ibid.*, *M.B.*, Vol. VI, pp. 385-386.

33 Pietro Braido. *Il Sistema Preventivo di Don Bosco.* Pas-Verlag, Zurich-Schweig, 1964, pp. 140-149.

34 Lemoyne, *op.cit.*, Vol. III, p. 251.

35 The New Catholic Dictionary, *op.cit.*, p. 462.

36 Lemoyne, *op.cit.*, Vol. IV, pp. 452-457.

37 *ibid.*, Vol V, p. 583.

38 *ibid.*, *M.B.*, Vol. III, p. 166; *M.B.*, Vol. V, p. 515, See also Ceria, *op.cit.*, *M.B.*, Vol. XI, p. 232, p. 253; *M.B.*, Vol. XII, p. 605, p. 610.

39 Lemoyne, *op.cit.*, *M.B.*, Vol. VIII, p. 940, p. 942.

40 *ibid.*, Vol. V, pp. 55-56. See also pp. 74-76.

41 *ibid.*, Vol. II, p. 164.

42 *ibid.*, pp. 198-199.

43 *ibid.*, Vol. IV, p. 233.

44 *ibid.*, Vol. III, p. 376. "In 1850 a delegation of older boys went to Don Bosco's room and for the first time formally presented their greetings and gift. Don Bosco then walked out to the balcony for a tumultuous ovation from a thousand boys outside, expressing their filial, sincere devotion, truly the fruit of Christian love."

45 *ibid.*, Vol. V, pp. 11-14; Vol. V, pp. 90-94.

46 *ibid.*, Vol. III, p. 77.

47 Auffray, *op.cit.*, p. 255.

CHAPTER 6

DON BOSCO'S PREVENTIVE SYSTEM: REASON, RELIGION, KINDNESS

KINDNESS

The third aspect of Don Bosco's preventive system—the others being "reason" and "religion"—was "kindness". Charity or kindness was used, by Bosco, as a pedagogical principle which connected the educational end, the salvation of souls, with the pedagogical methods centred in confidence, love, and friendship. Charity, which was both reasonable and kind, produced an educational environment between educator and educand based on filial and brotherly relationships. Kindness was therefore a necessary driving force in Bosco's pedagogy. Disciplinary problems were solved in love, educational reasons for doing things were motivated in terms of Christian kindness.

Bosco had learned, through experience, that kindness, tempered with patience, was an attractive trait, whereas rudeness, impatience, annoyance, and hypersensitiveness were not.[1] He realised, too, that to show equanimity to others, to have them interested in what was being said or done, one had to be friendly, kind, and charitable towards people. To speak unkindly about anyone, Bosco believed, was not only uncharitable but left a bad impression on "persons endowed with at least a minimum of good judgement."[2] And his educative mission depended, to a large extent, on his being able to attract both teachers and students to his ways. Hence, Bosco became aware, through his early ministry, of the magnetism of friendliness generated by kindness. The kindness he had shown to the inmates of the Turin jails, their friendly responses towards him, together with the influence he knew he exercised over them, and the co-operation he received from them,[3] convinced him of the necessity for having kindness as a basic characteristic of his preventive system.

In the early days of his educational work at Valdocco, it was largely his personal kindness which drew the boys to him.[4] When he had occasions to be absent from the Oratory, he was apprehensive about how the other teachers would treat the boys. In a letter written on 31st August, 1846, for instance, to Father Borel who was running the school in Bosco's absence, the latter showed some apprehension: "I am glad that Father Trivero is giving you a hand there; but tell him to take care lest he be too strict with the boys; I know that some of them resent that. Please see to it that the oil of charity renders all things agreeable at the Oratory."[5]

Don Bosco's idea of kindness, however, was based on personal directness, not maudlin sentimentality. He once said: "If a priest wants to do good, then he must combine charity with candid frankness."[6] It was his direct, amicable approach with adults that gained recruits for his schools:

> While making his way through the city's streets and squares and its outskirts, Don Bosco noticed such places as inns, taverns and hotels, where a priest would be unlikely to set foot. He would make it a point to enter, either to accompany some stranger.... Sometimes he would go in just for a hot drink, or a glass of water. These however were only pretexts. The mere appearance of a priest in such a place provoked a good deal of amazement. The proprietor would ask what he could do for him and surprised by the priest's affable manner he would strike up a conversation. Soon the customers would leave their tables to join them. At first, Don Bosco would amuse them with humorous stories, jokes, witty remarks anecdotes and the like; then he would bring the conversation round to the subject of eternal salvation.... Their answers were as forthright as his frank solicitude. Sometimes he had to debate a point, meet objections or dispel prejudices, but he did all with such grace that no one was ever offended; no tinge of bitterness ever crept into these peaceful exchanges. He assured us that he was never insulted in such places, nor was he ever the butt of any crude joke, though the lowest kind of characters could be found there. By the time he left, they had all become his friends and had invariably made him give his word to come again.... Finally he would beg the parents to let their children come to the Oratory service....[7]

His friendly and kindly attitude to people became well known. His kindliness towards rough coachmen[8] who housed their coaches next door to the Oratory was the same as he exhibited towards detractors who shouted abuse over the Oratory walls. Despite rebuffs, insults, and humiliations, he believed in maintaining a friendly disposition.[9] He was convinced that kindness, free from disparagement,[10] would in the final analysis gain the ends he desired: the education of youth, and the salvation of souls.

Kindness and friendliness were to be used, too, as tools for his educative job. An instance of this was when he welcomed back to his Oratory a group of teachers, who, had deserted him,[11] because he was "ever mindful of the valuable service that they had rendered him and the Oratory as catechists."[12] They had served him before, what they had done was past, and now, since he had extended the hand of friendship to them again, they would continue to serve him. But what was more important for Bosco was that his educational work was able to go on. Behind his affability there was always a motive: the continuation of his educative mission.

Acts of charity among the boys at the Oratories were encouraged by the pedagogist. John Villa, a visitor to the Oratory in the 1850's, testified that he heard Bosco declare: "that while the society aimed at doing good to others, the members should first aim at improving themselves."[13] With this in mind, Bosco trained the boys in citizenship and practical Christianity by having them undertake charitable works in the poorer districts of Turin:

> But before the end of 1854, not fully satisfied with the help then being given to the poor, Don Bosco established within the Oratory a small chapter similar to the St. Vincent de Paul chapters.... after carefully studying the regulations.... and the means suggested to achieve its purpose.... Every Sunday, in teams of two, the twenty or so members carried out their assignments; each team had to visit one or more poor families, bringing them material and moral assistance....[14]

To other clubs within the Oratories, Bosco extended invitations to engage in charitable works, both among themselves and neighbouring districts. Guidelines to their behaviour were reflected in a regulation of one of his clubs,[15] which urged its members never to be condescending or disparaging towards others, and to treat every person as they would themselves.

Don Bosco claimed that the methodological basis for "kindness" in his preventive system was based on the writings of St. Paul; for example:

> Charity is patient, is kind; charity feels no envy; charity is never perverse or proud, never insolent; does not claim its rights, cannot be provoked, does not brood over an injury; takes no pleasure in wrong-doing, but rejoices at the victory of truth; sustains, believes, hopes, endures, to the last[16].

Bosco's willingness to face every difficulty and to endure fatigue for the welfare of his pupils, was based on his understanding of what Christian "agape" entailed, an object in view: the civil, moral, and intellectual education of his pupils, the salvation of their souls.

To this end, rectors and assistants were to be as loving fathers who corrected and gave friendly advice to their pupils. If punished, the pupil was to be treated as a father would treat his son: the lines of communication were not to be closed but kept open for future dialogue. When a pupil deserved correction, he was to be given a reason why his behaviour was unacceptable, and then sent away knowing that he was still loved. Pupils were to receive friendly warnings; be offered friendly advice. There were to be no threats or enforcements in his schools. When it was time for the student to leave the Oratory, he was to be made to feel that he could return, at any time, to talk to his teachers who would still be interested in his welfare.

Bosconian pedagogy, therefore, gave an ex-pupil the opportunity to return to his old school and talk over with teacher advisers personal problems, and discuss frankly their plans for the future. In this way old-boys of Salesian schools were to be given an added dimension to their decision-making, and to have the extra advantage of adult friendly advice and encouragement when they needed it. On the other hand, it meant further demands upon the time of teachers, and added responsibilities to be accepted beyond the school situation.

In 1875 for instance, the pedagogist's advice to Father Bonetti, a teacher at the Oratory, was: "As regards yourself, behave in such a way that all those who speak to you may become your friends."[17] What he desired was that an atmosphere of kindliness would develop in his schools, that the pupils in them would sense that they were loved by their educators. And the teacher was expected to become interested in those things which interested the pupils. Bosco believed that the only way of having the pupils come to accept the educator's objectives was to like what they, themselves, liked.[18] Only then would the educator gain their respect and obedience. This was termed by the Salesians the "pedagogy of confidence" wherein both educator and educand were co-operating for the attainment of the same end. The fusion between teacher and taught was possible through the practice and observance of kindness in personal exchanges, and was based on teacher dedication in time and patience.

Don Bosco himself had early learned to be kind and cheerful with his companions when at the Chieri seminary in the late 1830's, winning "the esteem of all the seminarians by his unfailing good cheer, his pleasant way with people, and his willingness to be of help to anyone in need."[19] Later, in 1845, in a memorandum to his Salesians, he stressed that kindness ought to be shown to children during confession, too. He argued that priests who were patient, cheerful, discreet, and showed a pleasant disposition towards those being confessed, would win confidence and hence, respect.[20] And those who were respected were the ones who would be listened to, and obeyed.

From Father Bonetti's *Chronicle of the Oratory*, 1858-1863, Lemoyne reported Bosco's words on kindness, which suggest a warm, human attitude towards its development, rather than a pedantic concern for theological niceties:

> As regards young people, our charity must show itself in kindness. It must never be said of any of us, 'He is strict and tough!' No, never should our pupils think that way of us.... Above all, let us practise charity among ourselves too. If you have something against a companion of yours, get it off your chest right away without fear; do not hold a grudge. You may say something unwise, but it's a lesser evil. Say it and be done with it![21]

Student-teacher, and teacher-teacher exchanges were to be, therefore, less inhibited when they took place "in kindness". Lemoyne was of the opinion that the priest-educator's concept of kindness not only created a cheerful atmosphere in the school, but was "the strongest influence restraining the boys."[22] Peter Ricaldone supported this view, believing that the Salesian tradition of kindliness in looks, words, and manners, would always be "a most powerful attraction to the young. In many cases it will be the point on which the success of the Oratory depends."[23]

Since Salesian pedagogical success depends so largely on the nature of the teacher, it would appear that an inflexible, or unimaginative teacher, or one not able to sustain the demands of continuing supervision, or the traditions of patience and kindness demanded by their founder, would find the Salesian school difficult. The stress placed on all Salesian teachers who are not only responsible for students' schooling, but also for daily supervision, would seem to work against the demands for maintaining a serene and friendly disposition towards pupils. To be a Salesian educator carrying out teaching duties in the manner prescribed by Don Bosco, would appear to demand good health, energy and patience, courage and conviction. Salesian educators would have to be particularly dedicated people, for it seems it is more than a profession they are called to, it is a religious vocation. This could, however, affect laymen, too, who teach in Salesian schools. If, for instance, authorities within the schools were not able to ensure, in the face of a shortage of religious vocations, the suitability of each lay teacher, to the Bosconian atmosphere of kindness, that atmosphere could be strained. The failure of even some teachers, lay or religious, to practise the pedagogy of kindness with all its challenging, fatiguing, and persistent demands, could lead to the failure of the system within that school.

It followed, too, that if kindness was to be an integral part of Bosconian pedagogy, then its offshoot, cheerfulness, was to be its corollary. The family-spirit atmosphere of the Oratories it was claimed, gave expression to cheerfulness because its characteristics were those of love, freedom, and joy. Because the pupil knew he was respected by his educators who, in turn, had the educand's confidence and trust; and because, in that Salesian family environment, he could never be lonely or sad for long; he was cheerful.

Kindness and cheerfulness, for Don Bosco, were logical extensions of a Christian theology, which, because of its inherent optimism and hope, could only provide a thesis diametrically opposed to defeatism, pessimism, and despair. Thus, to be cheerful and kind, he reasoned, were necessary and sufficient conditions of being a Christian.

Cheerfulness was, moreover, a powerful educational means to growth and development. Work, study, play, religion, were more natural in a relaxed and happy atmosphere. A cheerful student, too, was more amenable to correction in such an environment. In this sense, Bosco's schools were happier, and most probably, sounder places for learning than many schools found elsewhere, particularly those in England, in the 1850's. Learning takes place more effectively if the child is securely placed in a happy environment. Bosco, too, believed in the efficacy of a happy environment and had his schools operating this way years before psychology became related to learning, and approximately one hundred years before any schools of pedagogy wrote on happy-ways and play-ways theories of education.[24] Nevertheless, again this idea placed great responsibility on teachers and administrators, and on those who selected them.

The means to cheerfulness, as suggested by Bosco, were to be found in free and guided activity, in "singing, music, and great freedom in games."[25] Other activities he advocated for the promotion of happiness were excursions, acting, reciting, and gymnastics. Then there were the various clubs, and the cadet units, and the camps. And the playground was to be the place where children could give full rein to their surplus energies while exchanging pleasantries with their teachers, and where much of the give-and-take of Bosconian pedagogy was to occur.

It was understandable that Don Bosco, who from his earliest years[26] and later as a seminarian was concerned about the formality and reserve of most of the clergy with whom he came into contact,[27] should resolve upon a course of action which stressed familiarity, friendliness, and cheerfulness in human relationships, particularly in the field of education. His early experiences as a chaplain of the jails of Turin, too, had been useful to him in formulating ideas which were to be applied, later, to his pedagogy in the Oratories:

> In his visits to the convicts, Don Bosco learned many previous lessons for the successful education of the young. He grew

more and more convinced that it was essential to treat these unfortunates, as well as all the young people, with great charity if any good result was to be obtained. He was later to insist upon this point with all his co-workers, assuring them that even a rough and rebellious boy easily yields to amendment when he finds himself treated with loving kindness.[28]

Bosco took issue, in 1847, with saturnine Christians in Turin, and elsewhere, when he wrote a young people s guide *Il Giovane Provveduto* (The Companion of Youth) particularly to inform youth that Christianity could be fun. He was against those ideas which led youngsters to believe that "obeying God's laws means having a miserable time with no fun at all."[29] He went on to say:

> As this is absolutely false, I should like to teach you how to lead a Christian life which will make you happy and contented. I will show you what true enjoyment and fun are, so that you make your own the words of.... David and say: "Let us serve the Lord with gladness".... This then is the purpose of this little book: to teach you how to serve God and be always happy.[30]

Don Bosco believed that the tenets of Christianity were compatible with life, that the practising of religion could lead to contentment, joy, and an inner peace, these qualities being useful conditions for learning. For his followers then, similar beliefs were also essential.

In his schools the theatre was used as a vehicle for cheerfulness. Bosco understood the creative value of dramatic work and the felt needs met by the participation of students in all forms of playwriting, acting, and presentation work. He believed that the aims of the theatre were to entertain, to educate, and to instruct in as pleasant a way as possible. Such entertainment, he argued, produced an atmosphere of joy in the school. On the other hand, violent or distressing themes for plays were discouraged as they tended to upset the equanimity of the boys. Besides being a means to happiness and cheerfulness, the Salesian theatre was, in essence, a school of morality which reflected Christian social modes of living, at the same time keeping the pupils occupied.

Similarly, music and singing were viewed by Bosco as means to happiness, a condition of learning. He declared: "An Oratory without music is a body without a soul."[31] Music helped in creating a serene atmosphere, and was, Bosco believed, both an attractive item which appealed to the majority of students, and conducive to a learning atmosphere.

Excursions and outings, too, were utilized by Bosco to promote cheerfulness not only during school time, but serving, too, as means of occupying the pupils during the holidays when, as is often the case nowadays, there were periods when through boredom and lack of something to do, boys became social nuisances. Don Bosco, an innovator in this field of holiday-time educational excursions, kept young people happily occupied, and at the same time, off the streets. Because these outings were supervised by Salesians, they gave rise to friendly social exchanges, and helped to keep the pupils free from exposure to moral danger.

In what has come to be called by Salesians, Don Bosco's 'pedagogy of praise', another practice aimed at producing an atmosphere of happiness within the school, a reward which was particularly esteemed by the pupils was official praise from the Rector, with the resultant complimentary letter sent by him to the parents. Other rewards were prizes given at various times throughout the year, and invitations to deserving students to dine with the head teachers. However, the pedagogist was aware of the harmful effects of praise unwisely bestowed. He warned his teachers that too much praise often ruined the best boys, and that it should never be given for physical attractiveness or natural talents. Bosco realized that the more moderate students should receive their turn, as too, should those who were lagging behind.[32]

Corrections, on the other hand, were to be given in a kindly manner: they were to be in private and at propitious times. Because of this, the Salesians were to begin a tradition of pedagogy which used corrective techniques involving charity and respect for the uniqueness and dignity of each person. Public admonitions were rare: the 'Word in the Ear', private talks with students, and the 'Goodnight' became keynotes. Bosco himself said: "If you have to give any correction, do it privately, in secret, and with the greatest sweetness."[33]

The Salesian 'Word in the Ear' or 'parolina' when used as an intimate corrective method, mainly during recreation time in the playground, was viewed as a communication link between teacher and taught, as well as an opportunity to offer help, or to sound warnings. It was father to son: it was personal, intimate, and in confidence. Above all, the 'Word in the Ear' was to be empathetic.

Besides that of confession, the Salesians utilized private talks with the students for more general purposes as well. Spiritual and other matters were subjects for friendly discussion. An important feature of these talks was that they were not prescribed: they were spontaneous and natural outcomes of socio-religious curiosity. Often the talks became occasions when the teacher, acting as a father, would advise the pupil on his future. In effect, the teacher was doing the work of the modern careers adviser or school counsellor, except that it was essentially personal and subjective.

The 'Goodnight' was another method within the framework of the preventive system which aimed at friendly advice and direction to youths at bed-time. The practice, according to Lemoyne, began with Margaret Bosco who gave the first Oratorians motherly bed-time talks on work, honesty and religion.[34] Later, in 1850, Bosco used this time for short talks on life, religion, for the telling of edifying stories, or incidents that happened during the day, for portraits from history, or even for puzzles and problem-solving.[35] By 1858, according to Joseph Reano, Bosco had almost perfected his 'Goodnight' technique,[36] his anecdotes becoming "inexhaustible".[37] The 'Goodnight' became, for Bosco, a vehicle for creating interests, maintaining discipline and promoting thought.[38] Other themes for his 'Goodnight' were school happiness, study, conduct, and how to acquire knowledge.[39] Adolf L'Arco, a writer, described the 'Goodnight' as "an essential part"[40] of Salesian education. In practice the 'Goodnight' was sound psychology: it created a sympathetic bond by strengthening communal ties between teachers and pupils.

Through various methods based on kindness, cheerfulness, and happiness, within the framework of religion and reason, Bosco had introduced a preventive system of pedagogy the end or goal of which was the civil and Christian education of underprivileged youth. Only later was this extended to general education.

Angelo Franco in his work *A Lamp Resplendent*, wrote, in 1958, of the preventive system in the light of Bosconian conditions for a good life: clear conscience, a frugal and active life, and good companions; applying these generally to all types of youth:

> Here indeed is a full and up-to-date program of sound Christian education. We say up-to-date for never as these days has educational psychology been insisting on the importance of serenity of mind, good fellowship and vigorous activity to insure the child's normal development both physical and moral. Of course in Don Bosco's mind what comes first is a clear conscience—that is a conscience which is at peace with God and alive with grace. To foster this life of grace in a boy, to protect it and strengthen it by all available natural and supernatural means—this was the aim of all his efforts. He was untiring in urging his boys to make good confessions and good communions, to keep active at all times and interested in wholesome pursuits, to play strenuously, and to avoid bad companions as they would a plague. It is this beautiful integration of natural and supernatural means—all directed to the one end of preserving sanctifying grace—that is the glory of the Preventive System.[41]

But there was apparently more to his system than this; Paul Albera, a former Rector Major of the Salesian Order, whom Franco quotes as saying that Salesian educators were like fathers as well as teachers, understood that they were to be pious as well. He said: "Our system of education is wholly grounded on piety. Without it our Schools and Oratories would lose their brightest ornament and prestige."[42] E.B. Phelan, writing in 1963, agreed, stating that Bosco "considered it the primary duty of the teacher to bring Christ to the boys" and that "books have been devoted to Don Bosco and his educational system. But to him teaching was only an expression of his love of Christ in the person of neglected boys...."[43]

Modern Salesian, A. Auffray, writing in 1964, in *Saint John Bosco*, explained further:

> This Preventive System, as he called it, opposed to the other, the Repressive System, based upon punishment, endeavours to dry up the evil at its source, by cutting off the occasions or by neutralising it, or by putting boys on their guard against it. .... This system whispers: 'Look out! Here is the dangerous

temptation: keep steady, and overcome the difficulty; and if it is too hard, in your weakness rely upon my strength, for I am close by you.'
The first is based upon reverential fear, the second by loving vigilance. The first keeps the superior at a distance in splendid isolation, which he leaves only to show severity and provides the well-known parallel lines along which masters and boys move without any risk of ever meeting; the second lifts authority from its pedestal without compromising it, and breaks down all the barriers between teacher and pupil, thus becoming all things to all persons.[44]

Another modern Salesian commentator, Gino Corallo, in his article entitled *Don Bosco's System of Education*, in 1965, wrote:

....his idea was to persuade the boys to want to be good: he wanted discipline to come from within, not from without. Hence Don Bosco was not greatly put out by faults of levity proper to youth and to inconstancy; neither was he dismayed by noise or high spirits.... Providing boys with healthy outlets for their surplus energy is the best way to 'prevent' faults: not giving them, that is, time to think about committing them. This surely is of far greater educational value than mere repression or the infliction of a penalty for evil already done, and which is not likely to benefit the delinquent in any way.[45]

Don Bosco's preventive system of education and his pedagogical methods had begun to attract the attention of Protestant churches and foreign departments of education, from 1876 on. Ceria mentioned, in his autobiographical works on Bosco, for instance, that certain Protestant groups in Nice, France, were interested in his methods and educational ideas.[46] By 1881, British printers had made available to English schools the translation, by an inspector of schools, J.D. Morell, of Don Bosco's school text, which had been adopted by the Italian authorities for use in schools, *Storia d'Italia* (History of Italy), under the title of *A Compendium of Italian History from the Fall of the Roman Empire*. In the Foreword to his translation, Morell, alluded to Bosco as a "learned priest" and commented favourably on the presentation and technique of the pedagogist's writing style.[47] And Norman F. Potter, an English Protestant clergyman, wrote, in 1902, an article entitled *Don Bosco of Turin, The Redemption of Boyhood*, which was an acknowledgement of Bosconian pedagogy:

The present sketch would be incomplete without some slight reference to Don Bosco's method of education. He was the first to define and act on the preventive method.

The Teacher, in Don Bosco's opinion, should be father, adviser, friend, more than master, and should aim to gain the child's assistance in united efforts to achieve the same end— his improvement. Thus baffling evil makes it unsuccessful; natural inclinations are directed and fixed in the strict path of virtue, which if neglected, might follow the broad path of vice; faults and consequent punishments are prevented. Infinite gentleness, unalterable patience, vigilant attention and ceaseless watching, are essential in the masters. Carrying out the preventive system exacts a course of action in accordance with St. Paul's saying "Charity is patient, is kind, suffers all things, hopes all things, and endures all things." The master should completely belong to his pupils, devote his time to precede, assist, and follow them everywhere, or depute others equally capable to do so, never leaving them alone nor allowing idleness. With this method it is difficult for bad companions to find occasion to corrupt innocence.

Don Bosco concealed this surveillance from the knowledge of its objects, and called the masters who, with him presided at recreation, in workshops, or classrooms, assistants—not superintendents. They mixed among the groups of boys during their play: nothing escaped notice....[48]

It is a matter of history that from 1902 onwards, Bosco's preventive system of education embraced many countries. By 1923, the first group of Salesian missionaries had reached Perth; fifty years later, Bosconian schools had been established in Victoria, Tasmania, South Australia, and New South Wales. At the same time, Bosconian pedagogy became an international movement.

Don Bosco's preventive system, based on prevention rather than repression, on kindness and love rather than on fear and indifference, was in some of its methods, unusual from the point of Catholic orthodoxy. His teaching concepts were however within the general framework of Catholicism.

Perhaps the most demanding aspect of the preventive system was its method of supervision, in which the educator continually present among his students, involved himself in their world; they in turn adopting his because they were aware of his love for, and interest in, them. While Bosco's system excluded corporal punishment; and appeals to reason, within the context of a religion which claimed to be reasonable, replaced the cane, the fear of God replaced the fear of teacher authority. Teachers themselves were to be like fathers who advised their pupil-sons; student guidance was given through both established Church agencies such as confession and private talks, as well as the more innovatory 'parolina', and 'Goodnight'.

Bosco's methods of education were thereby based on moral, rather than physical coercion; on mutual trust, the development of happiness and confidence. Salesian teachers were urged to be tactful and selfless, and were called upon to dedicate themselves to their work, within a multiplicity of social and religious groupings: clubs, retreats, recreations, holiday camps, hikes, excursions, church services, religious discussions, public performances in the arts and crafts, choirs, bands, sports, gymnastics, drama, as well as the classroom and the playground.

In addition, Bosco, aware of the dangers of mass education, insisted on a person-to-person relationship between students and their teachers. While his sodalities fulfilled the purposes of group processes in counselling, and gave rise to initiative, self-discipline and an overall spirit of freedom and enterprise, they made, as well, further demands on the Salesians who staffed them. These men were, however, primarily religious, who understood, in a sense, Don Bosco's preventive system of education incorporating reason, religion, and kindness as an extension in degree and application of the Pauline trilogy of faith, hope, and love. The faith was a knowledge and application of Catholicism; hope was the optimism arising from the reasonableness and salvation promised by that religion; love was charity exercised in Christian kindness, human understanding, and joy.

On the other hand, the very nature of the extensiveness of Salesian supervision, the restrictions imposed on teaching personnel due to the rigorous and exhausting demands made on the time and energy of the individual Salesian teacher, together with those aspects of their vocation which are essentially religious in nature, imposed limitations on the system. Salesian personnel today are expected to follow in

Don Bosco's footsteps and carry out, in a spirit of love and charity, his Regulations and Constitutions, some of which demand personal sacrifice, dedication, and humility. It is therefore not surprising to expect that Salesian vocations, in the light of modern materialism and non-acceptance of Christian morality, will probably fall off in numerical strength. Salesian administrators, already faced with the problem of admitting larger numbers of lay teachers into their ranks to compensate for the decline in Salesian vocations, will have the burden of training these non-clerical educators in Salesian methodology, preserving, and expecting of them, Bosconian idealism, perseverance, and dedication. Whether these could be expected of people other than those who have chosen the particular life-style of the religious, did not arise to this extent in Don Bosco's own time.

Notes to Chapter 6

1 Lemoyne, *op.cit.*, Vol. I, p. 371.

2 *ibid.*, p. 77.

3 *ibid.*, Vol. II, p. 83. See also his popularity with inmates and warders: pp. 137-145; p. 174.

4 *ibid.*, Vol. II, pp. 351-355.

5 *ibid.*, p. 393.

6 *ibid.*, Vol. III, p. 37.

7 *ibid.*, pp. 39-40.

8 *ibid.*, p. 60.

9 *ibid.*, Vol. IV, p. 7.

10 *ibid.*, p. 259.

11 In 1851, Father Rodrigo set up an Oratory in opposition to Bosco. Although he envied the pedagogist's methods in teaching he disagreed with his administration. Rodrigo bribed some of the catechists from Valdocco to join him. However, after a time, the disenchanted teachers returned to Valdocco because they missed the happy Bosconian atmosphere. Bosco welcomed them back and carried on as if nothing had happened. See: Lemoyne, *op.cit.*, Vol. IV, pp. 254-263.

12 *ibid.*, Vol. IV, p. 263.

13 *ibid.*, Vol. V, p. 307.

14 *ibid.*, pp. 306-307.

15 A regulation of the Sodality of St. Joseph reads: "Let us never look down on, or run down our companions. Regard all as our true brothers." See Lemoyne, *op.cit.*, *M.B.*, Vol. IX, p. 713.

16 *The New Testament of Our Lord and Saviour Jesus Christ.* (Trans. Knox, Ronald A.) I Corinthians, 13: 4-7, p. 175.

17 Amadei, *op.cit.*, *M.B.*, Vol. X, p. 1022.

18 Ceria, *op.cit.*, *M.B.*, Vol. XVII, pp. 107-114.

19 Lemoyne, *op.cit.*, Vol. I, p. 287.

20 *ibid.*, Vol. II, pp. 119-122.

21 *ibid.*, Vol. VI, p. 525.

22 *ibid.*, Vol. XI, pp. 204-206.

23 Ricaldone, *op.cit.*, p. 183.

24 For example the work of the English educationist, Percy Nunn who in his book, *Education: Its Data and First Principles,* advocated the play-way in education. No doubt he was influenced by Montessori's fun methods. There is also a possibility that Montessori could have gained these kinaesthetic ideas from her mother who was a Salesian co-operator.

25 Ceria, *op.cit.*, *M.B.*, Vol. XI, p. 222.

26 Lemoyne recorded that Bosco had said to his mother, in 1831: ". . . . If I ever become a priest, I will give my whole life to youngsters. They'll never see me looking stern and forbidding. I'll always be the first to speak to them." Lemoyne, *op.cit.*, Vol. I, p. 170.

27 *ibid.*, Vol. I, p. 281.

28 *ibid.*, Vol. II, p. 84.

29 *ibid.*, Vol. III, p. 8.

30 *ibid.*, p. 8.

31 *ibid.*, *M.B.*, Vol. V, p. 347.

32 Ceria, *op.cit.*, *M.B.*, Vol. XIV, p. 847.

33 Lemoyne, *op.cit.*, *M.B.*, Vol. VII, p. 506; Vol. VI, p. 890. See also: Ceria, *op.cit.*, *M.B.*, Vol. IX, p. 17, p. 346.

34 *ibid.*, Vol. III, p. 142.

35 *ibid.*, Vol. IV, p. 9.

36 *ibid.*, Vol. V, p. 606.

37 *ibid.*, Vol. VI, p. 46.

38 *ibid.*, pp. 46-47.

39 *ibid.*, Vol. VI, pp. 171-172; pp. 194-196; Vol. VII, pp. 480-487.

40 *Don Bosco in the World*, op.cit., p. 22.

41 Franco, *op.cit.*, pp. 16-17.

42 *ibid.*, p. 151.

43 E.B. Phelan. *Don Bosco, A Spiritual Portrait.* Doubleday, N.Y., 1963, p. 119, p. 249.

44 Auffray, *op.cit.*, p. 247.

45 *Don Bosco in the World*, *op.cit.*, p. 20.

46 Ceria, *op.cit.*, *M.B.*, Vol. XII, p. 118.

47 *A Compendium of Italian History from the Fall of the Roman Empire.* Trans. from the Italian of Giovanni Bosco, and completed to the present time by J.D. Morell, L1D. London, 1881. See: Foreword.

48 Lemoyne, in his appendix of Vol. IV of his *Biographical Memoirs of Saint John Bosco*, pp. 568-569, quoted an article, Don Bosco of Turin. *The Redemption of Boyhood* by Norman F. Potter taken from *The Commonwealth*, Vol. VII, No. 4, April, 1902, Alabaster and Spikenard, England.

CHAPTER 7

THE SOURCES OF HIS THOUGHT

Part I: Past Influences.

Throughout the nineteen volumes on the life of Don Bosco written by his biographers, Lemoyne, Amadei, and Ceria, and in other writings on him, there are references to other Catholic educators, before and during Don Bosco's lifetime, who, for various reasons, had appealed to him and to his outlook on education. Some of their ideas were incorporated in his own pedagogy based on reason, religion, and kindness.

Don Bosco, for instance, made reference, to his clerics, to the lives of Ignatius Loyola, Philip Neri, Alphonsus Rodriguez, Charles Borromeo, Francis de Sales, Aloysius Gonzaga, and Vincent de Paul, in relation to educational work. He gleaned from them ideas which were to have practical value and application in the course of his work among under-privileged youths. The men from whom Bosco drew inspiration were Catholics of the Renaissance and Counter-Reformation from Spain, Italy, and France, who had experienced problems similar to those encountered by Bosco two centuries later. Bosco's unsettled revolutionary Piedmont of 1848 seemed similar, in many ways, to the rapid social, political, economic and religious changes brought about by the Reformation and Renaissance in the world of say, Loyola, or Philip Neri. The revival of the old learning from Greece and Rome, together with the separation of Church and State in Loyola's and Neri's times had produced changes in religious values among the people. Similar shifts in attitude towards the Church, due particularly to the awakening of nationalistic and economic revolutionary forces with concomitant emphasis on the importance of the role of the individual in society, were being experienced in Bosco's Piedmont. Thus many of the men referred to in Bosco's writings and conversations were those who had adapted and successfully established their ideas in times of flux and uncertainty. Bosco had gathered from the past ideas to help him found a pedagogy which would survive social change in an age of resurgent liberalism and nationalism.

It was from Philip Neri, 1515-1595, that Don Bosco most probably developed his own vocation as an educative mission. Like Neri, Bosco was to become a priest-educator. Neri had sought to re-educate the Romans in their religion, and in their moral obligations after the sacking of Rome in 1527. Neri had used the street corners and market places of the Sant' Angelo quarter to speak to the young. "He had an attractive personality with a notable sense of humour, and he readily won a hearing,"[1] gathering around him followers who were called Oratorians "because they rang a little bell to summon the faithful to prayers in their Oratory." Later his followers had "shared a common table and spiritual exercises under his obedience, but he forbade them to bind themselves to this state by vows or to renounce their property if they had any."[2] Neri's room, which was built over the nave of San Girolamo, had been frequented by princes and cardinals as well as ordinary Catholics who came to learn from him. "Rich and poor mounted the steep steps that led to his apartment at the top of the house, with its loggia looking out above and beyond the roofs.... and to each person he gave advice suited to his special needs."[3]

Don Bosco, according to the testimony of Father Borel who worked with the priest-educator at Valdocco, was capable of predicting future events, as was claimed for Neri before him.[4] Bosco, therefore, appears to have felt that he had a special affinity of spirit with Philip Neri and repeatedly referred his students to Neri's maxims, such as: "Sin and gloom, away from my room";[5] or, "Run, jump, have all the fun you want at the right time, but, for heaven's sake, do not commit sin."[6] It seemed reasonable, to Don Bosco's biographers, that Bosco, through his reading of Father James Bacci's work on Philip Neri,[7] should have come, not only to understand, but also to adopt some of the techniques which Neri had employed. Bosco, like Neri for instance, used the square or piazza to communicate with some of the populace; he attracted people to his room at the Oratory and dispensed advice according to needs; he gathered about him Oratorians who were to carry out an educative mission; and his personality, too, was an attractive one, used to the fullest to bind people to him. Similarly, his sense of humour was used for his educational work, until, like Neri, the 'Apostle of Rome', Bosco became a well-known Turinese identity, not only because of his educational and humanitarian work for the underprivileged, but because of his charismatic personality as well.

J.B. Lemoyne reported that Don Bosco, like Ignatius Loyola, 1491-1556, regarded money and property as means to an end, at the same time he regarded work and personal effort in Loyola's terms, too, as expressed in this maxim of Loyola's: "Work as though the outcome of any undertaking depended entirely upon your efforts, and at the same time distrust yourself as though everything depended on the Lord."[8] As Bosco was conversant with Loyola's life, he had been attracted to reports of his modesty and humility, and to the Jesuit's work for education in the Counter-Reformation. Bosco, moreover, would have been familiar with Loyola's *Spiritual Exercises*, published in Rome, 1548, the scope of which was "to induce a state of interior calm and disinterestedness',[9] two characteristics which the pedagogist incorporated in his educational rationale because they were regarded as important factors in the processes of decision-making. Consequently, in his Oratories, largely through personal example, Don Bosco attempted to establish behavioural patterns among his boys which placed importance on detachment and personal equanimity. Like Loyola, too, he shunned displays of learning, encouraged visits to the poor and distressed, and made clear his understanding of those who held other beliefs.[10]

Another influence affecting the formation of Bosconian pedagogical ideas was that of Alphonsus Rodriguez, 1533-1617. It was at the Convitto Ecclesiastico in Turin where Bosco was furthering his theological studies, that he had become acquainted with the life of Rodriguez, through the Convitto's spiritual director, Father Joseph Cafasso. The most important idea taken by Bosco from his life was that of the dignity which the saint had attached to routine acts of duty. Bosco apparently was attracted to the Rodriguez concept of the holiness of duty, an idea which he instilled in his Salesians, who later became known for their hard work and responsible acceptance of onerous duties, particularly those in connection with the supervision of children. This tradition of time-consuming 'assistance' is regarded today[11] as still applicable, even to a modern, co-educational High School within the Catholic system, as to the more traditionally Salesian schools. This new type of school would rely, at least to some extent, upon lay staff. Since lay teachers normally would not remain with students out of school hours, and since it is believed that Bosconian methods of teaching are applicable to ordinary classroom students, not only to abandoned youth, 'assistance' would be available during school hours only, for some students and for some teachers.

This would appear to be a departure from Don Bosco's original position. Nevertheless, as Bosco borrowed from Alphonsus Rodriguez, adapting and applying his concept of routine acts of duty to his own times, so modern Salesians appear confident that their methods and traditions are flexible by nature, and can, therefore, encompass a new situation: a different period in time; a different country; co-education; numbers of trained lay-teachers helping; a modern multi-purpose school.[12] Nevertheless, while feeling that Bosconian 'reason, religion, kindness' can be relevant today, and that the demands of 'assistance' can be met under changing circumstances, most Salesians assume a Christian situation.

Lay teachers would, in this type of modern, but Salesian, school, require some training in Salesian methods and traditions first, to retain the distinctive atmosphere of a Salesian community. This suggests, again, a sense of still being involved in Bosconian ideals, and that there should be some distinctiveness in a Salesian school. That the traditions of the Salesian communities should tend to be acknowledged as the strongest influence on many modern Salesians' teaching careers, emphasises, again, both the continuing importance of that intangible atmosphere or "style of thought and feeling, of life and activity in our mission as sons of Don Bosco",[13] and, the essentially religious nature of the dedication of Salesian teachers.

From the life of Alphonsus Rodriguez, Don Bosco also became convinced of the importance of the college hall-porter, "a link between the public world without and the private world within"[14] for the successful running of a boarding school. Don Bosco modelled his ideas on the role of the college porter on that of Alphonsus Rodriguez, who for 45 years had developed relations between college and community as porter of Montesione College on the Island of Majorca.

Much of Don Bosco's work in connection with his Festive Oratories was based on the organizational efficiency he had learned to admire in the life of Charles Borromeo of Milan,[15] 1538-1584. Bosco learnt too, from Borromeo's educational ideas, in relation to the use of Sundays and Holydays for the purposes of catechetical instruction:

> St. Charles directed that children in particular should be properly instructed in Christian doctrine. Not content with enjoining parish priests to give public catechism every Sunday and holydays, he established the Confraternity of Christian Doctrine whose schools are said to have numbered 740, with 3,000 catechists and 40,000 pupils. Thus St. Charles was an originator of 'Sunday Schools', two hundred years before Robert Raikes, whose great work for Protestant children has naturally been better known in England.[16]

Bosco's early Festive Oratories were based, then, on Borromeo's concept of using Sundays for public instruction in the catechism, for children who otherwise might receive little or no education at all.

Bosco, like Borromeo, had to deal with the ravages which a plague brought to cities unprepared to face crises. In Milan, in 1576-8, Borromeo had personally inspired and organized his lay-helpers to care for the dying, administer to the sick, and build relief shelters to house the homeless. In 1854, Bosco's Oratory boys, led by the priest-educator, had performed similar duties during the Turin plague. Both Borromeo and Bosco had used up personal church effects to help alleviate the sufferings of plague victims.[17]

Presumably, therefore, while Bosco had included Borromeo's 'Sunday-school' idea in the organization and administration of his Oratories, he had also learned from Borromeo the need for personal leadership and the setting of good example in times of crisis. It was largely through the roles played by Bosco and his Oratory boys in the 1854 cholera plague in Turin, that favourable publicity was given to his Oratories and to his pedagogical ideas, and that others, again, were inspired to help those found in compelling circumstances. Thus Bosco had learnt from Borromeo that a pedagogy of catechetical instruction was only one aspect of education; another dimension of it was social: rendering assistance to the community in times of emergency.

Since, however, Don Bosco chose to name the Society he founded "Salesian", and not "Bosconian",[18] the pedagogist must have had a personal attraction to the life and work of St. Francis de Sales, 1567-1622. Although more mention was made of Francis de Sales by Bosco and his biographers than of any other saint, there was little evidence to show that the priest-educator had read any life on the man, or that he had personally owned or kept any copies of his writings.

Braido,[19] when confronted with this problem, was of the opinion that there existed in Bosco's native Piedmont a strong 'Salesian' tradition due to the fact that Francis de Sales had visited that region on at least three separate occasions. Another possibility was that the Chieri seminary in Piedmont, in which Bosco studied for the priesthood, passed on strong spiritual and devotional oral traditions of the saint to the incumbents. Joseph Cafasso, the Spiritual Director, who guided the pedagogist through his further theological and philosophical courses at the Convitto Ecclesiastico in Turin, suggested to his ex-pupil that his first Oratory at Valdocco be placed under the patronage of St. Francis de Sales.[20]

Don Bosco agreed to Cafasso's suggestion and added that the Oratory would bear the Bishop of Geneva's name for the following reasons: Marchioness Barolo,[21] who had helped Don Bosco in housing his first groups of ragamuffin boys, was an admirer of St. Francis de Sales, so Bosco named his Oratory after him to please the Marchioness; the work he "had undertaken for the welfare of boys required unruffled calm and forebearance, and therefore he wished to place himself under the special protection of a saint who had been a perfect model of these virtues";[22] because of the confusion among some of the working class in Turin, following the dissemination of Protestantism there, Bosco, mindful of St. Francis de Sales' work among the Chablais,[23] and anxious about what were regarded as heretical ideas becoming prevalent among the Turinese workers, "believed that the spirit of St. Francis de Sales was the best suited, at the time, to the education and upbringing of the working classes."[24]

Not long after Don Bosco had decided to adopt Francis de Sales as his Oratory patron, clerics who were closely associated with him at the Oratory observed that the priest-educator, in some respects, seemed to be consciously modelling his own behaviour on that of the saint. Fr. John Bonetti, one of these observers, stated:

> .... yet we now saw him a model of meekness, peaceable, and so self-controlled that he seemed never to be pressed by problems. We were convinced that he must have exercised continual self-control to such an heroic degree as to succeed in becoming a living copy of St. Francis de Sales' love for his fellowmen.[25]

In his regulations for Festive Oratories, published in 1852, Bosco wrote: "This oratory is placed under the patronage of St. Francis de Sales, because those who intend to dedicate themselves to this kind of work should adopt this saint as a model of charity and affability. These sources will produce the fruits that we expect from the oratories."[26] The charity referred to was that "supernatural, infused virtue, by which we love God above everything for His own sake, and our neighbour as ourselves for God's sake", not the generally understood idea, "outside of the Catholic Church", of "any good turn done to the needy, regardless of the motive...."[27] Thus the dedicated Salesian was necessarily a Christian, motivated by "Divine revelation"[28]. He was to be a Christian moreover, who would do more than "talk much" of charity, turning it into "smug sentimentality".[29] Charity inferred rather, "the adherence of the will to Love, to the Good, as that energizing, expansive love of God and his creatures which issues, by inner impulsion, in loving actions...."[30] Don Bosco's pedagogy was thus founded upon the Christian concept of love.

Earlier, while still at school, Bosco had decided that he would follow the idea set down by de Sales about prayers, and not let them prevent him from doing good works at the time most needed for them, since like de Sales, Don Bosco "did not wish to be a slave to personal devotions."[31] As a young man he had been influenced, too, by de Sales' maxim: "Ask for nothing, refuse nothing,"[32] and prior to saying his first Mass in 1841 Bosco wrote: "The charity and gentleness of St. Francis de Sales are to be my guide."[33] Lemoyne believed that

Don Bosco's determination to help humanity was based, to a large extent, on another statement of Francis de Sales: "A sincere love of one's neighbour is one of the greatest and most excellent gifts which Divine Goodness can give to man."[34] At the same time, eager and determined as he was to press on with his educational work, Bosco was to bear in mind another saying of de Sales: "Follow in the footsteps of Divine Providence; do not lead."[35] In 1847, Don Bosco was reported to have said: "If one is to do good, he must have a little courage, be ready for sacrifice, deal affably with all and never slight anybody. By following this method I have always had significant success.... Anybody else, even today, could achieve just as much by emulating the simplicity and gentleness of St. Francis de Sales."[36]

When the Oratory at Valdocco was in its infancy, Bosco had the motto of de Sales "Da mihi animas caetera tolle" (Give me souls; away with the rest) on one of the walls,[37] emphasising again the essentially religious nature of his educational work, an essential of all Salesian schools, still. Nevertheless, Don Bosco, like de Sales, in order to attract boys to his classes, was not afraid to use unorthodox methods. He often....

> ......used a rather curious method. Taking his cue from St. Francis de Sales, he had a boy go through the main streets of the neighbourhood vigorously ringing a good sized bell. Its clanging was a reminder to both parents and boys: to the former to send their sons and to the latter to attend. Within minutes, swarms of youngsters would appear from all over, tag behind the young bellringer, and help him call other lads to join them. In half an hour, the Oratory was filled with boys......[38]

When discussing with his co-workers the principles of his pedagogy, Bosco often began by referring to the words of St. Francis de Sales: "More flies are caught by a spoonful of honey than by a barrel of vinegar."[39] Thus Bosco's preventive system based on love and kindness, and the innovative methods employed by the pedagogist, reflected ideas of St. Francis de Sales,[40] who had scorned corporal punishment and encouraged methods involving interest, gentleness, and humour. He had been charitable towards those who needed help, witty, skilled in argument, iron-willed when the occasions demanded it.   Above all, he had been concerned with the welfare and education of deprived people.

In 1845, Don Bosco, inspired too by the life and work of St. Aloysius Gonzaga, 1568-1591, wrote a booklet on this saint entitled: *Le sei Domeniche e la novena in onore di S. Luigi Gonzaga, con un cenno della vita del medesimo Santo* (Six Sundays and a Novena in Honour of St. Aloysius Gonzaga, with an outline of the Saint's life).[41] In the preface Bosco wrote: "Here, beloved boys in Jesus Christ, is a model and an example for you to look up to in setting a pattern of life that will lead you to true happiness."[42] This booklet went through eleven editions and was handed to every Oratory boy from 1845 on.   Gonzaga's virtuous life of penance and prayer, his faithful adherence to his vocation which was devoted to the physical and spiritual welfare of his fellow men, Bosco saw as a model to place before all young people.   Don Bosco's experience of the inspiration or guidance afforded by other Christians' lives, was thus extended to his students, and this biographical pattern was further extended to include other short lives, for instance one on Dominic Savio a contemporary of the boys themselves.   Modern Salesians still claim a "superiority of real-life education over doctrinaire theories"[43] in this method, denying any aspect of anti-intellectualism in it, and arguing rather that it emphasises flexibility; learning by experience, our own and others; and human values; rather than theoretical organizational ideas.   Modern Australian Salesians for example, while not feeling limited by their founder's small written output on educational theory, do feel their methods are appreciably different from those of other Catholic teaching orders,[44] perhaps for this reason.   Familiar with the works of other educationists, they still regard the Salesian approach as significantly different; as apparently, does Pope Paul, who has been reported as saying that Don Bosco had left "a living flexible organism assimilating from every new era, rather than a rigid institution."[45]

Don Bosco named his second Oratory, opened in 1847 and located on the southern side of the city of Turin in the Piazza Castello, Piazza San Carlo, Borgo Nuova, and San Salvario districts, after St. Aloysius Gonzaga.   Prior to the opening of the St. Aloysius Oratory, Bosco had told his boys at Valdocco:

As we did in Valdocco, we shall open our second oratory on a day sacred to the great Mother of God, thus placing it under her protection. What shall we call it? We shall call it the St. Aloysius Oratory for two reasons: first, to provide a model of purity and virtue for boys, as the Church herself has done; secondly, as a gesture of appreciation and gratitude to our beloved Archbishop Fransoni, who bears the name of this saint ....[46]

In a short time "over five hundred boys attended the St. Aloysius Oratory."[47]

It was from Gonzaga, as from Borromeo, that Don Bosco drew inspiration in dealing with a public catastrophe. He would have been familiar with the part played by Gonzaga in the 1591 plague in Rome; again, a life-situation from which to learn:

In 1591 an epidemic of plague caused great ravages in Rome. The Jesuits opened a hospital of their own, in which the father general himself and many members of the order rendered personal service. Aloysius, at his own entreaty, was one of the number. He instructed and exhorted the patients, washed them, made their beds, and performed with zeal the lowliest offices of the hospital.[48]

Gonzaga was to become, in another way, a means for communication with the outside community. The priest-educator invited outside college boys who came from well-to-do families, to join his Oratory boys in joint celebrations of the feast day of St. Aloysius Gonzaga.[49] In this way, Bosco attempted to show the youth of Turin that Gonzaga, the official Church patron of students, was a model for all youth, whether rich or poor; and that Christian values were not just for the affluent classes, but were ideals towards which all could aspire.

Lemoyne, commenting on Salesian spiritual life, stated that the life and work of St. Vincent de Paul, 1580-1660, also had a strong influence on Don Bosco and hence on all Salesians:

Don Bosco not only sketched the life of St. Vincent de Paul, but carefully studied the saint's practice of the cardinal and theological virtues, and from that he drew guidelines for his own spiritual life. Apart from the adaptations demanded by the needs of his time, Don Bosco so faithfully copied St. Vincent de Paul that a reader personally acquainted with Don Bosco would feel a strong inclination to substitute his name for that of St. Vincent.[50]

While reflecting the views of a cleric, and one who had virtually made his life's work the biographical memoirs of Don Bosco, Lemoyne's comment nevertheless suggests something of the respect, even awe, held by members of his own faith, for the priest-educator. In likening him to so renowned a saint as Vincent de Paul, Bosco's contemporary and fellow priest was suggesting more than an explanation for some of Bosco's attitudes and ideas; he was making a deliberate comparison. The cardinal virtues, from which the rest of the Catholic moral virtues flow, of justice, prudence, temperance (moderation), and fortitude, were imputed to the educator, as well as those theological virtues of faith, hope, and charity. Don Bosco was compared, then, with a Catholic saint, rather than with other educators. The Catholic Church canonized Don Bosco in 1934, thus universalizing this view for Catholics. The Salesian tradition is, therefore, built on the life and teachings of a man who is recognized by his followers as a saint. Since, according both to available written evidence and the oral tradition, Bosco attempted to live according to these Christian concepts of virtue, Salesian pedagogy could represent a return to simple, practical Christian ideas rather than a complete break with the past. Bosco lived in relatively modern times compared with men such as Vincent de Paul, and he created a Society which has adapted to demands in different communities from his own, suggesting a certain flexibility in those basic ideas.

In 1850 Bosco played an active part in the foundation of Turin's first St. Vincent de Paul Society, and later was instrumental in helping found similar societies in Piedmont, as part of his active work within the general community. "Don Bosco continued to attend the annual general assembly of the Society for many years.... On those occasions he always spoke to the assembly."[51] In honour of St. Vincent, and again forming a link with society beyond the Oratory, he introduced into his first Oratory at Valdocco[52] a club which he named the Conference of St. Vincent de Paul, another purpose of this type of sodality being to instil a sense of Christian responsibility and solidarity among his students.

It was the fourth vow of the Vincentians, that of "stability", which appealed to the pedagogist. Vincent de Paul's stability, his founding of many institutions under stable regulations and constitutions, influenced Bosco in his search for simple, clear and practical guidelines and regulations in moral, theological and educational matters which would give stability amid change for his intended Society. Flexibility was not to suggest instability, for also like Vincent de Paul, Don Bosco knew what it was like to have to train himself to be patient and gentle; both men originally had explosive types of natures. It was de Paul's deliberate cultivation of the gentler human attributes, despite his more aggressive traits, which appealed to Bosco and which correlated with the need to cope with many types of people and situations in the establishing of a new educative system:

> Astonishing as it may seem, Monsieur Vincent was 'by nature of a bilious temperament and very subject to anger'. This would seem humble exaggeration but that others besides himself bear witness to it. But for divine grace, he tells us, he would have been 'in temper hard and repellent, rough and crabbed'; instead, his will co-operated with grace and he was tender, affectionate, acutely sensible to the calls of charity and religion. Humility he would have then to be the basis of his congregation, and it was the lesson he never ceased to repeat.[53]

John Ayers, in an unpublished paper entitled, *A Salesian Education*, writes that a Salesian priest and historian, Fr. Pietro Stella, stated that Don Bosco could have relied, too, "on followers of the Port-Royal school ....for crystallizing or formulating his own educational ideas".[54] Ayers quotes Stella who listed, among others, Fenelon, Rollin, and de la Salle, as adherents to the Port-Royal School[55] who influenced in some way Bosconian pedagogy.

It was probable that Francois de Salignac de la Mothe-Fenelon, 1651-1715, Archbishop of Cambrai, author of educational works: *Traite de l'Education des Filles, les Fables, les Dialogues des Morts*, and *Telemaque*, and who adopted a quietistic religious philosophy[56] which prompted his advocating a gentleness of manner and a pedagogy based on entreaty rather than compulsion,[57] affected, to some degree, Don Bosco's educational ideas. Don Bosco probably would have been aware of, and influenced by, Fenelon's distrust of "la contrainte"[58] in relation to teaching. Bosco, moreover, may have had some working knowledge of Fenelon's educational treatises, particularly the one dealing with the education of girls, which in itself was an unusual concept for the times.

Furthermore, it was possible that Don Bosco may have had some knowledge of Charles Rollin's (1661-1741) work: *Traite des etudes*, and most probably was familiar with Jean-Baptiste de la Salle's[59] (1651-1719) educational treatise *Conduct of Schools*, an exhaustive manual which "revolutionized elementary education" by replacing "the old method of individual instruction by class teaching.... in French.... not through Latin."[60]

But to generalize that Don Bosco's educational ideas were crystallized by Fenelon, Rollin, de la Salle, and others of the Port-Royal School, could be misleading, and in the case of de la Salle, the argument that he was associated with that school is tenuous, since de la Salle strongly opposed Jansenism.[61] Because of this, Bosco had more reason to be interested in de la Salle's educational work, rather than that of the Port-Royal School. Particularly in the field of educating deprived children, and in de la Salle's Sunday academy, 1698, "in which more advanced instruction was combined with religious teaching and exercises",[62] Bosco's own particular circumstances, and his response to them suggests that they may have helped him, later, in his Oratory work. It is possible, however, that Bosco could have been influenced by the innovatory breadth of the matter of the syllabuses used by the Petites-Ecoles de Port-Royal.[63]

Nevertheless, Bosco, while possibly considering the pedagogical matter of the Port-Royalists, could not have been greatly influenced by their manner of education. The atmosphere of Port-Royal, which was likened by Mme de Sevigne in her letter to Mme de Grignan, 1674, to a profound silence, a desert inhabited by hermits,[64] was a far cry from Philip Neri's words: "Run, jump, have all the fun you want at the right time...."[65] which Don Bosco frequently quoted in connection with his work, and the traditional Salesian atmosphere of work, fun, and 'joie de vivre'.

The manner of Bosconian pedagogy was based, according to the educator himself, on Christian Pauline theology and on the life and work of Christ. Don Bosco, in his treatise: *The Preventive System in the Education of the Young*, wrote: "The practice of this system is wholly based on the words of St. Paul who says: ....'Love is patient and kind.... Love bears all things.... hopes all things, endures all things.' "[66] It was more from the Pauline spirit of the early Church, together with the work of such men as Loyola, Neri, Rodriguez, Borromeo, Gonzaga, de Sales and de la Salle, than from the quietism of Port-Royal Jansenism, that Bosconian thought was influenced, and that the manner of Salesian education was evolved. This manner, recognizable today, determines the direction of the matter, and heightens the spirit of Salesian pedagogy.

Part II: Contemporary Influences.

As well as past influences which had bearing on the formation of Bosconian pedagogy, there were contemporaries of Don Bosco, all of whom he loved, admired or respected, who contributed in a number of ways towards his educational rationale. While there were probably those whose names biographers and others have not mentioned, who influenced Bosco in the education of deprived youth, the records have preserved the names of many others who, in different ways, contributed to his work and to his pedagogy.

These people, sometimes together with the institutions they represented, and sometimes as organized groups, had some bearing on the shaping of Don Bosco's methods, from Mamma Margaret, Don Bosco's mother, to the humanistic public schools of Piedmont of the 1820's. The Societa dell' Allegria; the various jobs and skills Bosco secured prior to his entry to the seminary; the seminary itself at Chieri; the work undertaken at the post-graduate theological college, the Convitto Ecclesiastico in Turin; Joseph Cafasso, lecturer in moral and pastoral theology, and later the Convitto's spiritual director; the Rifugio, where Don Bosco first began his mission in educational work; Archbishop Fransoni, the man who encouraged and supported Bosco's ideas at a time when other clerics doubted the worth of what Bosco was doing, all influenced him. Dominic Savio, the first exceptional product of Bosco's preventive system; Michael Rua, John Cagliero, among others, pupils of Bosco's came to influence their own teacher. The radical thinker Vincenzo Gioberti played a part, as did Anthony Rosmini's Congregation; the Boncompagni Educational Bill of 1848; and an educational review entitled: *L'Educatore Primario*. Fr. Girard and fellow clerical educationists; Ferrante Aporti and his Method Schools in Turin; Professors Rayneri and Allevio, who helped in pedagogical matters in the Oratories; the Cavours, Camillo and Gustavo, who both gave of their time to help Don Bosco; Louis Pavoni, whose work with artisans was well-known by the priest-educator; Urban Rattazzi, Minister of Justice, Minister of Interior, and later, Prime Minister of Piedmont were among public personages who influenced him. Bosco's visits to Rome and subsequent encouragement from Pius IX, and his later connections with Leo XIII were important to him; and lastly, the French theologian and educator, Felix Dupanloup was said to have impressed him.

Don Bosco's mother, affectionately known as Mamma Margaret, was instrumental in giving her son charitable attitudes towards people and work, which were to influence him in the education of young adolescents; and a practical down-to-earth knowledge of his religion based on her faith in God, which was manifested in what she did in the course of each day. Her daily Christian charity towards her family and neighbours was to extend, later, to the family-like life of early Salesian establishments. The young widow with long hours at work in managing a farm and raising a family impressed upon young John Bosco the concepts that the sweat of man's brow could be honourable, that duty was something holy if it were done in the right spirit.

Lemoyne, equally impressed by Margaret Bosco, was of the opinion that "John modelled himself on his mother."[1] Bosco was to exhibit "the same faith, the same purity, the same love of prayer.

Margaret's patience, fearlessness, constancy, trust in God, zeal for the salvation of souls, simplicity and gentleness of manner, charity toward all, untiring diligence, prudence in managing affairs, careful supervision of dependents and serenity in the face of adversity", claimed Lemoyne, were all to be characteristics of Don Bosco's.[2] Personal characteristics or qualities of character, rather than a detailed philosophy of education are still emphasised by Salesians. Australian John Ayers, for instance, refers to "a living history and a dynamic religious-spirit"[3] rather than a theory of education; to a response to "on-the-spot needs"[4] rather than a system. This tradition, based on Don Bosco's "evangelical simplicity and pragmatic awareness"[5], reflect his peasant mother's practical charity and hard work. Mamma Margaret's watchword: "God sees you" became, later, a maxim of Oratorians; her work ethic became the one Bosco used at the Oratories where routine chores became honourable duties. According to Lemoyne, Bosco transferred his mother's ways into his own pedagogy:

> Without realizing it, he was storing up for the future her effective pedagogical method based on love and sacrifice.... We saw reproduced in him his mother's teachings and examples: that constant vigilance, that desire to be as much as possible with his boys, that patience in listening to everything they had to tell them, that solicitous and prudent, gentle questioning with which he invited them to give an account of their conduct. All this he had learned from his mother.[6]

Perhaps the earliest Bosconian ideas about a preventive system were developed, Lemoyne believed, "under the guidance of his mother" for "John was absorbing that remarkable gentleness of manner that forestalls trouble and enables the educator to conquer the hearts of his pupils,"[7] within the family situation.

The young Bosco learned from his mother that a home was a place in which neighbours, "even bandits, carabinieri, peddlers, beggars, or stray travellers"[8] were extended hospitality. In return, they were expected to join in the family prayers; "this was the sole payment she exacted for the hospitality she extended to them."[9] Don Bosco, in connection with his educational work later, showed the same charity and hospitality towards those who called in on him. From them, too, he extracted a prayer and before taking their leave they invariably were given a short religious maxim to reflect on.

Don Bosco had many occasions to reflect on his mother's sacrifices made in order that he could study for the priesthood,[10] on her difficult decision to leave her farm and family in 1846 and spend the remainder of her life with him at the first Oratory at Valdocco,[11] on her loving work and sacrifices during the early days in the running of the Oratory.[12] In some ways, Don Bosco's counselling techniques were similar to those of his mother's who, "whatever the circumstances ....somehow always found the right words, either in public or in private, according to the individual's needs."[13] Margaret Bosco was not literate, but Don Bosco's respect for his own peasant origins and for the practical Christianity practised by his mother, is reflected both in the admiration expressed for her by the chronicler, Lemoyne, and in the "simple familiarity and free-flowing life-style that could be caught only by experience"[14] in early Salesian establishments.

Bosco, too, would have learned from his peasant mother's practical all-round efficiency: her ability to run the Oratory during his absence; her orderly ways; her astuteness in dealing with impending difficulties, in forestalling disorders, and in her business-like alertness.[15] Her friendly and sympathetic handling of domestic problems both in her own home, and later, while at the Oratory, were lessons rarely learned by men of the times, but which Don Bosco learned and later taught others, so that Bosconian pedagogy reflected that practical Christian charity which Mamma Margaret had instilled in her son as a youth, and later, from 1846-1856, as the mother and guide to so many boys in the difficult early pioneering days at the St. Francis de Sales Oratory in Valdocco.

By 1823 when young Bosco was eight years old, his mother, due to opposition from Anthony, young Bosco's step-brother,[16] had temporarily abandoned the idea of sending him to Castelnuovo[17] where there was a public school which offered "reading, writing, the essentials of arithmetic, the rudiments of Italian grammar and the catechism".[18] In the winter of 1823-4, however, John stayed with his mother's sister, Marianne Occhiena, who was housekeeper to a

Fr. Lacqua in the village of Capriglio, Don Bosco's mother's birthplace. Lacqua offered to teach John Bosco the rudiments of reading and writing, and by 1824, young Bosco had "learned to read and spell tolerably well."[19] By Christmas 1830, Mamma Margaret had finally managed to have her son, now fifteen, attend the local school at Castelnuovo:

> Municipal schools were then prevalently religious in character in accordance with the decrees of King Charles Felix issued on July 23, 1822. Boys and girls attended separate classes.... Classes began with morning prayers.... and closed with night prayers. The first half-hour of class was devoted to catechism instruction, as was the entire afternoon session on Saturday....[20] Teachers had to agree with the pastor concerning the pupils attending Mass before class and going to confession once a month. Further, on holy days, pupils were bound to attend catechism class and religious services in the parish church....
> There was only one Latin class for all the boys in all the various high school grades. The teacher was Fr. Emmanuel Virano of Castelnuovo d'Asti.... a very learned man and an expert teacher, much respected by his pupils....[21]

After some schooling here, Bosco went on to Chieri, a larger industrial town of 9,000 inhabitants, some 15 kilometres east of Turin where he attended the Chieri public school from 1831 to 1835. Whilst at Chieri, Bosco, now a young man, studied subjects and observed people with a view to his future work as an educator among youth:

> At Morialdo, Capriglio, Moncucco and Castelnuovo, he had had frequent opportunities to observe the tendencies and failings, the ways and habits of boys in lonely farmhouses, in hamlets, in villages, small and large. Now he would find himself in a town (Chieri) where crowds of boys, attending school or working, would provide him with new material for observation and give him an opportunity to learn better the field of his future work....[22]

It was from such a secondary school as the one in Chieri that Don Bosco was introduced to pedagogical ideas associated with institutions, such as school curriculum and organization. The secondary public schools flourishing in Piedmont in the 1820's with their balanced programs of secular and religious instruction, enjoyed a legal status guaranteed by royal decree of King Charles Felix. Aiming at a wide curriculum to educate the complete citizen, these schools were humanistic after the fashion of Vittorino da Feltra (1378-1446), encouraging the study of the humanities and accepting, at the same time, the existence of God. They were to form a nucleus of pedagogical ideas in relation to the incorporating of religious instruction[23] into a school curriculum which later Don Bosco used in his own educational establishments, for, as a young man brought up in the Piedmontese public schooling system, he had had impressed upon him, as upon others, that there was a strong link, a basic relationship between the principle "that education should have a religious character since God is the source of all knowledge and morality"[24] and the royal assent which Charles Felix had placed upon it. This was borne out later, as the curriculum and practical religious education of Don Bosco's Oratories were largely those characteristic of the humanistic public schools of Piedmont.

It was while still a student at the Chieri public school that Bosco, in an attempt to find a solution to some students' problems, first thought up the idea, and consequently put into effect, his students' social group which became known the Societa dell' Allegria (Happiness Club). The practical school problems encountered by some of Bosco's classmates could now be discussed openly and in a spirit of cheerfulness in this club. Typically, Bosco used his Societa dell' Allegria not only to promote communication among his fellows and to help them develop as persons but for religious purposes as well:

> ....John tried a better way of helping them, namely, to review their lessons with them and tutor them, if necessary. This way everybody was happy and he gained their goodwill, affection and esteem. Little by little, they began coming to him, first to play with him, then to hear his stories or to do their homework. Finally, as in Morialdo and Castelnuovo,[25] they just came for no special reason. It was like a club of their own and they started calling it Societa dell' Allegria, a most appropriate name because each one was expected to bring in only these books, topics or games that would add to the general cheerfulness.... John was the acknowledged leader of these boys. By common consent membership in this club was

dependent upon two basic conditions: (i) the avoidance of every word and deed unbecoming a Christian; (i) the exact fulfilment of one's duties whether scholastic or religious.[26]

Bosco took his club members to hear the Jesuit fathers conduct catechism classes in St. Anthony's church, already using the excursion method, and here became increasingly aware of the advantages of apposite illustrative religious educational material[27] which the Jesuits used in their teaching. Bosco would also amuse club members by organizing hikes and outings:

> On Sundays, after they had all fulfilled their religious duties, and also on school holidays, he would entertain them with suitable games and sleight-of-hand tricks, which they loved and which he had mastered for their sake, to keep them busy, away from idleness and bad companions. Thus they accepted him as their leader.
> Often he would suggest a walk, preferably outside the city.... Among the lovely hills surrounding Chieri they would roam from village to village, having so much fun that they did not mind getting home long after their dinner hour.
> Sometimes they would set out at daybreak to search for mushrooms in the woods around Superga.... Toward evening, they returned home, tired, flushed and soaked with perspiration, but happy and hungry.
> At other times they would plan to hike as far as Turin.... to see the bronze horse in San Carlo Square, or the marble horse in the Royal Palace.[28]

Later, the club members would meet on a voluntary basis once a week in one of their homes to discuss various topics and then to enjoy some recreation, reading, and prayer. Feelings of mutual confidence and personal trust became so developed that club members freely engaged in appraisal and evaluation programs: they "advised one another and mutually pointed out personal faults" which they "had observed or had heard others mention...."[29]

In this way it was among fellow students that many of Don Bosco's pedagogical ideas were evolved in his Societa dell' Allegria. The club, formed initially to meet needs which arose at the time, the solving of personal, educational problems, developed along lateral communication lines, with free discussions taking place in a relaxed and happy atmosphere. Members were free to come and go as they pleased, and rules were made by common consent. The club had a leader, who was acknowledged as such, not self-appointed, who guided, advised, rather than directed, them. The Societa engaged in matters of members' mutual interest concerning their welfare and the welfare of others. Its aims were directed towards social, physical, mental, and, spiritual health and led to educational efficiency, better citizenship, more effective Christianity. Self-activating, the club became a dynamic centre for students motivated by mutual respect and common interests.

Fourteen years later Don Bosco was to employ many of the features of his Chieri happiness club in his first Oratory at Valdocco, Turin. These Salesian characteristics of being adaptable to real-life situations, and of avoiding the dogmatic in educational theory while assuming the dogmatic in religious belief, are still reflected in modern in-service training.[30] "The Salesian approach" is still "to set up the most positive, attractive, evocative situation possible...." which will draw out "a free, spontaneous response."[31] All the various methods are only "means, it is rather an atmosphere, a way of life that embraces all" that is "the raison d'etre of our very existence."[32]

Another institution which influenced the priest-educator's pedagogy was the seminary in Chieri which he attended from 1835 to 1841, and where he came under the aegis of its regulations and organization. Bosco responded to the security that the systematic theological and ascetic formation offered. The institution's program of orderly divisions of studies with the practices of piety, strengthened Bosco's determination that order and the feeling of security it offered were valuable items in any educational planning. On the other hand, orderliness as contrasted with the haphazard, was not confused with formality, and seminary experiences of aloof teachers and formality in pedagogical methods led Bosco to a realization that personal relationships could be more relaxed: relationships with other teachers and students less formal than those exhibited by the superiors in the Chieri seminary:

> I loved my Superiors very much and they were always good
> to me, but I was not happy because they kept themselves aloof
> from us. We seminarians called on the Rector and on the
> other Superiors only when leaving or returning from vacation
> .... This was my only regret in the seminary. Often I would
> have liked to talk with them and ask their advice but I could
> not.... [33]

When Don Bosco himself came to be Rector, at Valdocco, he attempted to change such a situation, being a father to the boys: friendly, approachable, a teacher who offered advice and who let students know that he was available to them, no matter what the day or hour. Having experienced the results of aloofness while a student himself, Don Bosco determined that Salesian teachers would be always approachable; social intercourse always possible and open between teacher and taught. "The Salesian tradition expects teachers to mix freely with their pupils, in the classroom and outside, in common rooms and sports fields and playground", according to a modern Provincial Advisory Council on Education,[34] "true friendship" being "at the very heart of the Salesian educational environment",[35] since "there is nothing the Salesian might do, no effort he might expend, no sacrifice he might make that will possibly substitute for his 'attentive loving presence'. "[36]

An old school friend of Bosco's and fellow Chieri seminary student named Luigi Comollo[37] who studied for the priesthood from 1834 to 1839, and who died in that same year while still at the seminary, influenced Don Bosco's ideas on the practices of piety. Comollo was intensely pious but tended to make outward manifestations of piety, and was inclined to give himself unusually harsh penances. Bosco thus had his own thoughts on the practices of piety thrown into sharp relief, with the result that he came to value the more down-to-earth and practical approach for young people. In Bosco's schools, pious practices were to be in conformity with daily life, rather than harsh or too demanding. Fitted into the Oratory timetable as another part of the school day and not as exclusive ends in themselves, they included attendance at Mass and other sacraments, ejaculations or short prayers, always keeping to "simple things", but never getting "tired of doing them."[38] Newcomers were often "moved to profound conversion"[39] by vivid stories, portico maxims, the goodnight message, the word in the ear. According to the individual, religious expression ranged from "the primitive, instinctive fear of a vague Transcendent Power to that of a loving, mystical union with a revealed Personal-God".[40] Salesian houses today still "hope for this religious optimum", while being "duty bound to achieve the minimum",[41] within the particular local culture, and moving with the catechetical innovations of the times.

While still a student, and in order to pay his way whenever he could, Bosco took on a number of jobs, applying himself in such a way that he had a working knowledge and appreciation of what was entailed in them. Before his ordination in 1841, he had worked in various capacities as a farmer, wine-grower, saloon rouseabout, tailor, bootmaker and repairer, blacksmith, carpenter, joiner, printer, and bookbinder. He had acquired a knowledge of musical composition and skills as well: he played the violin, organ, piano, and could sing Gregorian chant. Armed with this practical knowledge, by 1853 Don Bosco had begun to realize the need for professional schools for young workers. "Thus there arose the first artisan school for tailoring and shoe-making (1853) and this was quickly followed by similar establishments for bookbinding (1854), carpentry (1856), printing (1861), metal work (1862) and such other undertakings as need and opportunity indicated."[42] In addition to these, Bosco had put his working knowledge of music into effect: by 1853 the Oratory band was established "as another means which he judged suitable to keep his boys from harm."[43]

His pedagogy was shaped, therefore, through his earlier practical experiences in arts and crafts, and later, through his conviction that artisans having been suitably prepared for their trades by skilled Oratory teachers, and having been trained in a Salesian atmosphere, would be equipped to take their places in an urbanized and largely technological environment without forfeiting their Catholicity:

> Don Bosco saw the problem in all its entirety. Youth must be given material security from misery, tyranny and ignorance; it must be given religious security from irreligion, atheism, and violence; it must be given professional security by provid-

ing the young worker with a training that is technically and theoretically perfect.[44]

Salesian teachers, who today still attempt to provide the means whereby youth can gain these forms of security, have been called "milieu modifiers", the "most significant factor"[45] in the environment of students. Since, it is argued, all are influenced by the environment, it is both reasonable and kind to "make it as healthy as possible."[46]

The institution which largely crystallized the educative mission and the future pedagogy of Don Bosco, however, was the Convitto Ecclesiastico of St. Francis of Assisi in Turin. It was there that Bosco came under the direction and influence of Fr. Joseph Cafasso, a lecturer in pastoral theology. Rather than go into pastoral work straight after his ordination in 1841, Bosco was advised by Cafasso to further his studies in moral theology and homiletics: "It was to this school, run by model priests and exceptional teachers, that Don Bosco was invited. Father Cafasso's advice was excellent. Outside the Convitto Ecclesiastico, it would have been extremely difficult for Don Bosco to acquire a sound and profound knowledge of pastoral theology, such as he would need in his future diversified mission."[47]

Bosco's plans for the education of youth were clarified and intensified when he saw at first hand the slums of Turin and "the misery and neglect of so many young people in the Piedmontese capital."[48] Bosco visited prisons, hospitals and the homes of the poor while staying at the Convitto, thus increasing "his ardent zeal for the welfare of the young."[49] At this time, too, he met Joseph Cottolengo, founder of the Piccola Casa della Divina Provvidenza (The Little House of Divine Providence),[50] a hospital which housed nearly two thousand hopeless and appalling cases of both sexes, observing there the gamut of human suffering and misery.

The Convitto Ecclesiastico also afforded Bosco experience in meeting and conversing with dignitaries: "Besides the Archbishop's residence, the Convitto of St. Francis of Assisi was a meeting place for the cream of Piedmontese society".[51] Many of these aristocrats who had met Bosco while at the Convitto, and who had indirectly heard of the priest-educator's aspirations, were to help him financially when he set up his first Oratory.

The first crowds of boys, who were to begin with him his educational work, milled in the grounds of the St. Francis of Assisi church which was adjacent to the Convitto Ecclesiastico. Lemoyne has quoted Bosco who wrote of it later: "No sooner did I enter the Convitto than a crowd of boys began to follow me through the streets and squares, even into the sacristy of the Convitto church."[52] When an opportunity came for him to leave the Convitto, he preferred to stay on, the pretext being that he had to give evening lectures there. But the real reason was that he had a preference for the Convitto "for he did not know where else he could gather his young friends."[53] The majority of clerics at the Convitto, including Father Joseph Cafasso, were satisfied to have him stay, and encouraged Bosco in his educational apostolate with the young ragamuffins who flocked to the St. Francis of Assisi church to be with him.

While facing up to the problems and deprivations of abandoned youth, Bosco was modelling himself on Cafasso: his confident, optimistic spirit; his learning,[54] punctuality and piety.[55] Cafasso in turn implored those who were unconvinced about Bosco's "goings-on" with grubby urchins, to "leave him alone"[56] and allow him to develop his own style. Indicating something of the suspicion in which the Bosconian approach was held by others, Cafasso's plea also encouraged the young priest: "Don Bosco has extraordinary gifts. No matter what you think of his ways, he is inspired from above...."[57]

By 1853 Bosco regarded Cafasso as his guide and mentor;[58] on another occasion readily admitting his importance in directing him at this stage of life.[59] When Joseph Cafasso died in 1860, he had cancelled all Bosco's previous debts to him and had left him 5,000 lire. Bosco also acquired some land adjacent to the St. Francis de Sales Oratory in Valdocco, an essential to the educator's plans, and through Cafasso's generosity, he then became the sole proprietor of land and buildings purchased from Francis Pinardi.[60] It was possible, then, for Bosco's pedagogical work to reach out to others.

Thus the Convitto Ecclesiastico gave Bosco varied opportunities and experiences to help him conceptually and financially to begin his educational work. By bringing him into contact with a man of great optimism and confidence, the Convitto provided Bosco with an influencial clerical friend who understood what he was setting out to do, thus allowing the pedagogist to continue his educative mission when the criticisms and doubts of others would have ended it. Lastly, Cafasso, until his death in 1860, was a source of advice, another opinion, a ready voice of encouragement which often spurred Don Bosco on in his educational work.

Don Bosco later wrote of Cafasso: "If I have done some good in my life, I owe it to this worthy priest, into whose hands I entrusted every decision, every deliberation, every plan, every undertaking of mine."[61] Reflecting the traditional Salesian interpretation of Administration and leadership, Cafasso's approachability, positive help and understanding set the pattern for relationships between teaching staff and Administration within the Salesian school. The Rector and his Council, some members of which may be deputised by the Rector or by Provincial Superiors to take departments such as Prefect of Studies or Bursar, are responsible for policies, "flowing from long-standing Salesian traditions based on the Society's educational philosophy"[62] and usually of a "broad and General" nature, "allowing the individual teachers great scope and flexibility".[63] Both the Rector, and any member of his Council, are always to be available to any member of staff, for professional or personal help, or simply to receive a complaint. "This 'open-ness' on the part of those who administer our schools, is an essential part of Salesian tradition",[64] still. Thus the Salesian ideal of the school being "a global unit" in which "no division should exist",[65] is based on accessibility and assistance.

In 1844 Don Bosco left the Convitto and was appointed chaplain to St. Philomena's Hospital. Nearby was the Pia Opera del Rifugio, an institution for delinquent girls. St. Philomena's, another of Marchioness Barolo's institutions, and intended for the care of crippled girls, was nearing completion and the Marchioness was so keen to secure Bosco's services as chaplain there that she allowed him to continue his work among his poor boys in the grounds of the yet uncompleted hospital. Bosco's other duties beside that of chaplain were to help out in Barolo's other endowed institutions: St. Mary Magdalen Convent; the Maddalenine (Little Magdalena) for problem girls under twelve; and, the Rifugio itself. Bosco's room was located in the Rifugio, whose director, Fr. Borel, quickly recognized the worth of Bosco's educative mission to street urchins. Allowing Bosco to use the room assigned to him, as well as a corridor and stairway, Borel permitted Bosco to assemble his boys for their lessons in these unorthodox areas:

> Boys were everywhere: in Don Bosco's room, along the corridor, and on the stairs. In his room, Don Bosco taught catechism and explained the Gospel, while on the stairs Father Borel, who had offered to help, did the same for the boys crowding each step. Their recreation.... was quite a comedy ....[66]

Bosco's stay at the Rifugio saw the continuation of his pedagogical work among the underprivileged Turinese youth; his work with the many unfortunate girls housed and cared for in the Marchioness Barolo's institutions nearby, alerting him to the needs of neglected girls, so that he began to realize that it would be necessary to extend his work eventually to include not only the throngs of boys, but girls also,[67] who, in their hundreds, were to be seen in various states of deprivation in the slum areas of Turin.

Don Bosco's pedagogical work in Turin was further to be encouraged when given official church approval by Louis Fransoni, Archbishop of Turin who, in 1847, authorized Bosco to admit to first communion and confirmation the boys attending his Oratory. Later, Fransoni declared: "The chapels of the Oratories shall be considered the boys' parish churches"[68] thus allowing Bosco more scope in the education of many young Turin workers who had come from outlying districts, seeking work, but who subsequently had no parish in which they could feel at home, and no opportunity for furthering their education. Fransoni, in an 1847 address to over 300 boys being confirmed at Bosco's St. Aloysius Oratory, expressed his gratitude to the pedagogist whose educational work in evening schools was fulfilling a felt need for many Turinese youths.[69]

Later, due to Fransoni's opposition to Piedmont's political liberalism, the Archbishop was banished from Turin by the secular authorities and subsequently exiled to Lyons in 1850. During the

Archbishop's absence from Turin, Don Bosco kept up a regular correspondence with the prelate, who was to be one of the first persons to suggest to Bosco the need to begin clerical and legal procedures to ensure the future security of his work: "Though far away, Archbishop Fransoni never ceased to protect and help the Oratory. Likewise he kept pointing out to Don Bosco the need to provide for its future...."[70] It was in Fransoni's experiences that Don Bosco saw what embroilment in tenuous political questions could lead to, removal from his diocese; which could mean, for a pedagogist, the possible end to a school system. Thereafter, although showing public allegiance to his archbishop,[71] Don Bosco decided to embark upon a pedagogical career which was free from political allegiances. In this way his work would be relatively safe and would survive the political uncertainties in Italy, particularly Piedmont, in the late 1840's and early 1850's. The Salesian way of life was thus traditionally to be noninvolved with politics.

On the other hand, because of Bosco's love and respect for the popes of the Church,[72] he made visits to Rome, the first in 1858, the second in 1867, both times receiving encouraging audiences with Pius IX; and his pedagogy reflected this respect for, and loyalty to, the papacy. From Rome Bosco wrote letters which were read out to the Oratory boys, much of the news in them concerning their pope. Later, when he had returned to Valdocco, he told many anecdotes about the pope to the Oratory boys, showing them how fatherly and loving was the papal concept, how human was the pope himself.

Don Bosco knew of Cardinal John Ferretti's strong interest in poor boys,[73] a fact which largely helped him in his first audience with Ferretti, after he became Pope Pius IX. Bosco was seeking recognition and approval of his newly-formed Salesian Society whose work was largely educational. Pius IX, after having been satisfied with Bosco's ability to successfully preach a mission, including a mission to women prisoners,[74] was assured that the pedagogist was the man "he himself had thought him to be at their first meeting."[75]

Pius IX subsequently aided Don Bosco in the recognition of his Congregation and gave his blessing to Bosco's Oratory work. By

1869 the Salesian Society had gained papal approval for a further ten years, the same year in which the Vatican decreed the approval of the Confraternity of Mary, Help of Christians. Meantime, the Constitutions of the Salesian Society were approved in 1874; by 1878 Don Bosco's Salesians had another pope, Leo XIII who, in 1884 became a Salesian Co-Operator. This was significant; Don Bosco's educational work was now canonically recognized; the Pope had personally joined Salesian ranks.

Since Leo XIII's times, succeeding popes have addressed themselves to the Salesian Society. At the 19th General Chapter of the Salesian Society, Pope Paul VI, for instance, thanked the Society for its continued support in education, then offered words of encouragement and advice:

> Have great faith in the aims of your Society. Could they be nobler, more modern; could they possibly be more in line with the apostolic programme of the Church today? You have chosen well. The Church confirms both the certainty of it and its merit. And finally, have confidence in those forms which give to your activity its particular character. Now the discourse becomes cautious, on account of that invitation to aggiornamento which the Church is both preaching and putting into practice. But one must be clear regarding the essentials as distinct from the accidentals: the interior forms which animate your pedagogy and your art as educators from those which are exterior and per se susceptible to some experimentation; the forms which are forever valid from those which the changed condition of the school today, of qualifications, of culture and of the didactic methods, as also the changes in social life demands these distinctions and those new choices which are already going on in the field of your practical pedagogy, which nevertheless will ever find its primitive nucleus its vital root, the knowledge and love of youth.[76]

Improvements and experimentation have always been a part of the Salesian tradition, since "the Preventive System is not a system of education so much as a way of life for use that forms in us those attitudes that make us natural followers of Don Bosco",[77] rather than followers of a prescribed system. Since Don Bosco is believed to have "pinned all his hopes in education on endurance and forebearance

—on living experiment....",[78] modern Salesian educators are expected to enrich their Society "by that very diversity and flexibility which naturally flow from the unregimented Salesian spirit",[79] while, at the same time, keeping abreast of modern developments in educational theory. On the other hand, no "contrary spirit" is to alter the "flexibility and adaptation to all forms of good"[80] which the Salesian Constitutions permit, and certain concepts, such as assistance, cannot be changed: "In assistance is to be found the compendium of Salesian pedagogy",[81] for "a teacher, according to Salesian tradition, is not enthroned in his classroom.... A Salesian classroom is a student-based classroom".[82] Thus, while heeding the pope's call to the 'aggiornamento', many modern Salesians warn against an interpretation that would lead to prescriptivism, even in modern terms, rather than to a rededication to that "way-of-life based on constantly —assimilating experience and the ongoing Breath of the Spirit"[83] which moves with the times.

Bosco's first journey to Rome in 1858, besides bringing the pedagogist to the pope's notice, also provided examples of other schooling systems which were of value to him. An educationist with an open mind, Bosco was continually on the lookout for pedagogical ideas which could be put to use back home in Turin.

For example, when Don Bosco was invited to look over the Tata Giovanni, a boys' hospice in the Via Sant' Anna dei Falegnami, a school founded at the end of the 18th Century by a bricklayer, Giovanni Burgi, who took in street urchins and provided a home for them in a rented house, he was delighted to find similarities between the Tata Giovanni in Rome and his first Oratory in Turin. Bosco observing these similarities, reasoned that "all charitable undertakings more or less resemble one another because God is their unchangeable prime mover...."[84] Always anxious to observe and learn from other educational enterprizes Don Bosco visited several at about this time. The running of the Tata Giovanni has been described by Lemoyne:

> The age-limit for admission is from nine to fourteen. The boys remain there until the age of twenty. The older and more dependable boys monitor the dormitories, while the more educated teach elementary reading, writing, and arithmetic

to the younger ones. A few clerics and laymen give lessons in the evening. Most boys learn a craft of their own choosing. Since there are no workshops on the premises, they learn their trade in town, just as the custom was in our Oratory during its early years. A few are given a liberal arts education, but only after unquestionable and long-standing proof of excellent moral character and keen intelligence....[85]

Soon after his tour of inspection of the Tata Giovanni, Bosco had occasion to visit the St. Vincent de Paul school for boys situated at Santa Maria dei Monti. "About sixty boys attended the school, all on free tuition. Their teacher had them read aloud, answer catechism questions, and do some problems in arithmetic. The pupils were unabashed, alert, and sure of themselves. Curious to know if they understood what they were reading, Don Bosco questioned a few of them and found that they had not grasped very much. He then courteously gave the teacher some suggestions which he accepted gratefully. The curriculum consisted of grammar, arithmetic, catechism, and bible history...."[86]

In the same year Bosco visited the well-known St. Michael's hospice which was under the patronage of the pope. He looked into its administration, work-shops, and boarding facilities. He found that the spirit or tone of the school tended to be repressive, so, when an opportunity arose, and using a real situation between a master and student there, he demonstrated the advantages and efficacy of his system based on understanding and kindness. Subsequently, most of the teachers at St. Michael's were impressed with the pedagogist from Turin.[87]

On another occasion he visited two festive oratories in Rome and found that they concentrated too much on recreational activities, and that the educational programs were neglected. In Bosco's view they were more like 'recreation centres', not oratories which, he believed, had to have a balanced program of work and play.[88] Another festive oratory which he visited was found to be, in Don Bosco's eyes, almost empty. After handling large numbers in Turin, he could not approve of a school which had 80 boys in an area large enough for 400 or more, thus denying many an opportunity to learn.

It was in his own students, too, that Don Bosco saw the effects of his pedagogy; and the interpersonal relationships, on a number of levels, which Salesian education fostered, tended to modify in small ways the Bosconian educational rationale.

Dominic Savio, 1842-1857, a product of Don Bosco's preventive system, and who, unlike Rousseau's masterpiece on paper, Emile, was a real person, has since been proclaimed by the Catholic Church "as the perfect model and fruit of Salesian education".[89] Savio put Bosco's work ethic into practice: "Daily work, regularly and conscientiously performed was a sure stepping stone to sanctity."[90] It was Dominic's willingness to work hard at his scholastic and religious duties in his first year at the Oratory in 1854 that attracted attention,[91] his reverence for his religion being noticed by Mamma Margaret who pointed him out to the already impressed Don Bosco; she had appreciated both his devotion and personality. Among fellow students, too, Dominic became known as an entertaining storyteller, a sought after companion, and a peacemaker. He organized a student group which was to remain close knit, till in 1859, after Savio's death, it became part of the Salesian Society newly formed by Don Bosco. Savio's methods intrigued his teacher:

> ....in a very short while he won over the difficult ones, and he spent most of his free time with them.
> But these were not his only friends; he also sought another type of boy. Among the boarders and day boys were some who—because they were clumsy, ignorant, or ill-bred—were shunned by the others. Dominic would eagerly seek them out as if they were the most likeable....[93]

Don Bosco, who later was to write Savio's life-story, saw in him a boy who was deliberately cultivating the friendships of students who in the eyes of their fellows were misfits within the Oratory. Perhaps, more importantly, here was a boy of twelve years of age, among his peers, who could give Bosco an opportunity of watching the results of such youthful charitable behaviour. According to Lemoyne Bosco found that "Dominic Savio caught more fish with his methods than preachers with their sermons,"[94] so that it was as if in Savio's methods, and in the favourable results they achieved, Don Bosco saw justification of his own, and gained added encouragement to continue with them. It was in Savio's spiritual development, "to the very heights of mystic union,"[95] rather than his not inconsiderable intellectual development, or his social competence, however, that the Salesian ideal was to be found.

Another two among the many pupils of Don Bosco, Michael Rua, 1837-1910; and John Cagliero, 1838-1926; both temperamentally different from each other and from Savio, were interesting products of the Bosconian preventive system. Don Bosco met Rua in 1848 when the latter was eleven and had watched his pedagogical methods at work with a person who was considered to be by nature saturnine, stiff, almost for a child, stern. Yet this was the person who was to succeed him, as Salesian leader, in 1888. Cagliero, who came to Bosco's school in 1852 with a reputation as being almost unmanageable, who was boisterous and belligerent, was successfully handled by Bosco's methods which put Cagliero's talents—when others, apparently, could not see them—to work and won for the Salesians, a gifted musician, capable organizer, and future Cardinal. That these two different natures could respond to the same educational philosophy resulting in their effective citizenship and Christian humanitarianism, was of value to both the men already working with Bosco, and to the educator himself in his evaluation of his pedagogical 'raison d'etre'.

Vincenzo Gioberti, 1801-1852, a cleric who played an important part in influencing Italian national feeling during the Risorgimento, had an influence on the educator, too. His contentious work, *Gesuita Moderno* affected a section of public opinion helping to develop further hostility towards the Church. However, the thesis that the Church should forfeit to the State its right to the education of the young,[96] impelled Don Bosco to defend Catholic education and in so doing Bosco crystallized his own thinking about his educative mission. Gioberti, in many ways, served as a catalyst to Bosco's educational rationale, based as it was on scriptural simplicity of faith, on Catholic teaching and on the dedication of a Religious Society. By 1848, Gioberti had joined the Piedmontese Fabrio-Casati cabinet as Minister Without Portfolio, and was exercising considerable political power. There was talk that he would become the next Foreign Minister.[97]

It was at this time that Don Bosco called on Gioberti in a courteous but uncompromising fashion and defended the Church's position in pastoral matters, education being considered as a pastoral concern. Bosco, who "....could not bear Gioberti posing as self-appointed teacher and censor of the pope...."[98] parted on good terms with Gioberti, but was not impressed with his arguments. On the other hand, the pedagogist had come away sure of his own position in relation to the Church and its—and subsequently his—role in education.

Gioberti was one of those who, according to the resistant Pius IX, "would have the Roman Pontiff to be head and to preside over some sort of novel republic....',"[99] during the agitation and political upheaval of the mid-nineteenth century movement for the unification of Italy. Reform movements since the Napoleonic era had existed in Italy "among small sections of the educated and well-to-do" who wanted both "constitutional liberty and national unity. However, the great majority of nobility and clergy, let alone the illiterate peasantry, remained traditionalists",[100] and Don Bosco, to survive as an educator, had to deal with both sections. To him, as to many Catholics at the time, liberalism was anti-Christian in its application, though the reformers' demands for freedom of speech, religious toleration, and an end to privilege and censorship, found sympathetic response among members of both the nobility and the city workers. Mazzini's complaint, for instance, that " 'the intellect dies in childhood for lack of nourishment....' "[101] could have been Bosco's own, but his call for " '....insurrection'," the " 'only course; a general determined, rising of the multitude; a holy war of the oppressed',"[102] was different from the exuberance of the Salesians, to whom "a victory which could not be gained by kindness was not worth winning".[103] Similarly, Mazzini's belief that " 'the special mission of each man, to be accomplished in harmony with the general mission of humanity' "[104] would better the human condition, was close to the dedication and zeal of early Salesians, but in its application differed from their "educative-love", which "by its own intrinsic dynamism"[105] would fill the earth.

As early as 1849, when King Victor Emmanuel II, following the failure of the 1848 revolution, refused to abrogate the constitution granted by his father to Piedmont-Sardinia,[106] Don Bosco's work was made less uncertain because of the relatively liberal and stable government in Piedmont,[107] the most advanced of the Italian states. On the other hand, the assassination of Prime Minister Pellegrino Rossi, a layman, of the Papal States, in November, 1848, the incident of the shooting of the pope's secretary, and the flight of the pope, had the effect of creating among Catholics suspicion and distrust of liberal movements. Pius IX who, when he first came to power, had been widely acclaimed as a 'liberal pope', had planned to have other non-clerics form a government council, and had allowed fewer restrictions on newspapers, now appeared to become rigid and reactionary. The 1864 "Syllabus of Errors",[108] condemned " 'progress, liberalism and modern civilization' ",[109] and Pius IX has been described as an "indefatigable foe of all liberal ideas."[110] Don Bosco, loyal to the papacy, did not, however, make any political statement or stand; and a modern Catholic writer's attitude to the situation, reflecting perhaps a more general Catholic attitude not unlike what could have been held by Bosco himself, contrasts with the usual estimate of the pope as a man who, once he was deprived of his territories, imprisoned himself in the Vatican from the fall of Rome and the Patrimony in 1870: "disillusioned by the results of his overtures and concessions to the liberals,"[111] Pius IX had realized that his enemies "were firmly resolved not to make peace with any wearer of the tiara".[112]

His successor, Leo XIII, was both "less emotional" and "prepared to see other points of view",[113] and, according to a modern Catholic popular historian reversed the policy of Pius IX, refusing to condemn political liberalism, at least outside Italy.[114] From Don Bosco's viewpoint no change in loyalty or attitude was involved for Salesians in this reversal, since their loyalty to the pope was in the religious sphere. Thus in the new Italy which so disillusioned Mazzini,[115] and was "revolutionary in its opposition to the claims of the Church, yet conservative in representing the upper class establishment and confining suffrage to men of property and education",[116] the Salesian mission to neglected and deprived youth was still both accepted and esteemed.[117]

During these difficult times, while opposition from without the Church had helped Bosco confirm his religious and pedagogical position, support and encouragement from within the Church continued to help him develop it. Anthony Rosmini, for example, and his Rosminians who ran the Institute of Charity at Stressa, agreed with Bosco's insistence on a religious basis to education regardless of contemporary trends, and offered him financial help at a difficult time.

Other more personal influences upon Bosco's developing pedagogy included that of Fr. Ferrante Aporti, 1791-1858. In 1844, when Turin, as capital of Piedmont, was the centre of both political and educational philosophy in Italy, Ferrante Aporti, somewhat of a radical in educational thinking, was invited to take the Chair in Pedagogical Method at the Royal University of Turin. This appointment, together with an educational review, *L'Educatore Primario* which appeared about this time and which represented the views of foreign as well as Piedmontese educationists, among them Fr. Girard, an advocator of popular education; stirred up interest among clerics and laymen in Piedmont many of whom were reawakened to the need for education for the masses.

Aporti, who was not only a professor of education, but was also responsible for the formation of a Method School in Turin, 1844,[118] approved by Royal Decree, 1845[119] had studied pedagogy in Vienna at the Teresianum, a school of education dealing with all three levels of pedagogy, and subsequently became an authority on Asili d'Infazia (Infant Schools). Accredited with having introduced kindergartens into Italy;[120] he had opened the first at Cremona in 1830; Aporti also began a course of his own in methodology for elementary school teachers.

It was about this time, 1844, that Don Bosco began to attend Aporti's lectures in educational method.[121] Although Aporti's ideas were under suspicion from some sections of the Turin hierarchy,[122] Bosco recognized in Aporti a man concerned with modern approaches to children, and therefore did not take notice of conservative reactions, or accusations that were levelled at him at the time: that he did not include sufficient direct references to religion in his work Don Bosco:

> had plans for his own Sunday and evening schools to be opened in the future.... He needed a supporter on whom he could rely at the outset, should trouble develop, one who would help

him overcome whatever difficulties might arise, a person of standing among those controlling public education. At that time, Father Aporti was such a man, and he fitted into Don Bosco's plans. Don Bosco had gained his esteem by showing himself favourable to popular education, and by occasionally consulting him on teaching methods.... [123]

Aporti in turn had acknowledged Bosco's *Storia Sacra*, which he believed had greatly benefited the cause of popular education,[124] and was a keen supporter of Bosco's schools at the Oratory of St. Francis de Sales.[125] "If Don Bosco was able to conduct classes undisturbed and unhampered by red tape, interference, and government inspections from 1847 to 1860, it was due to the favourable public opinion prevailing among those in power. Father Aporti certainly had a hand in all this."[126]

Don Bosco and Ferrante Aporti were generally agreed that education was a work of dedication, an apostolate in which the teacher's love for the child was paramount. Aporti was sympathetic towards the preventive system, and upheld Bosco's teaching methods which he witnessed, periodically, as a guest at the Oratory.

Illustrated text books; interesting anecdotes and episodes to illustrate lessons; pupil-participation in questions and answers, were some of the approved methods. Don Bosco, an observer and analyser of Aporti's enlightened methods, including the reinforcing of factual work with appropriate stories, and the emphasis on conceptual explanations rather than the more traditionally sanctioned learning by rote, accepted and adapted them for his own particular needs among the largely socially deprived students at the Oratory. Early demonstration lessons, in which interested observers watched a class in action on a stage, were also accepted by Bosco as practical means for showing numbers of people that the new methods worked, as well as for teacher training. The preventive system today, based as it is on the eclecticism of its founder, is still claimed to be not only religious, reasonable and loving, but also essentially "active".[127] On the other hand, techniques and methods are not of the greatest importance, since it is expected that they will change with changing times and cultures:[128] "the Preventive System is not so much a technique as an attitude; ....of course, it has its techniques, but these are no better or worse than any other technique unless they are vivified by the attitudes underlying them."[129]

Two other educationists who had some minor influence in the shaping of Don Bosco's pedagogy were Professors G.A. Rayneri and G. Allievo, at the Royal University of Turin. Both these academics had dealings with Bosco in relation to the Oratories. Rayneri, who in 1847, advised his students to go out to Valdocco and observe the sound teaching methods there,[130] regarded Bosco's Oratory as a place where his students could observe educational practice, as distinct from the theory. To what extent Rayneri directly influenced Bosco was, according to Braido, uncertain, but there would have been some discussions between them on the subject of education, while Professor Allievo, on the other hand, stated that he agreed generally with Bosconian emphasis on the importance of kindness in education, on rewards, on punishments, and on the concepts of the preventive system.[131]

Aspects of Bosconian pedagogy which attracted professorial interest and led to student observation emphasized the practical, rather than theoretical, nature of Bosco's work in education. Reluctant to become prescriptive by theorizing, or by explaining his system in detail, Don Bosco did outline much later in 1877, in a "brief sketch",[132] what was planned to be developed into a "small book"[133] on the preventive system, its practical application, advantages "and why it ought to be preferred."[134] However, due to constant demands on his time, only "an admirable little treatise"[135] was written.

Two distinguished Piedmontese admirers of Don Bosco's educational work whose influence on the priest-educator was also incidental were Count Camillo Cavour, 1810-1861, and his brother, the Marquis Gustavo. Both brothers visited the Valdocco Oratory on special feast days; Camillo Cavour openly lauded Bosco's humanitarian work for the disadvantaged youth of Turin, there.[136] In 1849 Gustavo Cavour wrote in *L'Armonia*, a Turin newspaper, in praise of Don Bosco's work in the Festive Oratories.[137] Marquis Cavour and Anthony Rosmini, in 1850, both attended and enjoyed the presentation of a play, written by the pedagogist, and staged by the Oratory boys.[138] Although Camillo Cavour, by 1855, had embraced liberal principles and denounced clericalism and absolutism, and although he became, as a politician, one who "combined liberal doctrine with Machiavellian practice",[139] he, nevertheless, showed favour towards Bosco's institutions and still offered the pedagogist personal financial assistance which Bosco prudently refused rather than compromise himself or lose his non-political status.[140]   Yet Camillo Cavour, espouser of anti-clerical legislation, advised Bosco to take steps to place his educational work on a legal footing so that he might continue with his socially useful work.[141]   Don Bosco's encounters with Cavour confirmed in him the need to ensure that his pedagogical work was founded on a broadly non-political base, and at the same time that its involvement in largely humanitarian work was deemed socially efficient by a government largely anti-clerical.

Contemporary with Don Bosco's developing Oratories was the pedagogical work of Lodovico Pavoni who ran boarding schools in neighbouring Lombardy. Bosco sent one of his Salesians, Fr. P. Ponte, to visit particularly Milan and Brescia where Pavoni's schools were established, so it was probable that Bosco had a working knowledge of Pavoni's treatise, *Gli Artiglanelli*, and the regulations for this Institute after Ponte returned to the Oratory in 1850.

The Pavonians were particularly concerned with the dissemination of their work through the printing press, and it was likely that Pavoni's success in so spreading new educational ideas impressed on Don Bosco the necessity to set up similar printing shops and presses in Valdocco, this being accomplished eleven years later at the St. Francis de Sales Oratory.[142]   Today, there are one hundred and one Salesian printing schools in the world[143] which not only teach young men the printing trade, but also produce books of educational value for distribution in other schools.

Meanwhile another prominent political figure to influence Don Bosco's pedagogy, was a former Minister of Justice, Minister of Interior, and later, Prime Minister of Piedmont, Urbano Rattazzi, 1808-1873. By 1854 Rattazzi had visited Bosco's schools, was impressed with the tone and methods used there, and had consequently suggested to his government that Bosco's preventive educational methods could be used to advantage in secular institutions such as gaols, and in civic affairs.

Although largely anti-clerical, Rattazzi's government gave financial assistance to the Oratories.[144] In 1856, Rattazzi urged the government to safeguard Bosco's institutions as they helped to reduce Turin's juvenile delinquency rate. By 1857 Rattazzi was echoing Cavour's advice in urging Bosco to place his educational work on sound judicial and theological bases. Rattazzi was asking Don Bosco at a time when other Catholic Orders were being suppressed, to begin writing regulations and constitutions for the founding of an entirely new religious Congregation. Moreover, Rattazzi guaranteed his government's support for Bosco's work, mainly on the grounds that it was eminently humanitarian in its undertaking of socially useful work,[145] and he gave Bosco the hint that his new Society would be safe if its members had property rights similar to those of ordinary citizens. Don Bosco decided to begin proceedings to legalize his pedagogical work, but at the same time was careful not to lose his independence by becoming obligated to Rattazzi's requests.[146] Through Rattazzi, Bosco's work in education was allowed to continue despite the sentiments of the ruling political majority who were largely anti-clerical.

Towards the end of Don Bosco's educational apostolate, small influences may have been brought to bear on his work by Felix Antoine Philibert Dupanloup, 1802-1878, Bishop of Orleans, theologian, orator, political writer, and educational philosopher. Bosco met Dupanloup in 1877. Later, in 1883, in a sermon given in Paris, it was noted that Bosco freely quoted Dupanloup. This probably was politic: it showed that Bosco was cognizant of Dupanloup's reputation in his own country. It could also have meant that Bosco was genuinely interested in Dupanloup's work, including his three volumes, *L' Education*, a series of works, written between 1850 and 1862, defending the need for freedom from outside authorities and controls in education. Though, by this time, Bosco's educational ideas were already crystallized, at least he would have gained satisfaction in knowing that the methods incorporated in his preventive system were echoed in Bishop Dupanloup's writings which also endorsed kindness in education.

Bosco would have had knowledge, too, of the results of the dispute, resolved by Pius IX in 1855, between Dupanloup and Fr. Gaume, 1802-1879, author and theologian, over whether the study of Pagan Latin classics was to be combined with the Latin of the Church Fathers.[147] Pius had ruled that Christian concepts written in the Latin of the pagan classicists would be acceptable in the teaching and learning of Latin in schools. This decision had a confirming post-influence on Bosconian pedagogy, for in 1853, two years before Pius IX's encyclical, Don Bosco had already included studies of the pagan classicists with those of the Church Fathers in the curriculum at the Oratory. Thus his earlier innovatory step in the teaching of Latin had been sanctioned, indirectly through Dupanloup and Gaume, by Papal Encyclical in 1855.

Don Bosco had drawn upon diverse elements from historical and contemporary sources to formulate his pedagogy, yet had never elaborated beyond brief outlines and notes for the passing on of his own ideas. While he had brought to these sources his own dimension, the concept of preventive assistance, he had anticipated many of the contemporary educative ideas of others in his Oratories from as early as 1841. Influences upon his pedagogy, Pauline in its spirituality and its emphasis on the persons involved at all levels, were often incidental, the flexibility of his ideas allowing for adaptations according to circumstances or to evidence of successful methodology elsewhere, particularly as his work expanded and became more complex. From the little Oratories to a demanding system of schools, the education of boys, and later of girls, came to involve the pedagogist with the problems both of the street and of government.

Basic and unchanging in his pedagogy however was the Christo-centric educational environment which was to be "joyful", with "festive exuberance and dynamic activity. . . . geared to the here-and-now conditions of local culture. . . . informal, open-hearted. . . .", allowing for individual development "as spontaneity and creativity thrive on such freedom",[148] with the educator always in the midst of his boys. Professionalism was secondary to the dedication and good will of the

Salesians, and political involvement was almost on the level of diplomacy in order to maintain non-alignment and to survive.

Don Bosco's means of disseminating his pedagogy were, regardless of his few written explanations, nevertheless at least as successful as those used by other pedagogists. His religious Society passed on a living and oral tradition and began to build up "a small library of real-life studies in education",[149] based on the biographical, anecdotal approach: real-life stories, examples, situations, memoirs. Often written in flowery style with "the Italian fondness for neologisms and circumlocution", at which "an Anglo-Saxon mentality "may "balk",[150] the " 'way of doing things, taught us by Don Bosco,' " nevertheless has been handed down: "pastoral love, young and alive, is at the very heart of our spirit; just as it was for Don Bosco as seen in the very beginning of our Society."[151]

This pedagogy, based on the patience[152] and love of the educator, was concerned more with the behaviour of educators than with organization and curriculum, though he borrowed from many sources to keep abreast of successful developments in both. That a "touch of steel in the Salesian system"[153] was found in his attitude towards self-discipline, in both educator and student, was not, however, because he accepted coercion, but because he was convinced that voluntary self-mastery would come in the love atmosphere:[154] "There was nothing we would not do for him who loved us so tenderly."[155]

The Salesian educator, exhorted "at all times to show respect and gentleness to parents.... meeting them as persons rather than as adjuncts to be tolerated";[156] dedicated to the loving assistance of his students, with an "evenness of temperament.... poised, alert.... cheerful and pleasant";[157] dealing not only with local authorities but also with his own community, with whom the same behaviour involving patience, tolerance and confidence was expected; would seem to have faced a difficult task. Don Bosco's "paradoxical saying",[158] however, suggests a down-to-earth awareness of human limitations as well as an idealism that confidently assumed eventual success: " 'the best is the enemy of the good.' "[159] Reluctance to codify permitted Bosco's acceptance of a behavioural zeal, a willingness to learn, a dedication to children from his early teachers. They were not expected to produce a professional 'best';[160] but rather to enter upon a life-style which, demanding the very dedication and zeal they already offered, although non-inhibitory, non-restrictive and non-punitive, was to be willingly accepted for the welfare of others, in this respect being closer to early Christian philosophy than to the various contemporary influences affecting organization or method.

Notes to Part I of Chapter 7

1   *Butler's Lives of the Saints*, Vol. II, p.396.

2   *ibid.*, p.397.

3   *ibid.*, p.398.

4   Lemoyne, *op.cit.*, Vol. II, pp.226-7.

5   *ibid.*, Vol. IV, p.388.

6   *ibid.*, Vol. VII, p.100.

7   Don Bosco could have read this popular Life on St. Philip Neri, written by Fr. James Bacci in 1837.

8   Lemoyne, *op.cit.*, Vol. IV, p.174.

9   *Butler's Lives*, *op.cit.*, Vol. III, p.226.

10   *ibid.*, pp.225-6.

11   Informally questioned on their pedagogy and teaching, and on their attitudes to modern developments in education, representatives from Australian Salesian Houses at a Chapter called by the Provincial in Melbourne, December 1974, indicated these views.

12   *ibid.*,

13   Fascie—*Del Metodo Educativo di Don Bosco*, p. 32; quoted by J. Ayers, in his unpublished treatise, *A Salesian Education*, p.3.

14   *Butler's Lives*, *op.cit.*, Vol. IV, p.226.

15   Lemoyne, *op.cit.*, Vol. III, p.66.

16   *Butler's Lives*, *op.cit.*, Vol. IV, p.258.

17   Charles Borromeo used up coloured processional fabrics to make clothes for the needy; Bosco used altar cloths and vestments as bandages for cholera victims. *Butler's Lives of the Saints*, Vol. IV, p. 261; Lemoyne, *op.cit.*, Vol. V, pp.50-64.

18   Don Bosco could have had his Congregation named after himself. Other Orders and Societies within the Catholic Church had taken the name of their founder: Franciscans from St. Francis, Benedictines from St. Benedict, Dominicans from St. Dominic, Vincentians from St. Vincent de Paul. That Bosco's Congregation took the surname of another saint was an indication of the esteem and respect that Bosco had for St. Francis de Sales.

19   Braido, Pietro. *Il Sistema Preventivo di Don Bosco*, pp.81-82.

20   Lemoyne, *op.cit.*, Vol. II, p.196.

21   Marchioness Barolo was a wealthy Turinese benefactress who gave money to build schools, foster homes for working girls, hospitals, and convents. She helped the working classes and the poor.   She was responsible for the building of the Rifugio, an institution for wayward adolescents; for St. Philomena Hospital; and the Convent of St. Mary Magdalen; all of which were in Turin.   She was also responsible for the building of the Maddalenine, an institution for delinquent girls under the age of twelve.   When the Marchioness met Bosco who at that time was only recently ordained, she immediately took to him and allowed him to use the grounds of the yet uncompleted St. Philomena Hospital as a place where Bosco's boys could gather and play.   These were the days before Bosco had established a permanent place to start an Oratory. See: Lemoyne, *op.cit.*, Vol. II, pp.182-188.

22   Lemoyne, *op.cit.*, Vol. II, p.197.

23   The Chablais were a people of the Savoy alpine region in France who were influenced by Calvinistic theories and threatened to break with the Catholic communion in Savoy.   Francis de Sales was sent to the Chablais region and from 1594 to 1598 he laboured to convert these people who were, at first, obdurate, but later became willing followers of de Sales.   Because of his success in converting the Chablais, de Sales was, in 1599, appointed coadjutor to the Bishop of Geneva, and in 1602 he became Bishop of that See.

24   Lemoyne, *op.cit.*, Vol. II, p.197.

25   *ibid.*, p.197.

26   *ibid.*, Vol. III, p.68.

27   *The New Catholic Dictionary*, p.196.

28   *loc.cit.*

29   Gerald Vann. *Morals and Man*, p.114.

30   *loc.cit.*

31   Lemoyne, *op.cit.*, Vol. I, p.271.

32   *ibid.*, p.297.

33   *ibid.*, p.383.

34   *ibid.*, Vol. II, p.36.

35   *ibid.*, p.47.

36   *ibid.*, Vol. III, p.39.

37   *ibid.*, Vol. II, pp.409-411.

38   *ibid.*, Vol. III, p.124.

39   *ibid.*, Vol. IV, p.385.

40   St. Francis de Sales, for instance, was not in favour of corporal punishment.   He believed that fostering confidence through love was a means which did away with the need for threats.   He, too, was methodical, charitable in outlook, gentle in his manner, yet possessed, when necessary, an iron will. He engaged others in dialogues to arouse interest, used humour to attract people to his cause, was vitally concerned with the education of the young, particularly those of the working classes.   He visited the sick, the lonely, provided shelter for the homeless.   He was well-versed in argument, possessed a rapier wit. It was as if Don Bosco had modelled himself on the man whom he valued so highly that he declared him patron of his first educational enterprise and later took his surname to name his own congregation.   Butler's Lives, Vol. I, pp. 195-201.   Margaret Trouncer, *The Gentleman Saint, St. Francois de Sales and his Times*, 1567-1622, The Catholic Book Club, London, 1963.

41   Lemoyne, *op.cit.*, Vol. II, p.281.

42   *ibid.*, p.282.

43   Ayers, *op.cit.*, p.4.

44   Informal questions, Melbourne Australian Chapter; December, 1974.

45   Ayers, *op.cit.*, p.27.

46   Lemoyne, *op.cit.*, Vol. III, pp.187-188.

47   *ibid.*, p.200.

48   *Butler's Lives, op.cit.*, Vol. II, p.605.

49   Lemoyne, *op.cit.*, Vol. IV, pp.472-473.

50   *ibid.*, Vol. III, p.270.

51   *ibid.*, Vol. IV, p.50.

52   *ibid.*, M.B., Vol. V, pp.469-473.

53   *Butler's Lives, op.cit.*, Vol. III, pp.143-144.

54   Ayers, *op.cit.*, p.24.

55   Port-Royal, formerly a convent situated in the Chevreuse Valley near Versailles, became a centre for adherents of the doctrine prescribed by Cornelius Jansen, 1585-1638, Bishop of Ypres, Flanders.   Jansen's doctrine,

later called Jansenism, was a form of Calvinism as it precluded the human will as a partner in God's love; God chose and converted whom He pleased; this was strongly opposed by the Jesuits.

56 Quietism, a mystical doctrine of a Spanish priest, Molinos, 1640-1696, was taken up by Mme Guyon, 1648-1717, a widow of means who subsequently influenced Fenelon who read her devotional works, the substance of which was that the role of the Christian was a passive one. Only through devotional contemplation and the abandonment of the will to God was salvation possible. Fenelon, imbued with the tenets of Quietism, wrote *Maximes des Saints*, which was condemned by Rome, 1699.

57 Lagarde and Michard, in their study of French Literature of the Seventeenth Century, wrote of Fenelon: "Sans etre un apotre de la tolerance a la maniere des 'philosophes', comme on l'a cru au XVIIIe siecle, il prefere agir par la douceur et user de sa seduction naturelle, car il doute de l'efficacite de la contrainte." Lagarde, A et Michard, L. *XVIIe Siecle Les Grands Auteurs Francais du Programme*, Vol. III, Bordas, Paris, 1960. p.423.

58 *loc.cit.*

59 St. Jean-Baptiste de la Salle, 1651-1719, was the founder of the Brothers of the Christian Schools. Braido, in his work: *Il Sistema Preventivo di Don Bosco*, pp. 110-115, pointed out that Bosco's pedagogy was similar in some ways to that of the Brothers' whose ideas were based on de la Salle's work.

Braido also suggested that there were ideas from de la Salle's *Le dodici virtu' di un buon maestro* (Ed. Agatone, 1835) that Don Bosco used, particularly in relation to evening schools and the personal dedication of the teacher.

De la Salle was also founder of the first teachers' training college, Rheims, 1687. Parish priests sent suitable candidates to la Salle who trained them in pedagogy then sent them back to their parishes as fully trained teachers.

"The Church has shown her appreciation of the character of this man, a thinker and initiator of the first importance in the history of education, by canonizing him in 1900.... in 1950 Pope Pius XII declared him.... patron of all school-teachers."
Butler's Lives, op.cit., Vol. II, p.318.

60 *ibid.*, p.317.

61 *ibid.*, p.318.

62 *ibid.*, p.317.

63 Les Petites-Ecoles de Port-Royal: "Ouvertes sous le nom modeste de Petites-Ecoles, les ecoles de Port-Royal furent tres peu nombreuses; l'une d'elles avait ete etablie a Paris en 1647 rue Saint-Dominique d'Enfer; les autres furent creees vers 1650 a la compagne, a Port-Royal-des-Champs et dans quelques maisons voisines, aux Granges, au Chesnai, pres de Versailles,

et au chateau des Troux, pres de Chevreuse. La persecution les fit fermer on 1660. Mais, si au cours de sa breve existence comme maison d'education Port-Royal n'eut le temps de former qu'un millier d'eleves tout au plus, la plupart apparentes aux religieuses ou aux Solitaires, l'enseignement qu'il donna fut tres brillant et, si l'on peut dire, deja tres moderne.

"Ses innovations pedagogiques ont surtout consiste a developper l'enseignement du grec et du francais, a faire meme une place aux langues etrangeres, espagnole et italienne, a simplifier les etudes grammaticales en y introduisant plus de logique, a donner le pas aux exercices oraux sur les exercices ecrits et a mettre le plus possible entre les mains des eleves les textes complets des auteurs." Marcel Braunschvig. *Notre Litterature Etudiee Dans Les Textes*, Tome I, *Des Origines a la Fin du XVIIe Siecle*, Harrap, Paris, 1949. pp.723-724.

64 "Ce Port-Royal est un Thebaide." (The first Christian hermits retired to the Thebaide desert in Upper Egypt). Braunschvig. *op.cit.*, p.578.

65 Lemoyne, *op.cit.*, Vol. VII, p.100.

66 *Constitutions and Regulations of the Society of* St. Francis de Sales, *op.cit.*, p.200.

Notes to Part II of Chapter 7

1 Lemoyne, *op.cit.*, Vol. I, p.31.

2 *ibid.*, pp.31-32.

3 Ayers, *op.cit.*, p.20(c).

4 *ibid.*, p.20(c).

5 *ibid.*, p.20(c).

6 *ibid.*, p.43.

7 *ibid.*, p.49.

8 *ibid.*, p.119.

9 *loc.cit.*

10 *ibid.*, pp.160-161; p.215.

11 *ibid.*, Vol. II, pp.403-405.

12 When the running of the Oratory became financially difficult, Mamma Margaret sold the remainder of her land together with part of her bridal trousseau to raise money in order to buy food and clothing for the first boys who stayed with them. The remainder of her trousseau was used to make vestments for the chapel, chasubles, albs, surplices, altar cloths. Lemoyne, *op.cit.*, Vol. II, p.414.

13 Lemoyne, *op.cit.*, Vol. III, p.261.

14 John Ayers. *Blessed Michael Rua*, Pauline Fathers and Brothers of the Society of St. Paul, Homebush, N.S.W., 1974, p.13.

15 *ibid.*, pp.264-267.

16 Margaret Occhiena had married the widower Francis Bosco who already had a son, Anthony, from a previous marriage. Margaret subsequently had two children, Joseph and John, by Francis who, on May 11th, 1817, died of pneumonia, aged 33 years. The young widow was now left with three children to raise, and a small land holding to manage. As Anthony was considerably older than the other two boys, Joseph and John, it fell to his lot to help his step-mother manage the farm. When John showed a desire to go to school, Anthony placed obstacles in his step-brother's path; he believed that schooling was unnecessary for John and that he should take his place on the farm. Mamma Margaret therefore faced a dilemma about John's education, but she bided her time until an opportunity presented itself. Meantime, John helped at home and on the farm and did not shirk his duties at either place.

17 Castelnuovo was a town some five kilometres from Becchi.

18 Lemoyne, *op.cit.*, Vol. I, p. 73. The school at Castelnuovo was typical of the public humanistic schools in Piedmont. Religious instruction was a requisite subject of the curriculum in the public school system in Piedmont at that time.

19 *ibid.*, p.75.

20 In Piedmont, schools closed on Thursdays and Sundays.

21 Lemoyne, *op.cit.*, Vol. I. p.166.

22 *ibid.*, p.185.

23 An account of what constituted religious education, which was considered as a basic factor in education appears in Lemoyne, *op.cit.*, Vol. I, pp.196-197.

24 *ibid.*, p.197.

25 Wherever Bosco went he had groups of youngsters around him who would come to hear stories and be instructed in their faith. Bosco would also devise games for them to play and help them in their schoolwork.

26 Lemoyne, *op.cit.*, Vol. I, pp.194-195.

27 *ibid.*, pp.195-196.

28 *ibid.*, pp.199-200.

29 *ibid.*, p.196.

30 For example, the 1964 translation of Father Eugene Valentini's "The Salesian Assistant", a conference given at a Refresher Course for teachers of philosophy and pedagogy on the 28th August, 1959. (Circular).

31 Provincial Advisory Council on Education: *Treatise on the Preventive System* (No date), p.4.

32 Valentini, *op.cit.*, p.10.

33 Lemoyne, *op.cit.*, Vol. I, p.281.

34 *Treatise on the Preventive System, op.cit.*, p.17.

35 *loc.cit.*

36 *ibid.*, p.14.

37 Luigi Comollo, 1817-1839, was a close school friend of Don Bosco's. He later joined Bosco at the Chieri seminary and because of his character and piety gained Bosco's admiration. Earlier, at school, Bosco's strength and courage had come to Comollo's rescue when he had been assaulted by some bigoted schoolboy larrikins. From that time their friendship continued until 1839 Comollo died at the early age of twenty-two. Bosco was impressed by Comollo's courage and Christian piety. In 1854 he wrote *Notes on the life of the youth, Luigi Comollo*, and much later, in 1884, he wrote a small book entitled: *New Stories of Luigi Comollo.*

38 Valentini, *op.cit.*, p.8, quoted Don Bosco's writing on the life of Michael Magone.

39 Ayers, *op.cit.*, p.23(a).

40 *ibid.*, p.23(a).

41 *ibid.*, p.23(b).

42 Dino Cavallino, "Technical and Agricultural Schools", *Don Bosco in the World, op.cit.*, p.152.

43 *Don Bosco in the World, op.cit.*, p.197.

44 Cavallino, *Technical and Agricultural Schools, op.cit.*, p.152.

45 Provincial Advisory Council, *op.cit.*, p.5.

46 *ibid.*, p.15.

47 Lemoyne, *op.cit.*, Vol. II, p.35.

48 *ibid.*, p.45.

49 *ibid.*, p.48.

50 The Piccola Casa, run by Fr. Joseph Cottolengo, cared for those cases which the other hospitals in Turin could not admit. There, were hospitalized "forsaken orphans, disabled men, cripples, paralytics, mental defectives, epileptics, people afflicted with ulcers and incurable diseases in all stages of gravity and loathsomeness—and rejected by other hospitals, whose rules barred their admission." Lemoyne, *op.cit.*, Vol. II, p.52.

In Turin, today, the now famous Cottolengo Hospital still caters for those cases which other hospitals, for aesthetic reasons, cannot admit to their wards.

51 Lemoyne, *op.cit.*, Vol. II, p.150.

52 *ibid.*, p.54.

53 *ibid.*, p.178.

54 *ibid.*, p.67.

55 *ibid.*, pp.97-98.

56 *ibid.*, pp.274-275.

57 *ibid.*, Vol. III, p.38.

58 *ibid.*, Vol. IV, p.410.

59 *ibid.*, pp.413-414.

60 *ibid.*, Vol. VI, p.373.

61 *ibid.*, Vol. II, p.39.

62 Provincial Advisory Council, *op.cit.*, p.16.

63 *ibid.*, p.17.

64 *ibid.*, p.17.

65 *ibid.*, p.16.

66 Lemoyne, *op.cit.*, Vol. II, p.192-193.

67 Don Bosco's pedagogy was officially extended to girls in 1872 with the foundation of the Institute of the Daughters of Mary, Help of Christians, with Mother Mazzarello as their first Superior. She used Don Bosco's preventive system of education.

Today, there are over 18,000 Salesian Sisters in the world whose educational works include: 1,071 Oratories, 843 kindergartens, 687 elementary schools, 278 secondary schools, 398 professional schools, 690 work rooms, 131 evening schools, 108 tertiary institutions, and 120 mission schools. *Don Bosco in the World*, *op.cit.*, p.387; p.390.

68 Lemoyne, *op.cit.*, *M.B.*, Vol. III, p.196f.

69 *ibid.*, Vol. III, p.264.

70 *ibid.*, Vol. IV, p.77.

71 Don Bosco had shown loyalty to Fransoni, and had displayed some courage by visiting the prelate in Lyons during his exile there. Lemoyne, *op.cit.*, Vol. IV, p.77.

72 Lemoyne, *op.cit.*, Vol. II, pp.258-260.

73 Cardinal John Mastai Ferretti, Bishop of Imola, was president of

Giovanni Tata and St. Michael institutions for poor boys. Later, as Pope Pius IX, he continued to show an interest in underprivileged children. Lemoyne, *op.cit.*, Vol. II, pp.369-370.

74 Bosco was invited through Monsignor Merode, Chamberlain to Pius IX, to give a retreat to 260 women prisoners. Later he was to give another retreat for men at St. Michael's. Bosco did well and earned the respect of Pius IX. Lemoyne, *op.cit.*, Vol. V, pp.571-572.

75 *loc.cit.*

76 "The Discourse of His Holiness Pope Paul VI to the Members of the 19th General Chapter of the Society of St. Francis of Sales.", 21st May, 1965, in *XIX General Chapter of the Salesian Society*, Rome, 1965, pp.298-299.

77 Provincial Advisory Council, *op.cit.*, p.2.

78 J. Ayers, *A Salesian Education*, *op.cit.*, p.16.

79 Rinaldi, "Conferenze", p.105; quoted by Ayers, *ibid.*, p.17.

80 Aubry, "*The Salesian Spirit*", quoted by Ayers, *ibid.*, p.20(b).

81 Valentini, *op.cit.*, p.2.

82 Provincial Advisory Council, *op.cit.*, p.18.

83 Ayers, *op.cit.*, p.20(d).

84 Lemoyne, *op.cit.*, Vol. V, p.542.

85 *ibid.*, p.541.

86 *ibid.*, p.545.

87 *ibid.*, pp.549-551.

88 *ibid.*, pp.570-571.

89 Piero Bargellini, "St. Dominic Savio", in *Don Bosco in the World*, *op.cit.*, p.97.

90 *ibid.*, p.96.

91 Lemoyne, *op.cit.*, Vol. V, p.82.

92 *ibid.*, p.134.

93 *ibid.*, p.136.

94 *ibid.*, p.137.

95 Ayers, *A Salesian Education*, *op.cit.*, p. 23(a). The mystical union "consists in the experiential love of God, so intimate that the soul, without losing anything of its physical and natural being, is divested of its own affection and is wholly lost in God." (*The New Catholic Dictionary*, *op.cit.*, p.980). It is considered under that branch of theology which deals with the higher forms of mental prayer, Mystical Theology.

96 Lemoyne, *op.cit.*, Vol. III, p.164.

97 "On December 16, 1848, Vincenzo Gioberti was appointed president of the cabinet and foreign minister. In a desperate attempt to find support for the new war which was being planned against Austria, Gioberti went to Paris to seek help from the French Republic. His mission was a failure.... Gioberti decided to send Piedmontese troops into Tuscany, the scene of republican agitation, to restore that region to the Grand Duke, but the other ministers opposed the plan. As a result, Gioberti permanently lost his ministerial post on February 22, 1849." Lemoyne, *op.cit.*, Vol. III, p.326.

98 *ibid.*, p.302.

99 E.K. Bramsted, "Italy, 1815-1914." *The West and the World,* 1789-1914. (Ed. N.K. Meaney), Science Press, N.S.W., 1972, p.165.

100 *ibid.*, p.162.

101 A.G.L. Shaw, *Modern World History*, Cheshire, Melbourne, 1961, p.121.

102 *ibid.*, p.121.

103 Ayers, *A Salesian Education*, *op.cit.*, Attributed to St. Francis de Sales, p.7.

104 Bramsted, *op.cit.*, p.164.

105 Ayers, *Blessed Michael Rua*, Pauline Fathers and Brothers, Homebush, N.S.W. 1974, p.41.

106 Also referred to as the Kingdom of Sardinia, as Piedmont-Sardinia.

107 J.J. Cosgrove and J.K. Kreiss, *Two Centuries*, Whitcombe and Tombs Pty Ltd, 1969. The king nominated the Senate and Council of Ministers; there was a narrow franchise for the Chamber of Deputies, less than one percent of the population voted, p.144; A.G.L. Shaw, *op.cit.*, p.159.

108 This was attached to the encyclical, *Quanta cura.*

109 Shaw, *op.cit.*, p.288.

110 Bramsted, *op.cit.*, p.166.

111 J. Farrow, *Pageant of the Popes*, Catechetical Guild Educational Society, St. Paul, 2, Minnesota, Sheed and Ward, N.Y., 1950, p.350.

112 *ibid.*, p.348.

113 Bramsted, *op.cit.*, p.170.

114 D. Meadows. *A Short History of the Catholic Church.* All Saints Press, Inc., N.Y., 1960, p.210.

115 Bramsted, *op.cit.*, p.170.

116 *loc.cit.*

117 Lemoyne, *op.cit.*, Vol. IV, p.68.

118 *ibid.*, Vol. II, pp.148-149.

119 *ibid.*, p.169.

120 *ibid.*, pp.165-167.

121 *ibid.*, pp.167-168.

122 *ibid.*, pp.169-171.

123 *ibid.*, p.171.

124 *ibid.*, p.311.

125 *ibid.*, p.312.

126 *loc.cit.*

127 Valentini, *op.cit.*, p.1.

128 Don Cimatti, a Salesian missionary to Japan is reported to have asked: "Unless we Salesians become Japanese to the marrow—understanding their character and customs, transforming ourselves into them to make them see our love—then our apostolate will remain without fruit." (L'arco, Don Cimatti; a character sketch, quoted by J. Ayers, *A Salesian Education, op.cit.*, p.23(b).)

129 *Provincial Advisory Council on Education, op.cit.*, p.14.

130 Lemoyne, *op.cit.*, Vol. III, p.21.

131 Braido, *op.cit.*, pp.127-128.

132 *Constitutions and Regulations of the Society of St. Francis of Sales, op.cit.*, p.195.

133 *ibid.*, pp.195-196.

134 *ibid.*, p.196.

135 *ibid.*, Footnote, p.195. Bosco's written output, however, included: textbooks; works on theology, religious philosophy; almanacs, and lives of saints and popes.

136 Lemoyne, *op.cit.*, Vol. III, pp.288-289.

137 *ibid.*, p.360.

138 *ibid.*, Vol. IV, p.26.

139 Bramsted, *op.cit.*, p.167.

140 Lemoyne, *op.cit.*, Vol. IV, pp.73-77.

141 *ibid.*, p.74.

142 Printing presses and a printing shop were first established at the St. Francis de Sales Oratory, Valdocco, in 1861.

143 *Don Bosco in the World, op.cit.*, p.272.

144 Lemoyne, *op.cit.*, Vol. V, pp.34-39.

145 *ibid.*, pp.459-461.

146 *ibid.*, pp.281-283.

147 *ibid.*, Vol. IV, p.443.

148 Ayers, *A Salesian Education, op.cit.*, p.30.

149 *ibid.*, p.4.

150 *ibid.*, p.20(b).

151 Article 40. *S.D.B.: New Regulations,* quoted by Ayers, *A Salesian Education, op.cit.*, p.20(b).

152 "But above all else I recommend to you prayer and patience, without which all rules are useless." Don Bosco, quoted by E. Valentini, *op.cit.*, p.3.

153 Ayers, *op.cit.*, p.19.

154 *loc.cit.*

155 Bishop Costamagna, quoted by E. Valentini, *op.cit.*, p.8.

156 Provincial Advisory Council on Education, *op.cit.*, p.18.

157 *ibid.*, p.19.

158 Ayers, *op.cit.*, p.15.

159 *loc.cit.*

160 "....If I had aimed at perfection, I should have achieved little or nothing." Don Bosco, quoted by Auffray, *Saint John Bosco, op.cit.*, p.280.

CHAPTER 8

CONCLUSIONS FOR TODAY AND TOMORROW

The Salesian educational movement today is international. Don Bosco's preventive system of education embraces, to some extent, every continent. Salesian educational internationalism is, in part, therefore, an indication of the relevancy of Bosco's educational ideas in modern times. His methods are used in the teaching of both boys and girls at pre-school, primary, secondary, and tertiary levels of education; Salesian schools cater for various educational needs: general, commercial, technical, agricultural, vocational, and academic.

Pertinent to each Bosconian institution, regardless of country or nationality, are the threefold Salesian educational criteria of Don Bosco's preventive system: "reason", "religion", and "kindness". All three criteria emphasize a way of life, a manner rather than a matter in teaching, the focal point of which is qualitative, with reference to both the educator and the individual pupil for whom he is responsible. This qualitative approach is not limited to Salesian pedagogy today; it has been proposed by modern educators who hold differing philosophies from Bosco's; but its wide acceptance again suggests a continuing relevance in Salesian pedagogy. Professor L.M. Brown, for instance, has written: "It is the man who counts, and the way he goes about performing his work."[1] The Salesian educator is primarily a man who is living Christian, humane values, among educands who in his view are inalienably worthy of them. Salesian methods are largely practical not theoretical: though these are based on a particular interpretation of man it is how the educator and the pupil work that counts. The consistency between that which is taught and that which is seen to be done by the educator, by those under his charge, is a measure of the Salesian's worth. He may talk about reason, religion, and kindness, but more importantly, he must be seen, and known, to be reasonable, religious, and kind in his dealings with those whom he teaches. In this sense the Salesian teacher must exhibit "a relatively high degree of personal dignity and self-mastery"; and exercise a "calm rationality in human relations."[2]

The work of the Salesian teacher is a labour of love, for Don Bosco's preventive system asks of each teacher hard, demanding, unremitting work; long hours of constant and committed assistance. For the Salesian, teaching is a vocation, a calling, a profession which demands dedication: in its ranks there is little room for the uncommitted, inept, unsure or indecisive. A Salesian's love for children must show, for pupils must know they are loved; a love for children is fundamental; without it there is no effective Salesian education. Educands in recognizing this love their teacher has for them will in time, reciprocate it. Reciprocal love and mutual respect are basic in Bosconian pedagogy, foreshadowing in this, Buber's[3] dialogic relationship and triadic communion, but in this case, Christian in its nature.

Don Bosco's preventive system is, however, as effective as the quality of its 'assistance'. While this may be true of many educational systems where, if supervision is lacking, or ineffective, the atmosphere of student society tends to lose vitality, it would be more so in the case of Bosco's preventive system where assistance is the key to both the educational environment and to its efficiency. The term 'preventive' however, does not infer anything 'prohibitive' or 'restrictive', as it has come to mean in the modern sense, rather, derived from the Latin word 'praevenire' which means 'to set up beforehand', 'to go before', 'to support', 'to provide' or 'to foresee',[4] it suggests sensitive and predictive educators.[5] In Salesian educational philosophy a gram of prevention, through intelligent assistance is, figuratively speaking, worth a kilo of cure.

Salesian 'assistance' is never simply an arbitary line drawn across a playground supervision roster: it is the hub of Bosconian pedagogy. Every member of staff of a Salesian school is 'at assistance' from the Rector and Headmaster down to the most junior teacher or senior student; and assistance is an on-going, round-the-clock, built-in permanent feature of each Salesian's educational acceptance. Rectors, Heads of departments, teachers old and young, strike up conversations with students in the playground; lines of communication are vertically and horizontally opened up so that the recreation period becomes as it did with Don Bosco, an extension of the educational processes begun in the classroom, those processes centred in relaxed, informal, reasonable, respectful and kind exchanges between educator and educand.

Salesian 'assistance' foresees problematical situations, provides support and direction for those who need them, is in itself a counselling technique without the restrictions, or inhibitory nature of the formalities of the counsellor's office with its four walls and closed door. Don Bosco's 'word in the ear', his advice 'on the run', his insistence on an informal, friendly, and kindly approach are all means to Salesian assistance, which is characterized by its active, participatory, personal involvement with students during playground recesses, according to the times and the culture involved. The rapport established between teacher and student in conversation or at play is transferred to the classroom to establish an educational work ethic based on mutual trust, confidence, respect and co-operation. Foreshadowing the work concept commented on by Mumford Lewis,[6] that work which makes man a master of the conditions in which he lives, rather than that competitive self-interest work ethic criticized by Karl Mannheim,[7] which is both repressive and ascetic; Don Bosco's interpretation was social and expressive. One result of Salesian 'assistance' was the making of a classroom situation in which work was not odious or tedious but something shared which was interesting, productive, worthwhile, and fun.

However, if so much of Salesian pedagogical effectiveness is dependent on the efficiency of its 'assistance'; then the quality of each Salesian and the quantitative worth of his assistance are of more importance than social organization if the preventive system is to work. Don Bosco's methods were concerned more with 'loving' and 'persons', than with 'reconstructing', and 'society',[8] though his ideal was the Christian social concept of the Kingdom of God[9] on earth.

Each teacher is as effective as the combined qualities of each individual; hence, it is the individual man who counts in the long run, not the theory. Given Salesians of mediocre standards, or possibly, given lay-teachers who do not subscribe to or share the enthusiasm of religious with regard to 'assistance', the preventive system could face the loss of its particular effectiveness, to change into a disrupted community characterized by a dichotomy of educational purposes. The ideal of Salesian 'assistance' is only possible where all members of staff genuinely share in its making. Only then will the students, who perceive the staff's common committed approach to their assistance, have the necessary confidence in their teachers to perceive them as Don Bosco had urged: foreshadowing in this respect Rogers'[10] concepts of 'congruence', of sensitivity and awareness of others, of warmth and caring, and yet of being separate in the Buber sense. For Don Bosco, however, the communication of this acceptance and love, is on both a communal and a personal basis, approaching the theological concept of "the communion of saints".[11]

Don Bosco had occasion himself to call his Salesians to task when he found that they had been neglectful in their assistance of the boys. He remedied such a situation by calling the staff to a meeting and exhorting each individual to go back to his former practice, joining the students in their games in addition to engaging them in conversation. In this way Salesian teacher participation became a part of student involvement and the peculiarly Salesian tone of the school developed. Don Bosco had shown that there was a distinction between active assistance and passive supervision and that the atmosphere of educative love was dependent upon each Salesian teacher fulfilling his role in preventive assistance.

The priest-educator's experiential teaching methods underlined an approach which was not aloof, superior or self-conscious, but aimed at reaching "beyond immediate or short-term objectives" and was "....characterized by ideals", and "a concern for a better quality of life".[12] Bosconian pedagogy thereby assumed the teacher's, love and respect for the dignity and worth of the individual pupil. It assumed that any method was valid if it allowed for initiative, movement, and versatility in an educational situation where the focal point was the child, unique in his growth and development. A balanced program of work and play, in this atmosphere of friendliness, relaxation, mutual respect and encouragement, would create a situation in which an important element for the learning process developed— the child's feeling of personal adequacy and self-esteem.[13] The

Bosconian pedagogy is imbued with a spirit of enquiry fostered through group work, pupil-participation and interaction, involving the same two-way educational process in which the pupil knows that he is loved by the teacher who, in turn, enjoys the educand's trust and confidence. Particularly in the case of the disadvantaged child, one whose environment had failed to provide him with the necessary experiences, skills and values for success in his society,[14] this warmth, the accepting and respecting atmosphere in which the teacher understood his student's background and attitudes, the Bosconian educators anticipated modern ideas.[15]

The long-range aims of Don Bosco's pedagogy were two-fold: to prepare an individual to take his place in corporate society; to give him an awareness, understanding and appreciation of his Catholic religion in order to help him take his place in the community as an effective Christian citizen. There were more immediate needs to be met, and short-range aims were concerned with the acquisition of the necessary vocational skills to enable a person to work satisfactorily and hence provide for his immediate and future family needs, Don Bosco seeing in vocational education a legitimate means to promote social betterment and alleviate suffering by developing economic efficiency as well as civic responsibility in his students. Other short-term aims of Bosconian institutions were: the development of such personal qualities as diligence; pride in, and respect for, work; concern for the welfare of others; patience, humour, restraint, perseverance, loyalty, courage, independence, tolerance, honesty, gentleness, forebearance, kindness, reverence, respectfulness, and humility; the ideal virtue in each case being consistently brought before the attention of each child through reasonable, respectful, and kindly Salesian example. For instance, each student was either shown in class, or more often, in the recreation period in the playground, in the presence of Salesian assistance, when the opportunity arose, an act which usually consisted in the solution of a pressing situational problem. Later, the educator usually followed up with a 'word in the ear' to ensure that the reasons given and actions performed by the teacher to solve the particular problem had been understood and appreciated.

Don Bosco's educational methods were flexible in that they stressed the utilization of the means available, according to cultural circumstances, and that they were based both on the accumulated experiences of the Society and on the teacher's own experience. The school, viewed as an instrument, a means to a better quality of life, both physically and morally, was, according to Albera, an historical adaptation of the "original pattern" of the Festive Oratory in which boys, "attracted by brief, animated recreation"[16] could learn something about their religion. It was the demands of his times that led Bosco to seek accommodation, to teach trade skills and 'the three R's', and to create at last the complex, permanent colleges. One of the preparations for a better quality of life was seen in the charitable involvement of students and staff in the works of assistance which invited both to act in a spirit of co-operation in accepting responsibilities inside and outside the school situation; as well as in the opportunities to become literate, or to improve other cognitive and social skills.

Bosconian institutions, due to the family spirit that is encouraged in them, still employ pedagogical methods which involve continued delegations of authority. For instance, senior students are asked to assist younger pupils in their work and play, to be responsible for some of the duties assigned to them, and to apportion work and duties to others. They in turn have been assigned duties from higher up, a vertical 'responsibility chain' of duties thereby operating alongside the lateral communication within peer groups. Don Bosco's teaching methods, based on authoritative rather than authoritarian lines, and on the principles of liberty rather than authority, are usually free from constraints or conditions, hence, suggestions take priority over enforcements in classroom or playground procedure, and are those which best meet collective and individual needs of teacher and students. For example, lessons are programmed to follow students' interests, games played involve free choice, boys are not regimented or treated en masse in spiritual matters, a reasonable or kindly act has priority over seniority, rank, or privilege. The classroom or playground became a microcosm of society from Don Bosco's time, in that it depended on a close co-operation and communication among students, teachers, parents, employers and employees. For instance the many social and educational events which were put on for the general public and which Bosco encouraged in his Oratories were practical examples of parent-teacher-pupil-ex-student-employer associations necessary for both student and school success; and examples of a community involvement, which has continued to develop throughout the world. A World Convention of Past Pupils was held in Turin in 1954-5.

Bosco's methods suggested that motivational techniques were necessary for promoting effective learning. Dealing largely with the underprivileged, neglected and deprived children of industrialism, Bosco's particular techniques were developed to meet their needs; and while modern Salesians explain[17] that all the means used then are not necessarily applicable today, Bosco's sustained attempts to arouse the curiosity of children produced an educational process which became an outgoing joyous experience such as could still be aimed at. Hence, teaching techniques were not static but differential; capable of modification in a changing society. These techniques, too, however, relied on the educator's personality and initiative to a large extent, so that while Salesian teaching methods were up-to-date and largely eclectic they did not have a step-by-step series of definitive directions which could be followed, without much personal effort, by the teacher. Wherever possible however, the 'high-light' technique was suggested for lessons which were to be carefully prepared by the teacher, dealing with concrete, one-step-at-a-time points, using pictures and examples the children understood. Most procedures of inference were inductive rather than deductive, ensuring a fuller use of material collected and used by both teacher and pupils. These methods again predicted those advocated by modern educators dealing with "culturally deprived children".[18]

In general, the Salesian school today is still run on family lines, with the Rector assuming the role of a father who is concerned for the welfare of the school. The preventive system with its emphasis on reasonableness, the practising of religion, and the necessity for friendliness and kindness in human relations is fundamentally an attitude of mind, a way of life rather than a collection of pedagogical methods and theories. Its essence is presence, an assistance which is personal and continuing. Bosco's 'system' as such, is a 'way' in which what is done is consonant with faith and reason, and how it is done involves personal attitudes and performances. The welfare of others in Bosco's 'way' is related to 'caring', which, to be effective, involves 'doing': a continuum of practical works of assistance, not performed abstractedly, but personally. Assistance is given and received because a person is loved. While the modern concern with "only the sentimental face of love",[19] has paradoxically accompanied that obsession with "the need to depersonalize (or impersonalize)",[20] 'love' has become an awkward term, "a mere epiphenomenon"[21] which could make the Salesian ideal appear vague and diffuse. Nevertheless, in the same century that "we have come to know man as he really is.... that being who has invented the gas chambers of Auschwitz" who "is also that being who has entered those gas chambers upright, with the Lord's Prayer or the Shema Yisrael on his lips";[22] it is still indisputable that man, for good or ill, is also "able to live and even to die for the sake of his ideals and values".[23]

In the Salesian ideal of the 'friendly presence' of the assistant is seen "the most readily discernible manifestation of the Preventive System; it is also its supreme technique. The Salesian must constantly have under review the motivation, the manner, the style and the frequency of his presence among the boys. The 'basic attitude' of our apostolic methods.... is one of 'sympathetic and willing contact with the boys'."[24]

The distinctive feature of Don Bosco's Salesian schools, as seen within the broad framework of Catholic education is their philosophy of preventive assistance.

Don Bosco's Pedagogy in Relation to Twentieth Century Educational Thought

The only account written specifically on education by Don Bosco was his treatise, of some dozen pages, entitled: *The Preventive System in the Education of the Young*. Compared with a prolific writer and educationist who bridged the nineteenth and twentieth centuries, such as John Dewey, or with more recent educational thinkers such as J. Brubacher, J.M. Rich or P. Nash who wrote works on various aspects of educational philosophy, Don Bosco was not an educational theorist. He was essentially a practical educator, a 'doer', one of those "sensible men" who "soon abandon 'saying' in favour of 'showing'."[1] Biographical memoirs are studded with examples of his pedagogy in action, hence they are more akin to case-histories than to pure research. If Gilbert Ryle's[2] view were applied, however Bosco's lack of written, formulated educational theory[3] would offer few problems: Ryle believed that we do not need a theory to account for a practice; the rationale can follow later.

Besides the anecdotes, the vignettes, recorded by men who worked alongside the pedagogist, and who had deliberately decided on a course of reproducing and recording the words and actions of Bosco because they believed that it was their duty to posterity; there is the small treatise about his preventive system which is a standard or measure alongside which the biographers' accounts when placed, show a certain correspondence. This treatise and the many recorded actions he carried out in his capacity as educator, together with other biographical, in-the-field works, make up the traditional Bosconian pedagogy.

From an analysis of what Don Bosco's biographers recorded in the life of the priest-educator, in relation to his work among youth in his Oratories and elsewhere, some general principles of Bosconian educational thought are inferred. These pedagogical principles grouped under broad headings, when examined and compared with pedagogical criteria of other educational writers of more recent times, show a foreshadowing of many twentieth century educational ideas.

Don Bosco's educational concepts based on 'reason', 'religion' and 'kindness', all three areas of which were interrelated and part of his preventive system of education, were largely concerned with educational processes which involved: training, instruction and learning by example and experience; teaching and learning principles; training and encouragement in problem-solving; training in the art of conversation through sodalities, clubs and 'assistance'. These were aimed at, in R.S. Peters' phrase, the "whole man",[4] who learned what was "worth-while"[5] for his material, intellectual, and spiritual benefit. Margaret Mead, at the sixty-second annual convention of the National Council of Teachers of English, in the U.S.A. in 1972, suggested that each child's learning "what it is to be completely human" was what was worthwhile in education, and while for Don Bosco being 'completely human' involved the religious experience, his students' collaboration "with the teacher in the educative process" had brought about a relating "to what has happened, what is happening and what will happen"[6] in the context of their times. What was educationally 'worth-while' lay not only in the developing of a useful citizen, one who could take his place in an efficient and competent manner at his employment, but also one who could be responsible to, and for, others in socially useful work. However, what was 'worth-while' was also to be found in the practising of his Catholic faith: 'knowing, loving and serving God'; and developing from this, his relationships with his fellows, these being based upon the Bosconian ideals of reasonableness, charity, and kindness.

Don Bosco's aims, then, were realistic enough: effective citizenship, useful work through education; a faith to live and die by. Bosconian values, too, were in agreement with his aims: a largely vocational education to meet the needs of people confronted with industrial urbanism; together with a Catholic philosophy of life; a preparation for living and for 'the life to come'.

John Dewey, pioneer of pragmatic instrumentalism[7] admitted of only naturalistic values; Bosco admitted of both naturalistic and supernaturalistic. Whereas both Dewey and Bosco were concerned with social efficiency, with education by participation, with play as a means to learning, with the efficacy of psychological and sociological educational bases, and with what Dewey defined as the 'reconstruction of experience' as worthwhile educational aims; Bosco would have regarded education, not as its own end, as Dewey did, but only as a means to an ultimate end: man's eternal salvation. While John Dewey regarded education as a process of living, Bosco saw it as a preparation for future living as well.

Don Bosco's educational aims prefigured in some respects those of A.N. Whitehead,[8] English educationist, since Whitehead in the 1950's described the educated person as one who was appreciative of culture but who had, in addition, expert knowledge in some special direction; and suggested that ideas presented to educands were to be as few and as important as possible: a priority concinnity of educational style. Don Bosco's boys particularly his artisans, would not have been unfamiliar with that form of education, the 'acquisition of the art of the utilization of knowledge' which Whitehead described. The secular educational concepts acquired by Bosconian pupils were utilized and tested, not inert or useless but practical and down-to-earth. In Bosco's Italy, though anti-clericalism was strong, the practicality of his students' acquisition of religious concepts too, could have had more than spiritual significance for young people living in a still basically Catholic society.

R.S. Peters, another English educationist, writing in 1963, in "Must an Educator have an Aim?"[9] argued that some educational systems followed a method in which experiential means were adopted to premeditated ends, resulting in a means-end model which was false. For Peters, values were principles involved in 'proceeding' or 'producing' rather than 'goals' or 'end-products'. He stressed that a term such as 'self-realization' was grandiose and was to be avoided. The crucial question for Peters with regard to educational aims was that they were to be in terms of what procedures were adopted: aims were, in fact, procedures. Quality of life lay in the activity of education, not its end. Don Bosco's pedagogy was in agreement with Peters', in that the manner of education was important; but was not in agreement with an educational rationale without a premeditated end. For how would one 'proceed', or 'produce' without direction? And where would these 'procedures' end? Principles involved in 'proceeding', for Don Bosco, would only be part of the argument, tending towards an educational amphiboly. Educational principles, for him, were in agreement with a process which was: that through diligent and purposeful work, and the practising of religion, all 'proceeding' and 'producing' would arrive at an end: man's salvation.

Don Bosco and Jacques Maritain[10] however, would seem to have agreed on the ends of education: the 'shaping' of 'dignified' Man, the fulfilment of his personality and individuality; on education as a 'human awakening', a liberation of man through knowledge, wisdom, goodwill and love. They both, as Catholic educators, would have regarded any pedagogical rationale based exclusively on science as spurious; that pragmatism, as Dewey understood it, was a form of scholarly scepticism, a cult of means which would end in a psychological worship of the subject. Don Bosco's views anticipated Maritain's conception of education as a process of constant, creative renewal, a spontaneity in and widening of the pupil's experience; and a need for adoption of methods to suit the times. Don Bosco would seem to have presaged Maritain's criterion that wisdom could not be learned as a subject, that it included both intuition and love.

Martin Buber's transcendental existentialism,[11] although denying Christocentricity, with its social conception of knowledge based on mutual relationships, was not unlike Don Bosco's Catholic spirituality as seen in his Sodalities. Here Bosco encouraged dialogical relationships between pupils and teachers with the 'inclusiveness' on the part of the educator assuming a disinterestedness so as not to destroy the relationship through familiarity, as in the case of Buber's 'I-Thou' relationship. While man's solitariness according to Buber was checked by communicative encounters between man and man, man and nature, man and God; Bosco had evolved communicative techniques in dealing with personal isolation and loneliness in his inclusive Salesian 'assistance'. Teachers as 'loving fathers' whose continued 'presence' foresaw problems before they arose were already behaving in the manner of Buber's conception of an educator: a 'teacher-artist'; for the effective implementation of Bosconian preventive pedagogy required teaching to be an art. The needs of children were being met with consistently applied methods centred in reasonableness, and kindness, in a communion of love.

An empiricist such as Herbert Feigl,[12] however, having no time for absolute values, would not find affinity with Bosconian pedagogy's being based on beliefs and valuations in the unknown and unknowable. Like Dewey, Feigl did not admit of revelation or supernaturalism, as Bosco did. On the other hand, Bosconian educational ideas differed little from Feigl's hypothesis that the educator should clearly guide people towards conduct which would yield a large measure of self-approval; the danger of egotistical subjectivism developing from this, which would be contrary to the ideals of Christian charity and humility, however, was acknowledged by Bosco, and was to be balanced reasonably against the need for the learner's self-esteem.

G.H. Bantock, in his work, *Freedom and Authority in Education*,[13] disagreed with empirical thinkers in relation to educational aims, arguing that Dewey's analogy between school and society was tenuous: school was concerned with learning in a way society was not; moreover, the role of the teacher as 'Big Friend' or 'Cheer Leader' was not true to life outside of the school situation. Bantock's concluding that ultimate questions could not be avoided, that educational aims, concepts of value and authority were bound up with the nature of man and his relation to the universe, could allow for the unequivocably Christian interpretation that Bosco made. His pedagogy assumed adequate ends, without which, according to Bantock, educational practice was directionless, pointless. To the Christian educator it would be like building an educational system without a plan, a beginning with no end, a causeless causality.

Don Bosco wrote in the first section of his treatise on the preventive system: "There are two systems which have been in use through all ages in the education of youth: the preventive and the repressive."[14] Further on Bosco stated that the repressive system was such that it depended on a Rector who "must rarely be found among his subjects, and as a rule only when it is a question of punishing or menacing" and that the system as such, being an enforcement of law, was "less troublesome.... especially suitable among adults and the judicious, who ought of themselves to know and remember what the law and its regulations demand".[15] Bosco then showed that the preventive system was "opposed to" the repressive in that having made school rules and regulations known to the students, the Rector and his assistants then accepted an added responsibility of active 'assistance'; they became as 'loving fathers' who "can converse with them, take the lead in every movement and in a kindly way give advice and correction" thus placing the pupils in the warmth and security of "the impossibility of committing faults".[16] In other words, the preventive system, although more difficult to put into effect because of its demands on teaching personnel who were to be continually present among their students, was still better than the alternative, some form of repressive system which was more quickly and easily applied. The main difference, in an important pedagogical sense, Bosco argued, was not so much in terms of time taken or immediate results, but in that the preventive system allowed his teachers to relate to student attitudes and levels of behaviour and to communicate with them, not in the capacity of overseers or outsiders but as insiders who were accepted there, to offer assistance when required.

The preventive system, as such, was free from pressures and disciplinary measures extrinsic to it; guidance, correcting, counselling forces being intrinsic, it could therefore allow for a significant freedom of action on the part of educator and educand. In effect, Don Bosco's preventive system aimed at being free from outside enforcement and allowed for more educational freedom from within. As in the case of a working democracy, however, speed of decision-making was slower, and the change over from an efficient repressive system to the more slowly working preventive system often entailed a lengthy period of adjustment to a changed environment for new students.[17] Bosconian solutions to educational problems, sought in a family-type environment where teachers, because of their continued presence were accepted as fathers or brothers who were 'on hand to lend a hand' at the logical and psychological moment, took time. It also assumed a Christian concept of the validity and worth of the family both as a social unit and as a prototype of the loving environment: "that common life, rooted in the self-forgetful attitude of mutual devotion, the undivided loyalty.... the inclusive love given by the whole person to the whole person....",[18] which can develop, through "the daily work, the daily drudgery; all the burdens.... the economic anxieties; the responsibilities...." of life, a "deep, underlying joy ...."[19] In this manner, Bosco's children being secure in the knowledge of continuing help in a communion with others, were not "isolated" or "anxious" in the sense that Fromm suggested was the situation for many people in the modern age:

> That modern man, freed from the bonds of pre-individualistic society, which simultaneously gave him security and limited him, has not gained freedom in the positive sense of the realization of his individual self; that is, the expression of his intellectual, emotional and sensuous potentialities. Freedom, though it has brought him independence and rationality, has

made him isolated, and thereby anxious and powerless. This isolation is unbearable and the alternatives he is confronted with are either to escape from the burden of this freedom into new dependencies and submission, or the advance to the full realization of positive freedom which is based on the uniqueness and individuality of man.[20]

As constituted members of a pedagogical family, each child's "uniqueness and individuality" had already been acknowledged by Bosco, together with the security that such an environment provided. Freedom was, however, to be understood in the Pauline sense: "where the Spirit of the Lord is, there is freedom".[21] While "it is not appropriate to say that we choose to be happy", since "choice is not the same as wishing",[22] Thomistic moral doctrine as Bosco understood,[23] did "not aim at the niggardly ordering of the individual's conduct in blind obedience to a code"[24] but did limit Catholics to the laws of the Church; on the other hand:

> It is not solely self-love, however sublime; it is not merely altruism, however grand; it is not merely obedience to a law; it is not the service, however disinterested, of an impersonal absolute, nor obedience to a capricious God; it is the communal striving, motivated by love which is.... 'congregativus', not, like selfishness, 'disgregativus', after the life of God....[25]

which was sought for in Bosconian institutions.

Thus, although Don Bosco's Oratories allowed for certain freedoms within the framework of the Christian, family-type environment, and although he spoke on free will in his talks to the boys, they were only partially free, in Mannheim's sense,[26] to influence the social conditions of the Oratories from within. Due to subtle and kindly pressures, they were acting voluntarily to the extent that they were making choices they had to make, given the factors of Salesian 'assistance', which influenced their development. Although the nature of free will was pointed out to Bosco's pupils by the Salesians and they were 'free' to either accept or reject their state, most of their choices were determined through preventive 'assistance' by educational and religious orientated conditioning processes. This is not to say that this basically deterministic approach could be applied exclusively to Bosconian pedagogy; it is a problem shared by many educationists today: that of free will and determinism. While many have become aware of their own freedom, but because of the mostly-beyond-our-control-framework in which we live, much of the time our responses are determined, and hence, only occasionally we are free to choose.

On the other hand, as R.S. Peters has pointed out, what is worthwhile can be "transmitted in a morally unobjectionable manner".[27] If then, "the concept of 'indoctrination' may be used to describe all sorts of processes" as J.P. White has argued,[28] "as long as they are seen by the indoctrinator as effective ways of enforcing belief",[29] then there appears to be an as yet ill defined distinction between that "all-out assault"[30] on a student which Bosco himself objected to, and that "danger that a pupil who identifies himself with a teacher who is himself a believer will be indoctrinated...."[31] Yet if "motivation is the key to any modern education policy"[32] and it is now being admitted that "the stimulus of ambition"[33] is not sufficiently strong, then Bosco's emphasis on the stimulus of "curiosity, the desire to understand, to know or to discover"[34] could be applied to religious as well as secular experience, so that religious belief could be transmitted in an 'unobjectionable manner' through 'a teacher who is a believer'.

Similarly, it has been argued that some modern educators who believe that "because the school should be in closer touch with everyday life.... it should simply be done away with", are not "progressive and even revolutionary", but rather leading to a "retrograde"[35] situation, such as Don Bosco struggled to remedy. Because Bosco's few regulations were "seen to be rational"[36] and since his students had confidence in him as a rule giver,[37] his system, free in the Pauline sense, worked.

J.M. Rich,[38] an American educationist, pointed out that any successful organization, such as a school, would largely depend on the harmonious relationship within it between two basic functions: control and innovation. If those in authority had few relations with teaching personnel who, in turn, had little communication with their students, then teachers and students would think that a 'faceless' authority was determining their future, and feelings of alienation resulting in inefficient teaching would follow. Such problems would be prevented, Rich concluded, if individuals had meaningful social contacts and interaction with their peers. Further, alienation would be diminished by involving teachers and pupils in forms of decision-making. Don Bosco, from 1847, had been involving the students in youth circles in decision-making in their clubs and sodalities; the 'presence' of the Salesian teachers during 'assistance' was encouraging 'social contacts' and 'interaction' among educators and educands; Don Bosco was meeting his staff weekly to discuss current pedagogical problems in connection with their and the students' work, and sought solutions on a harmonious and friendly basis. Bosco was already anticipating organizational methods of control which are, at times, still talking points among educationists. Further, Rich was of the opinion that one solution to the problem of organization lay in teachers identifying their own goals with the school, and, in most cases, the personality of the administrator had a direct bearing on this procedure.

There is little doubt that Don Bosco's dynamic personality enabled him to direct those teachers under his care along lines which were consonant with his educational policy, mainly due to the personal nature of his relationships with them. Each one knew that he cared for and about them; he was as a father to them, interested in their welfare. Pupils regarded their teachers in the same light; hence, school organization and control were on family lines in which independent interests and goals were enjoined to further the progress of the whole organism. Still today incoming Salesians "have been advised to steep themselves in the Salesian way of life, until such a simple life-style becomes part and parcel of their religious thinking and educational make-up",[39] rather than, "in the name of a counterfeit professionalism" becoming part of "a huge Educational Juggernaut".[40]

Nevertheless, complex educational establishments had to be managed and administered. The same spirit prevailed in this. Don Bosco made a point of explaining school rules, for instance, to the whole school, staff and students, at least once a term, giving the justification for each rule. In addition, the prospective duties of both teachers and pupils were read out and the reasons for such duties given. The aims of this procedure were: to ensure that all members of the school family were aware of their responsibilities, duties, and freedoms;

that the community would be aware, through the public airing and substantiation of regulations, of what they were choosing to abide by; and that these rules were meant to be effected in a 'fair' and 'impartial' manner. Again, the importance of the rule giver as well as of the bases of the rules themselves, was evident; but Salesian emphasis on what has been accepted or rejected traditionally, refers only to the 'spirit' of Bosconian pedagogy, not to a series or set of rules.[41]

Don Bosco's Oratories approximated to, in Israel Scheffler's terminology, the "rule model"[42] in which the school abided by rules or principles which were reasonable; wherein issues arising out of school business were assessed in the light of general principles; where concepts of 'principles', 'reasons' and 'consistency' went hand in hand in cognitive and moral spheres; where rationality was measured in terms of consistency, impartiality, universalizability of principles, and human dignity; and, in which the "job of education" was to "develop character in the broadest sense", a "principled thought and action" in which "the dignity of man" was manifested.[43] Bosconian Oratories, which anticipated many of these principles, had distinct advantages: knowledge was received, assimilated, used, after having been assessed and justified by the pupils by recourse to principles; there were possibilities for innovation and room for autonomy of judgement at least in the secular studies, through principled assessment; dialogue between educator and educand was possible using the common ground of an appeal to principles; this 'rule-model' allowed for independent thinking, freedom to accept or reject what was taught in the light of an objectivity and rationality in teaching procedure. On the other hand, this was possible within the acknowledged and accepted limits of a Catholic philosophy of life, where, if rejection of basic moral principles was freely made, no place could be found for that student within the society of that school or Oratory. While, on the one hand, Don Bosco always attempted to ensure the future elsewhere of such people, on the other, little possibility for that freedom which has been associated with a sort of 'plural society' within the school could be accepted.

The greatest advantage of the 'rule-model' type school was that other methods which were more impressionistic or intuitive could still be included as the rational judgement process of the 'rule-model' could apply accumulated ideas or insights to principled assessment. What was sometimes in question was that 'rule-model' establishments, similar to those of Bosco's, could become formalized or rigid, if principles were not continually under review and reasons for them were not forthcoming. Don Bosco attempted to overcome formalism in his Oratories by emphasizing the 'reasonableness' of what was being done there and by encouraging group relationships with accents on informal, relaxed, and joyous ongoing experiences in his classrooms, and through the recreations.

Bosconian charity produced an atmosphere of joyousness in Bosconian Oratories and schools. Preventive techniques, where so much was dependent upon rapport between educator and educand, are reported to have developed mutual trust and respect in "an atmosphere of friendliness and mutual understanding". A relationship which was described as "friendly, sympathetic, and helpful",[44] depended upon an educator who was charitable towards the educand, who, in turn, was appreciative of his teacher's concern for him, so that, feeling needed as well as loved, his self-esteem developed and he felt happy. Exuberance, joyfulness, excitement, even delight, may, however, have been the result of the change in the boys' physical environment, as well as a response to the caring of their teachers. "Rowdy, dirty, and undisciplined"[45] early students, while feeling they were "not in a boarding school but in a real family",[46] were from backgrounds sharply in contrast to that provided, however unpretentiously, by the Salesians. Similarly, the contrast with a formal educational atmosphere, such as that experienced by students at a De La Salle Brothers' school in Turin in 1848, for example, was productive of delight:

> Whenever Don Bosco entered the school chapel for Mass or confessions, as Rua later reminisced, the Brothers' proverbial discipline for once went out the window, 'There was always a mad rush to greet him.... Each one of us felt genuinely loved by him.' "[47]

Bosconian rapport was characterized by a continuing personal communion: its effectiveness consisting in what Buber later was to describe as the 'dialogic relationship' between teacher and taught, both personalized and individualized, carried into every facet of the preventive system, and underlining pedagogical policy in relation to correction; provision for the felt needs of the young; giving a sense of belonging and security to the student; promoting a sense of confidence between educator and educand as among the students themselves. Rapport was the basis of the Salesian 'assistance' in which educators communicated with and counselled students in class, at play, in games, clubs, dramatics, choirs; in the Sodality system itself. It was the presence of the Salesian educator which could make "a dull day suddenly hum with excitement; and re-create Don Bosco for us in a way that made our young hearts leap with joyful enthusiasm. (Father Joseph Ciantar)."[48]

Don Bosco established this rapport by using means centred in Christian charity, and which were eminently effective in winning confidence. First, "he made himself available always. He took a keen interest in the studies of his boys, their sports, their hobbies, dramatics, debates, and Sodalities. He kept himself posted on their home and school activities".[49] Bosco explained: "The young must not only be loved, they must be made to feel that they are loved".[50]

Second, the educator gained the confidence and respect of the pupil through love, not fear. This was achieved through "warm and expansive kindness, persevering and never-ending patience by avoiding harshness and sarcasm which hurt the young and weaken their self-respect".[51] Paradoxically, too, Don Bosco had written: "An educator should seek to win the love of his pupils if he wishes to inspire fear in them'.[52]

Third, a friendly, kind approach was used in counselling or correcting. "The pupil realizes that a friend is at hand. His heart will open and unfold anxieties and needs".[53] Don Bosco had advised his Salesians that on every occasion advice had to be given or a suggestion made, that it was to be done in such a way that the student felt happier for it.[54]

Fourth, a boy's confidence was to be won by overcoming 'generation gaps' or age barriers. "This is accomplished by a certain familiarity. Outside the classroom, mingle freely with the pupils. Enjoy their laughs and jokes. Such occasions give the students an opportunity to see us not as teachers but as interested friends".[55] Bosco explained further, that the teacher, "having once succeeded in gaining the confidence of his pupils" could "subsequently exercise a great influence over them, and counsel them, advise and even correct them, whatever position they may occupy in the world later on".[56]

Lastly, and encompassing all the methods or suggestions offered, it was through love in the Christian sense, in a charitable disposition towards his students, that the gap between educator and pupil would be bridged. "We know only too well that the heart of the young is like a fortress. Only love can find its way into it. When asked for the secret of his success in education, St. John Bosco replied: 'Love'. And on another occasion, 'Love the things the boys love!' "[57] He attempted to explain further what was, perhaps, indefinable, in figurative language: "By the preventive system pupils acquire a better understanding, so that an educator can always speak to them in the language of the heart, not only during the time of their education but even afterwards...."[58] The rapport so engendered, contributed towards the pupil's growth in personality and confidence and in happiness. The concept of happiness so often referred to by the biographers, however, was an extension of Christian charity based both on 'kindness' and the Pauline interpretation of joy: "Rejoice in the Lord always; and again I say, rejoice.... whatever things are true, honourable and just; whatever holy, lovable and good; if there be any virtue or anything worthy of praise, then ponder on these things."[59] The 'happiness' or 'joy' resulting was a fulfilment of the Thomistic interpretation of man, whose "natural innate desire for happiness" lay in the "possession of God".[60]

The religious atmosphere of Salesian education, characteristically based on family lines, involved boys in prayer, in singing anthems, and attendance at Mass as a Christian unit. A sense of 'belonging' thus came to permeate their religious lives: they worked together at the practising of Christian charity, and at developing diligence in their work. This was communal involvement; common purposes and aspirations rooted in mutual and collective relationships led to a sense of purposeful striving which was 'worthwhile' and gave rise to inner contentment and feelings of joy. Again, however, while considering the effect of contrast in the environment and in adult behaviour, upon young students, and while allowing ʌor the descriptions of youthful fun in Salesian schools,[61] the Catholic interpretation of 'joy' would have influenced those who recollected such an atmosphere. According to Aquinas, "the desire or love of the good",[62] motivates people regardless of "whatever they desire or seek", to "desire happiness", but this 'happiness' lies in the "actualization of a man's potentialities",[63] not in material goods or the acquisition of power. "Or one can put the matter in this way. 'Beatitudo' in the objective sense connotes that good which, being possessed, perfects the potentialities of man as man. Used in a subjective sense it connotes the activity of possessing this good and the satisfaction or happiness.... which accompanies this activity",[64] and "Aquinas had a quite definite idea of what constitutes the supreme good for man. And this idea was a Christian idea".[65] Thus the Salesian student who perceived himself as an important person, one who was loved, who mattered and who was asked to join in the corporate life of the Oratory, nevertheless had come to centre his values in Christianity. As much through new opportunities, and that concerted action based on an involvement with his fellows and teachers, as through the common fraternity of joyous purposes: 'to know, love, and serve God', did the Salesian student come to find 'happiness'.

Frauke Chambers, in an article entitled: "Education Through Ecstasy?"[66] which is a review and commentary on George Leonard's *Education and Ecstasy*,[67] wrote:

> Joy and delight are rarely the paramount feelings of students and teachers in our classrooms. From above and below, the school situation is deplored and only reluctantly accepted as an inevitable, necessary evil that must be somehow endured.... Therefore a book with the title *Education and Ecstasy*.... will meet with sceptical or even derisive incredulity.... Leonard states that the main purpose and goal of education is 'the achievement of moments of ecstasy' (p.17) and that 'education, at best, is ecstatic' (p.16)....[68]

The all important and most pervasive consideration in all attempts to reform our educational environments should be the association of learning with pleasure and joy, since that is the best motivation for further learning, which we recognize more and more as a lifelong process or, in Leonard's words, 'life's ultimate purpose'.[69]

One hundred and twenty three years before Leonard wrote his 'incredible' book, Don Bosco had established schools in which pupils were experiencing 'pleasure and joy' through a Salesian pedagogy which, though based on another interpretation of 'life's ultimate purpose', still produced a sort of 'ecstasy':

> 'It would be impossible', writes Canon Ballesio, himself a boy of that period, 'to give an adequate idea of the life of the Oratory in those memorable years. Hundreds of young students fulfilled their duties with ardour and exactness.... there flourished.... innocence, simplicity and Christian joy. One might be tempted to label this as legendary, but it is sober historical truth.'[70]

On the other hand, "such a liberal, accommodating attitude in education.... joy, freedom and magnanimity", never developed into what Salesians would see as "permissiveness".[71] Salesian students were never, in the George Leonard sense, 'free learners' who, "whilst on the school grounds—are *absolutely* free to go and do *anything* they wish that does not hurt someone else".[72] Rather, as Albert Schweitzer explained, with regard to his opportunity to fulfil his ambition to become a jungle doctor, both students and teachers, seeing their opportunities to learn, to become part of the Salesian family, were "so favoured as to be able to embark on a course of free personal activity" that it made them "accept this good fortune in a spirit of humility";[73] for "happy those who in the end are able to give themselves really and completely!"[74] To early Salesians, "the will for the ideal which exists in mankind" was "manifested in action",[75] so that for both educator and educand love for a person, and a personal idealism, embraced, rather than passively accepted, limitations on their freedom, this action, at least for the adult members of the Salesian Community, approximating Buber's 'Teshuba' or 'turning', a free decision.

Claiming free decisions on the part of students, too, Salesian educators admit that "mutual acceptance and understanding are absolutely necessary", making possible "that intercommunion of spirit which distinguishes education from.... instruction",[76] and from which decisions "reconstructed" out of their own experience and "justified" on the basis of their own experience, were made by boys like Dominic Savio, as well as by men like Paul Albera.[77]

Since, then, according to biographers, the priest-educator's educational institutions were, in a Christian context, happy and joyous places it could be assumed that students and teachers within his Oratories enjoyed, to a large extent, 'the good life'. Modern educational philosophers, examining this concept, have considered the grounds upon which an estimate of the 'good' life can be made. American educationist, Harry S. Broudy,[78] for example, after considering various historical levels of subjective and objective viewpoints on educational aims in relation to the 'good' life, came to the conclusion that although there was little agreement among teachers about 'aims' there was considerable agreement as to what constituted the 'good' life. According to Broudy, while the 'good' life did not include excessive pain, fear, insecurity, unfulfilment, and lack of interest, what it did include were physical well-being, love, security, self-realization, power in accomplishment, goals, and interest. Broudy did not define the particular meaning of 'love' or 'goals' or 'interest', but posited the 'good' in general and sociological terms: "....the group becomes the good society, and the individual not only meets its demands but is genuinely happy in doing so...."[79] The problem however, of adequately defining 'the good life' as he saw it, had a universal aspect: "....the task that confronts any view holding to an objective concept of the good life is to show that human nature has a structure that is everywhere the same, and that this structure demands for its own preservation the form of action characteristic of the 'good life'."[80] Don Bosco, in 1841, had no doubt as to what constituted 'the good life'. It was a life consonant with the Christian ideal: 'to know, love and serve God', and it included the attainment of an object: "the civic, moral and intellectual education of his pupils".[81]

Contrary to Theodore Brameld's[82] estimate of the purpose of

Catholic education in the 1950's, preparation for 'the afterlife' did not override all other purposes in Bosco's schools. That "justifiable optimism",[83] which Brameld felt for progressive education in the 1960's was not unlike the optimism, since justified by experience and time, of early Salesians who, though they tended to use "the quaint, ingenuous style of.... Fioretti",[84] expressed a similar confidence in their educational decisions. Pope Paul VI in a 1971 address claimed that for modern Catholics, too, the challenge of Salesian education continues,[85] and though modern Salesians cannot accept the pragmatic view of man, they can, as Paul Hirst says, accept similar educational principles,[86] while still holding that "there is no true happiness without interior peace",[87] based on the Christian life. The era of 'peace on earth, good will toward men', quoted in controversial translation by Thayer[88] becomes for them 'peace on earth to men of good will'.[89]

Influencing the concept of what constituted 'the good life' within Bosconian schools and Oratories, was the preventive system's corrective prescriptions and the view of punishments which was held by its followers.

Primarily, "if possible", Don Bosco wrote, "never make use of punishments".[90] He envisaged, instead, a method whereby the prevention of wrongdoing, through Salesian 'presence' and 'assistance' would preclude the need for punitive measures. Realistically, however, in order that punishments were at least reduced to a minimum he devised certain measures[91] which today, are still pedagogical features of Salesian schools. Based on the assumption that every member of the school was conversant with the rules and regulations of the school, and the reasons for such; on a "fatherly watchfulness'[92] on the part of the teacher, a striving to be loved and at the same time to let students know that they are loved; the approach was positive, and behaviour problems were minimized. Once the esteem of the pupils had been gained through 'inclusive' love it was then possible to temporarily withdraw 'affection and attention"[93] when offences occurred. On this point the pedagogist wrote:

> When he succeeds in doing this, (winning their love) the withholding of some token of kindness is a punishment which stimulates emulation, gives courage and never degrades.

With the young, punishment is whatever is meant as a punishment. It has been noticed that in the case of some boys a reproachful look is more effective than a slap in the face would be. Praise of work well done, and blame in the case of carelessness are already a great reward or punishment.[94]

Other preventive measures included patient counselling: " . . . . an educator should correct. . . . with the patience of a father" and "as far as possible in private" and at the "right moment",[95] that is after he himself had thought about what he had done; and, in having the teacher in full control of his own emotions and feelings so that he would, when correcting a fault in someone else, be setting an example for the person being corrected to follow. Don Bosco wrote:

> First of all, master your own character, and then you will succeed in mastering those of your pupils. Show them that uncontrolled emotion plays no part in your actions; they will respect you for that and their respect will prompt their obedience. But betray the least sign of weakness, of passion, of impatience, and your authority and prestige will not long endure. Besides, your punishment will not be taken as a remedy for the boy's fault, but as a vent for your own anger. . . . Even a slight flush of the countenance or a small change in the tone of the voice caused by anger is betraying and incites the boys to lose their esteem and confidence in us. Then all punishment is useless, because the boys feel that reason alone ought to be used in correcting them.[96]

If all else failed in correcting a pupil, Bosco advised the bringing in of a third party, some other teacher in the school who had the boy's confidence. These preventive techniques, on Bosco's admission, were sometimes difficult to put into effect, and where a point was reached where nothing could be done with a student, he was realistic, almost to the point of being ruthless: "Be exacting when it is a matter of duty, firm in the pursuit of good, courageous in preventing evil, but always gentle and prudent. . . . If any pupil gives scandal by word or action, and does not amend his conduct in spite of the advice given him, he must be dismissed without fail, but with all the kindness that circumstances permit."[97]

In 1966, P. Nash, writing on punishment, in *Authority and Freedom in Education*,[98] stated that punishment involved a sense of reverence for the child; that manipulative methods were better than coercive ones; that disciplinary measures were to be orderly, directed, and restrained for the good of the child. In addition, Nash indicated some general rules to be observed in relation to punishment: be genuine and honest with the child; be sure that the good flowing from the punishment be judged to be greater than the suffering experienced by the one punished; and, the practice of punishing the whole group cannot be morally defended. Education's life task, Nash believed, was based on a rigorous process of self-discipline achieved through the child's 'overcoming' himself. Moreover, effective discipline, a product of freedom, was both relevant and realistic; and the granting of unrestricted choice to the immature cut them off from the possibilities of future freedom.

Earlier, in 1883, in a circular written by Don Bosco and sent out to Salesian schools, the pedagogist set down suggestions about punishing which were as follows:

1. Before punishing ascertain all the facts.
2. Be sure that the guilty one knows why he is being punished.
3. Never turn a pupil out of the classroom. In more serious cases have the lad accompanied to the principal.
4. Justice must always be used when punishing.
5. Never make use of general punishments.
6. Never make use of corporal punishments.
7. Punishments must be few and never prolonged.
8. Written punishments are generally to be discouraged.
9. Never make use of the *reflection room*, where the pupil remains in idleness.
10. Always inspire the hope of pardon.[99]

Bosco, writing some eighty-three years before Nash on the subject of punishment had presaged much of what modern educationists have to say on the subject. Psychologist, B.Z. Friedlander's "second thoughts"[100] on the complexity of the teaching and learning process in which such a delicate balance between freedom and discipline is involved, also reflect Bosconian emphasis on the role of the teacher: "....it is to the teacher's credit for serving as a worthy model of rational intelligence, effectively and judiciously in action";[101] but the Bosconian approach, essentially Christian, has in the Salesian view the advantage of an "Exemplar"[102] to inspire both teachers and taught in matters pertaining to 'discipline'.

An essential feature of Bosco s pedagogy was the emphasis he placed upon play: free games, unrestricted and uninhibited as well as games with rules which balanced theoretical and practical work, and served as an outlet for students whose opportunity to learn and work demanded similar zest and enthusiasm in the classroom. It was during games that the teachers who joined in did much purposeful counselling in an informal atmosphere.

According to R.F. Deardon,[103] children's play has had a significance with educators beyond the certainty that it will appear. Frederic Froebel, German pedagogist 1782-1852, for instance, had placed a metaphysical significance on his kindergarten: a child's essential nature "unfolded",[104] like the petals of a flower; while Rousseau, "the non-metaphysician",[105] on the other hand, described twelve year old Emile as "just a rough, vulgar little boy".[106] Bosco's conception allowed for the 'unfolding' aspect of Froebel's child-garden, but saw the essential nature of the child as being not only innocent but also open to "temptations" to commit sin, in the Catholic sense,[107] rather than as being 'vulgar' in Rousseau's sense. Hence Bosconian ensistence on the company of dedicated teachers during recreation. Play was, nevertheless, for relaxation, engaged in "just for the satisfaction involved in it",[108] while at the same time it allowed teacher and student to communicate informally. Don Rinaldi (1856-1931), third successor to Don Bosco, saw Salesian education in terms of this communing but alert role of the educator:

> —Avoid the mistake of wanting to constrain all the young into an a-priori personality mould which we have created in our mind.
> —Don't crush the individual personality....
> —Respect for the liberty of the young must be traced to that inviolable zone of conscience to which only the youth himself has the key.
> —To give the youth the impression that we are inflexible is to cultivate hypocrisy....
> —A pre-conceived educational blue-print—no matter how wise—breaks down.... open-hearted spontaneity....

—The sacred dignity of the young should preclude snap judgements.... [109]

Don Bosco's pedagogy is not so much a system to be analysed as a way of life to be observed. Through recorded experiences, both oral and written, the Salesian Society has developed and maintained Bosco's rationale. The literature, often adulatory and personalized, is, together with 'living experience', the source of both information and motivation in the Salesian tradition. It involves educator and educand in a commitment to a Faith, both in God and humanity, which is practice rather than theory; expressed in terms of personal encounters; whose criteria are 'reason' and 'kindness'; whose object is the attainment of 'the civic, moral and intellectual education' of youth.

The Salesians of Don Bosco, with their model of "an educator in action",[110] use a preventive method which works. They offer a balanced program of creative and recreational activities, which together with "an awareness of the necessity of kindness in the training of the young",[111] and their method of 'assistance', engender ordinary, everyday opportunities for communication on many levels.

Don Bosco's techniques, though developed from his metaphysics, anticipated many of the principles developed later by educationists with different philosophical standpoints. A pedagogy offering the young a sense of contentment, joy and fulfilment, the basis of Salesian schools throughout the world, is not unlike many modern views of education.

Essentially Don Bosco's pedagogy is "a living tradition that is carried on from generation to generation.... something living; to be fully understood, it must be seen in action."[112]

Notes to Part I of Chapter 8

1   L.M. Brown, "Professional Considerations in Teaching," *Independent Education*, The Journal of the N.S.W. Independent Teachers' Association, (Ed. J.C. Nicholson), Vol. 4, No. 4, Autoprint, N.S.W., 1974, p.6.

2 *ibid.*, p.7.

3 Martin Buber, *Between Man and Man*, Collins, London, 1961.

4 *Provincial Advisory Council on Education, op. cit.*, p.3.

5 "What is the use, says Don Bosco, of punishing the boy after the offence has been committed." E. Valentini, *op. cit.*, p.5.

6 Mumford Lewis, *The Conditions of Man*, Mercury Books, London, 1963.

7 Karl Mannheim, "The Crisis in Valuation", *Diagnosis of Our Time*, Routledge and Kegan Paul, 1950. Mannheim argues that there are two sets of influences in modern democratic societies: self-interest in a competitive life; unselfishness in social life for common ends. The first influence is repressive and ascetic, he argues, the second is self-expressive.

8 John Dewey, "Education and Our Present Social Problems", *School in Society*, April 15, 1933; and C. Wright-Mills, *The Power Elite*, O.U.P., N.Y., 1959.

9 *The New Catholic Dictionary, op. cit.*, p.530. "Kingdom of God.... not only a place or goal to be attained, but an influence under which our minds come when we are one with Christ and acting under His ideals...."

10 Carl R. Rogers, *On Becoming a Person*, Constable and Co., London, 1961.

11 *The New Catholic Dictionary, op. cit.*, p.238. "Communion of Saints, an article of the Apostles' Creed, a spiritual solidarity binding together the faithful on earth, the souls in purgatory, and the saints in heaven, in the same mystical body of which Christ is the head, and in constant supernatural interchange. The merits of Christ are communicated to each one, and those of each one to the others. The faithful on earth mutually exchange merits and satisfactions. The souls in purgatory profiting by our suffrages, and the saints in heaven honored by our veneration, intercede for us in turn."

12 Brown, *op. cit.*, p.8.

13 A.W. Coombs and D. Snygg, *Individual Behaviour*, Harper and Row, N.Y., 1959.

14 James E. Myers and Kalil I. Gezi, "Teaching the Culturally Disadvantages", from *Teaching in American Culture*, (Ed. Gezi & Myers), Holt, Rinehart & Winston, N.Y., 1968.

15 For example, Frank Riessman, "Education of the Culturally Deprived Child", *The Science Teacher*, 32. Nov., 1965.

16 Quoted by J. Ayers, *op. cit.*, p.12.

17 Suggested by informal answers to questions. 1974 Melbourne Chapter of Australian Salesians. *op. cit.*

18   Riessman, *op. cit.*, After Riessman's title.

19   Pierre Teilhard de Chardin, *The Phenomenon of Man*, Collins, Fantana Books, London, 1965, p.290.

20   *ibid.*, p.283.

21   Viktor E. Frankl, *Man's Search for Meaning*, (Trans. Ilse Lasch), Hodder and Stroughton, 1964, p.114.

22   *ibid.*, p.214.

23   *ibid.*, p.99.

24   *Provincial Advisory Council on Education, op. cit.*, p.16.

Notes to Part II of Chapter 8

1   Max Black, "Rules and Routines", from *The Concept of Education*, (Ed. R.S. Peters) Routledge and Kegan Paul, London, 1967, p.102.

2   Gilbert Ryle, "Knowing How and Knowing That" from *Philosophy and Education*, Modern Readings, (Ed. I.   Scheffler), Boston, U.S.A., 1966.

3   It is interesting to note that in L. Arnaud Reid's article "Philosophy and the Theory and Practice of Education" from *Philosophical Analysis and Education*, (Ed. R.D. Archambault), Routledge, London, 1965; he questions the term "educational theory" and realizes that educational practice involves a fresh decision, apart from theory.   Reid is also unable to prove his belief that a study of educational philosophy is essential or valuable to the individual teacher.   In the same volume, Edward Best's "Common Confusions in Educational Theory" queries what educationists mean by the term "theory".

4   R.S. Peters, "What is an Educational Process?" from *The Concept of Education, op. cit.*, p.21.

5   *ibid.*, p.4.

6   Quoted from W.J. Crocker's "Learning to be Completely Human", from *English in Australia*, No. 25, November, 1973, p.14.

7   John Dewey argued that the hypothesis that worked was the true one.   He also held that the scientific method was the only worthwhile method; that democracy the only worthwhile political system.   Moreover, science showed the purely subjective character of value.   Dewey's evaluation standpoint was scientific.

8   A.N. Whitehead, *The Aims of Education*, Benn, London, 1950.

9   R.S. Peters, "Must an Educator Have an Aim?" from *Authority, Responsibility and Education*, Allen and Unwin, London, 1963.

10   J. Maritain, *Education at the Crossroads*, Yale University Press, U.S.A., 1943.

11   Martin Buber, *Between Man and Man*, Collins, Fontana Library, London, 1961.   Buber's philosophy was, in the main, existentialist.   He argued that concentration on subjective states of experience led to transcendence to God.   Buber posited an 'I-Thou' philosophy which was seen as a third possibility to traditional 'either-or' or 'good or evil', 'love or fear' 'alternatives'. Buber saw in the field of educational philosophy a battle between irreconcilable opposites: 'objective' education at issue with 'subjective' interests.   Truth was, then, neither subjective not objective but 'participation in being': a man gives himself to the truth subsequently proving it by leading a life of truth himself.

12   Herbert Feigl, "Ends and Means of Education" from *National Society for the Study of Education, 54th.   Yearbook*, Part I, University of Chicago, 1955.

13   G.H. Bantock, *Freedom and Authority in Education*, Faber and Faber, London, 1965.

14   *Constitutions and Regulations of the Society of St. Francis of Sales*, *op. cit.*, p.196.

15   *ibid.*, p.197.

16   *loc. cit.*

17   One such student, Michael Rua, later to become Don Bosco's successor, first experienced difficulties at Bosco's St. Francis de Sales Oratory after having come from another Catholic school where more rigid systems applied.   The more casual, relaxed atmosphere of Bosco's school gradually impressed Rua who went on to "marvellous progress and enthusiasm".   J. Ayers, Blessed Michael Rua, *op. cit.*, p.13.

18   Gerald Vann, *Morals and Man*, *op. cit.*, p.169.

19   Gerald Vann, *The Divine Pity*, *op. cit.*, p.162.

20   E. Fromm, *Escape From Freedom*, Holt, N.Y., 1941, quoted from Foreword, p.viii.

21   II Corinthians, 3:17.

22   Thomas Aquinas, quoted in *The Pocket Aquinas*, Selections from the Writings, (Ed. Vernon J. Bourke), Washington Square Press, Inc. N.Y., 1960, p.189.

23   Ayers, *A Salesian Education*, *op. cit.*, p.23(a).

24   Vann, *Morals and Man*, *op. cit.*, p.119.

25   *ibid.*, pp.119-120.

26   K. Mannheim, *Man and Society in an Age of Reconstruction:* Studies

in Modern School Structure, Routledge, London, 1940. Mannheim postulated that whether society be planned or otherwise, a man feels free if he thinks he has initiative and free will to influence social conditions.

27 R.S. Peters, "What is an Educational Process?" in *The Concept of Education*, *op. cit.*, p.5.

28 J.P. White, "Indoctrination" in *The Concept of Education*, *op. cit.*, pp.177-191.

29 *ibid.*, p.188.

30 *loc. cit.*

31 *ibid.*, p.189.

32 Edgar Faure, "Education and the destiny of man", in *The Unesco Courier*, Nov. 1972, 0.9.

33 *ibid.*, p.9.

34 *ibid.*, p.9.

35 *ibid.*, p.9.

36 Max Black, *op. cit.*, p.96.

37 *ibid.*, p.95.

38 J.M. Rich, *Education and Human Values*, Addison-Wesley, Massachusetts, 1968.

39 Ayers, *A Salesian Education*, *op. cit.*, p.21.

40 *ibid.*, p.21.

41 "In South America a heavy-handed superior in Father Borghino opened a parcel from Don Rua to find a small jar of honey with a note attached, 'Take a spoonful every morning, dear Father, to sweeten your community life.' " Ayers, *Blessed Michael Rua*, *op. cit.*, p.31.

42 Israel Scheffler, "Philosophical models of teaching" from *The Concept of Education*, *op. cit.*, pp.129-132.

43 *ibid.*, p.130.

44 Paul Avallone, *Reason, Re'igion, Kindness*, The Educational Method of St. John Bosco, Salesian Publishers, New Rochelle, New York, 1965, p.39.

45 Ayers, *A Salesian Education*, *op. cit.*, p.12.

46 *ibid.*, p.12.

47 Ayers, *Blessed Michael Rua*, *op. cit.*, pp.11-12.

48 Fr. John Ayers' own recollection of his education at an Oratory in Australia, and in particular the impressions he gained of one of his teachers there, Fr. Joseph Ciantar. In Ayers, *A Salesian Education*, *op. cit.*, p.23.

49 Avallone, *op. cit.*, p.47.

50 Ceria, *op. cit.*, *B.M.*, Vol. XVII, p.110.

51 Avallone, *op. cit.*, p.48.

52 *Constitutions and Regulations, op. cit.*, p.206.

53 Avallone, *op. cit.*, p.48.

54 Lemoyne, *op. cit.*, Vol. IV, p.395.

55 Avallone, *op. cit.*, p.48.

56 *Constitutions and Regulations, op. cit.*, p.199.

57 Avallone, *op. cit.*, p.48.

58 *Constitutions and Regulations, op. cit.*, p.199.

59 I Colossians, 4:4 and 8.   Quoted by Ayers in *A Salesian Education, op. cit.*, as having been read by Don Bosco, p.20(a).

60 F.C. Copleston, *Aquinas*, Penguin, Gt. Brit. 1955.

61 For example, some brief anecdotes collected on Salesian teachers. Ayers, *A Salesian Education, op. cit.*, p.22.

62 Copleston, *op. cit.*, p.180.

63 *ibid.*, p.180.

64 *ibid.*, p.181.

65 *ibid.*, p.181.

66 Frauke Chambers, "Education Through Ecstasy?" in *Education News*, June 1974, Volume 14, Number 9, pp.18-21.

67 George Leonard, *Education and Ecstasy*, Delacorte Press, New York, 1968.

68 Chambers, *op. cit.*, p.18.

69 *loc. cit.*

70 Terence O'Brien, *Dominic Savio*, Guild Publications, London, 1969. p.90.

71 Ayers, *op. cit.*, p.18.

72 Chambers, *op. cit.*, p.18.

73 Schweitzer, *op. cit.*, p.87.

74 *loc. cit.*

75 *ibid.*, p.87.

76 O'Brien, *op.cit.*, p.67.

77 Acknowledgement to C.D. Hardie's use of these words for different

purpose. "Pragmatism in Philosophy and Education." *The Educand,* Vol. 3, No. 2, Nov. 1958, pp.125-130.

78   Harry S. Broudy, *Building a Philosophy of Education,* Prentice-Hall, New Jersey, 1954.

79   *ibid.,* p.37.

80   *ibid.,* p.39.

81   *Constitutions and Regulations, op.cit.,* p.204.

82   Theo Brameld, "A Cultural Evaluation of Progressivism", *Philosophies of Education in Cultural Perspective,* Dryden Press, N.Y., 1956.

83   Theo Brameld, *Education for the Emerging Age: Newer and Stronger Means,* Harper, N.Y., 1961, p.157.

84   Ayers, *A Salesian Education, op.cit.,* p.4.

85   20/12/1971. Quoted from Aubry's *Apostoli Per I Giovani,* by John Ayers, *A Salesian Education, op.cit.,* p.131.

86   Paul H. Hirst, "Philosophy and Educational Theory", *British Journal of Education Studies,* Vol. XII, No. 1, Nov. 1963.

87   O'Brien, *op.cit.,* p.73.

88   V.T. Thayer, "The Relation of the School to the Social Order", *Formative Ideas in American Education, School and Society,* Vol. 93, No. 2258, 20/3/65.

89   ". . . .peace on earth to men that are God's friends", Ronald A. Knox translation, Luke 2: 14. Knox, *op.cit.,* p.55.

90   Ceria, *op.cit., M.B.,* Vol. XIII, p.920f.

91   These measures were described by Don Bosco in Ceria's *Memorie Biografiche, op.cit.,* Vol. XIII, pp.920ff.

92   Avallone, *op.cit.,* p.67.

93   *ibid.,* p.68.

94   *Constitutions and Regulations, op.cit.,* pp.206-207.

95   Avallone, *op.cit.,* p.68.

96   *ibid.,* pp.68-69.

97   *ibid.,* p.70.

98   P. Nash, *Authority and Freedom in Education,* Wiley, New York, 1966.

99   Avallone, *op.cit.,* p.71.

100   B.Z. Friedlander, "A Psychologist's Second Thoughts on concepts, curiosity and discovery in teaching and learning", *Harvard Educational Review,* 1965. No. 35.

101   *ibid.*, p.38.

102   Don Bosco had concluded his 1883 letter, dealing with the theme of punishment, in these words: "Remember that education is a difficult art, and that God alone is its true Master. We will never succeed in it, unless He teaches us the way. While depending humbly and entirely on Him, we should try with might and main, to acquire that moral strength that is a stranger to force and vigour. Let us strive to make ourselves loved, to instill into our pupils the high ideal of duty and the holy fear of God, and we will soon possess their hearts. Then, with natural ease, they will join us in praising Jesus Christ, Our Lord, Who is our Model, our Pattern, our Exemplar in all things, but especially in the education of the young. Quoted by Avallone, *op.cit.*, p.72.

103   R.F. Dearden, "The Concept of Play", in The *Concept of Education*, op.cit.

104   *ibid.*, p.75.

105   *loc.cit.*

106   *loc.cit.*

107   Don Bosco, Preface to "Part One, Dominic's Life as told by St. John Bosco", Terence O'Brien, *Dominic Savio*, op.cit.

108   Dearden, *op.cit.*, p.84.

109   Ayers, *A Salesian Education*, *op.cit.*, p.19. Quoted and translated from Rinaldi's "Conference".

110   Avallone, *op.cit.*, p.6.

111   *ibid.*, p.7.

112   *ibid.*, p.30.

A SELECT BIBLIOGRAPHY

Author's Note.

There are nineteen biographical volumes written in series by three biographers: Lemoyne, Amadei, and Ceria; on the life and works of Saint John Bosco. Recently Volumes I-VIII by Lemoyne, and Volume XI by Ceria were translated into English. The remainder, namely Volumes IX, X, XII-XIX are in Italian. In the course of this work, at times the Italian volumes were referred to because it was felt that their descriptions were more apposite, at other times the English translations were preferred. To designate when the original Italian version was used the letters M.B. (Memorie Biografiche) are used.

Amadei, Angelo. *Memorie Biografiche di Don Giovanni Bosco*, Vol. X, Societa Edutrice Internazionale, Torino, 1939.

Aubry, J. *The Salesian Co-Operator: A Real Vocation in the Church*, Sign, Madras, 1972.

Auffray, A. *Saint John Bosco*. Isag-Colle Don Bosco, Asti, Italy, 1964.

Auge, C. and P. *Nouveau Petit Larousse Illustre Dictionnaire Encyclopedique*, Librairie Larousse, Paris, 1954.

Avallone, Paul. *Reason, Religion, Kindness, The Educational Method of St. John Bosco*, Salesian Publishers, New Rochelle, New York, 1965.

Ayers, J. *A Salesian Education*. Unpublished Treatise, Boys' Town, Sydney, 1974.

Ayers, John. *Blessed Michael Rua*. Pauline Fathers and Brothers of the Society of St. Paul, Homebush, N.S.W., 1974.

Bantock, G.H. *Freedom and Authority in Education*. Faber and Faber, London, 1965.

Black, Max. "Rules and Routines", from *The Concept of Education*. (Ed. R.S. Peters), Routledge and Kegan Paul, London, 1967.

Bosco, John. *St. Dominic Savio*. St. Joseph's Technical School, Madras, India, 1954.

Braido, Pietro. *Il Sistema Preventivo di Don Bosco*, Pas-Verlag, Zurich-Schweig, 1964.

Brameld, Theo. "A Cultural Evaluation of Progressivism", from *Philosophies of Education in Cultural Perspective*. Dryden Press, N.Y., 1956.

Brameld, Theo. *Education for the Emerging Age: Newer and Stronger Means*. Harper, N.Y., 1961.

Bramsted, E.K. "Italy 1815-1914", *The West and the World, 1789-1914*. (Ed. N.K. Meaney), Science Press, N.S.W., 1972.

Broudy, Harry S. *Building a Philosophy of Education*. Prentice-Hall, New Jersey, 1954.

Brown, L.M. "Professional Considerations in Teaching", from *Independent Education*. The Journal of the N.S.W. Independent Teachers' Association. (Ed. J.C. Nicholson), Vol. 4, No. 4, Autoprint, N.S.W., 1974.

Buber, Martin. *Between Man and Man*. Collins, London, 1961.

Butler's Lives of the Saints. (Ed. H. Thurston and D. Attwater). Vols. I-IV, Burns and Oates, London, 1956.

Centenary 1872-1972. Daughters of Mary, Help of Christians, Isag, Colle Don Bosco, Asti, Italy, 1972.

Ceria, E. *Memorie Biografiche di Don Giovanni Bosco*, Vols. XI-XIX-Societa Edutrice Internazionale, Torino, 1930-1937.

Ceria, Eugene. *The Salesian Society*. (Revised by Joseph Hopkins). Salesian Publishers, Paterson, New Jersey, 1955.

Chambers, Frauke. "Education Through Ecstasy?" from *Education News*. Vol 14, No. 9, June, 1974.

Chardin, Pierre Teilhard de. *The Phenomenon of Man*. Pantana Books, London, 1965.

Chiavarino, J.L. *Smiling Don Bosco*. (Trans. L.M. Gallo), St. Paul's Press, Allahabad, India, 1957.

Colussi, John. *Don Bosco and His Preventive Method of Education*. Unpublished treatise, University of San Francisco, 1969.

Constitutions and Regulations of the Society of St. Francis of Sales. St. Joseph's Technical School, Madras, India, 1967.

Coombs, A.W. and Snygg, D. *Individual Behaviour*. Harper and Row, N.Y., 1959.

Copleston, F.C. *Aquinas*. Penguin, Great Britain, 1955.

Cosgrove, J.J. and Kreiss, J.K. *Two Centuries*. Whitcombe and Tombs Pty. Ltd., 1969.

Cuskelly, E.J. *A Summary of the Spiritual Life*. Mercier Press, Cork, 1964.

Dearden, R.F. "The Concept of Play", from *The Concept of Education*. (Ed. R.S. Peters), Routledge and Kegan Paul, London, 1967.

Dewey, John. "Education and Our Present Social Problems", *School in Society*. April 15, 1933.

Don Bosco in the World. (I. Giordani et al), Elle di Ci, Turin, Leuman, Italy, 1968.

Farrow, J. *Pageant of the Popes*. Catechetical Guild Educational Society, St. Paul 2, Minnesota, Sheed and Ward, N.Y., 1950.

Fascie, D.B. *Del Metodo Educativo di Don Bosco*, Societa Editrice Internazionale, Torino, 1927.

Faure, Edgar. "Education and the destiny of man", from *The Unesco Courier*, Nov. 1972.

Feigl, Herbert. "Ends and Means of Education", from *National Society for the Study of Education*, 54th Yearbook, Part I, University of Chicago, 1955.

Forbes, F.A. *Saint John Bosco*, Salesian Press, Tampa, Florida, 1941.

Franco, Angelo. *A Lamp Resplendent*. Salesiana Press, N.J., 1958.

Frankl, Viktor E. *Man's Search for Meaning*. (Trans. Ilse Lasch), Hodder and Stroughton, 1964.

Freemantle, Anne. *The Papal Encyclicals in their Historical Context*. The New American Library, N.Y., 1956.

Friedlander, B.Z. "A Psychologist's Second Thoughts on concepts curiosity and discovery in teaching and learning", *Harvard Educational Review*, No. 35, 1965.

Fromm, E. *Escape From Freedom*. Holt, N.Y., 1941.

Gheon, H. (Trans. F.J. Sheed). *The Secret of St. John Bosco*. Sheed and Ward, London, 1954.

Hirst, Paul H. "Philosophy and Educational Theory", from *British Journal of Educational Studies*, Vol. XII, No. 1, Nov. 1963.

Lagarde, A. et Michael, L. *XVII Siecle Les Grands Auteurs Francais du Programme*, Vol. III, Bordas, Paris, 1960.

Lemoyne, Giovanni B. *Memorie Biografiche di Don Giovanni Bosco*. Vols. I-IX, Scuola Tipografica Libreria Salesiana, Torino, 1898-1917.

Lemoyne, J.B. *The Biographical Memoirs of Saint John Bosco*. Vols. I-VIII. An American edition translated from the original Italian, Diego Borgatello, Editor-in-Chief, Salesiana Publishers, Inc., New Rochelle, N.Y., 1965-1974.

Leonard, George. *Education and Ecstasy*. Delacorte Press, New York, 1968.

Lewis, Mumford. *The Conditions of Man*. Mercury Books, London, 1963.

Mannheim, K. *Man and Society in an Age of Reconstruction: Studies on Modern School Structure*. Routledge, London, 1940.

Mannheim, K. "The Crisis in Valuation", from *Diagnosis of Our Time*. Routledge and Kegan Paul, 1950.

Maritain, J. *Education at the Crossroads.* Yale University Press, U.S.A., 1943.

Meadows, D. *A Short History of the Catholic Church.* All Saints Press, Inc., N.Y., 1960.

Morell, J.D. *A Compendium of Italian History from the Fall of the Roman Empire.* (Trans. from the Italian of Giovanni Bosco, and completed to the present time), Longman, Green and Co., London, 1881.

Myers, J.E. and Gezi, K.I. "Teaching the Culturally Disadvantaged", from *Teaching in American Culture.* (Ed. Gezi and Myers), Holt, Rinehart and Winston, N.Y., 1968.

Nash, P. *Authority and Freedom in Education.* Wiley, New Work, 1966.

Nunn, T.P. *Education: Its Data and First Principles*, Arnold, London, 1947.

O'Brien, Terence. *Dominic Savio.* Guild Publication, London, 1969.

Peters, R.S. "Must an Educator Have an Aim?" from *Authority Responsibility and Education.* Allen and Unwin, London, 1963.

Peters, R.S. "What is an Educational Process?" from *The Concept of Education.* (Ed. R.S. Peters), Routledge and Kegan Paul, London, 1967.

Phelan, E.B. *Don Bosco, A Spiritual Portrait.* Doubleday, New York, 1963.

Ricaldone, Peter. *Festive Oratory, Catechism and Religious Formation.* St. Joseph's Technical School, Madras, India, 1939.

Ricaldone, Peter. *Fidelity to Saint John Bosco.* St. Joseph's Technical School, Madras, India. (No Date).

Ricceri, Aloysius (et al). *XIX General Chapter of the Salesian Society*, Progress Press Co. Ltd., Valetta, Malta, 1965.

Rich, J.M. *Education and Human Values.* Addison-Wesley, Massachusetts, U.S.A., 1968.

Rogers, Carl R. *On Becoming a Person.* Constable and Co., London, 1961.

Ryle, Gilbert. "Knowing How and Knowing That", from *Philosophy and Education.* Modern Readings, (Ed. I. Scheffler), Boston, U.S.A., 1966.

Scheffler, Israel. "Philosophical models of teaching", from *The Concept of Education.* (Ed. R.S. Peters), Routledge and Kegan Paul, London, 1967.

Shaw, A.G.L. *Modern World History.* Cheshire, Melbourne, 1961.

Sheppard, L.C. *Don Bosco.* Burns and Oates, London, 1957.

Smith, Denis Mack. *The Making of Italy, 1796-1870.* Harper, N.Y., 1968.

Stella, Pietro. *Don Bosco Nella Storia Religiosita Cattolica.* Volume Primo, Vita E. Opere, Pas-Verlag, Zurich, 1968.

Tanquerey, A. *The Spiritual Life.   A Treatise on Ascetical and Mystical Theology.* (Trans. from French by Herman Branderis), Society of St. John the Evangelist, Desclee and Co., Tournai, Belgium, 1932.

Thayer, V.T. "The Relation of the School to the Social Order", from *Formative Ideas in American Education, School and Society.* Vol. 93, No. 2258, 20/3/65.

The New Catholic Dictionary. (Ed. C.B. Pallen and J.J. Wynne). Van Rees Press, New York, 1929.

The New Testament of Our Lord and Saviour Jesus Christ. (Trans. R.A. Knox), Burns and Oates, London, 1960.

Trouncer, Margaret. *The Gentleman Saint, St. Francis de Sales and His Times, 1567-1622.* Hutchinson and Co., London, 1963.

Valentini, Eugene. *The Salesian Assistant.* Unpublished Paper, Melbourne, 1959.

Vann, Gerald. *Morals and Man.* Collins, London, 1960.

Vann, Gerald. *The Divine Pity.* Collins London, 1945.

Villefranche, J.M. *The Life of Don Bosco.* (Trans. from the French by Lady Martin), Burns, Oates and Washbourne, Ltd., London. (No date).

White, J.P. "Indoctrination", from *The Concept of Education.* (Ed. R.S. Peters), Routledge and Kegan Paul, London, 1967.

Whitehead, A.N. *The Aims of Education.* Benn, London, 1950.

Wirth, Morand. *Don Bosco et les Salesiens, Cent Cinquante Ans D'Histoire.* Elle di Ci., Torino-Leumann, 1969.

Wright-Mills, C. *The Power Elite.* O.U.P., New York, 1959.

INDEX

NOTE: Parenthesis indicate *footnote*.

249

207, 210. See also: FLEXI-
BILITY; INTERNATIONALISM.
CURRICULUM: 64, 68, 80, 109,
163, 168-9, 181, 191, 208, 210.
See also: BALANCE.

– D –

DAUGHTERS OF MARY, HELP
OF CHRISTIANS: See CON-
FRATERNITY.
DEARDON, R.F.: 232.
DEATH and DYING: See PEDA-
GOGY.
DECISION-MAKING: 57, 153, 219,
221. See also: LIBERTY.
DEDICATION: 47, 60, 122, 138,
147, 148, 154, 157, 166, 184,
187, 191, 192-3, 206.
DE LA SALLE, John-Baptist: 163,
164, (196).
DELINQUENCY: See UNDERPRIV-
ILEDGED.
DEMOCRACY: 65. See also: LI-
BERTY.
DEMONSTRATIONS: 67-8, 79, 180,
187, 188, 210-11.
DE PAUL, Vincent: 49, (82), 151,
160-2.
DE SALES, Francis: 46, 47, 67,
151, 156-7, 164, (194), (195).
DEVOTIONAL LIFE: See PIETY.
DEWEY, John: 127, 212, 214, 216,
217, (235).
DIALOGUE-DISCUSSION: 51, 56,
62, 76, 143, 170, 171, 216, 222,
224.
DISADVANTAGED: See UNDER-
PRIVILEGED.
DISCIPLINE: Self-Discipline: 68, 90,

126, 157, 192.
Within the School: 54, 62, 69,
70, 93-4, 96, 97, 99, 123, 134,
137, 142, 145, 218, 225, 231-2.
DISCOVERY TECHNIQUES: See
METHOD.
DRAMA: See METHOD.
DUPANLOUP, Felix: 165, 190-1.
DUPRE, Joseph: 79-80.
DUTY: See PEDAGOGY.
DYNAMISM: 184, 191. See also:
FLEXIBILITY.

– E –

ECLECTICISM: 34, 35, 51, 55, 56,
80, 91, 151, 180, 187, 191, 211.
EDUCATORS: See TEACHERS.
ENDS-MEANS: 127-8, 173, 214, 215,
217. See also: AIMS.
ENDURANCE: 179. See also: ASSIS-
TANCE.
EQUALITY: 54, 94, 108. See also:
DEMOCRACY.
EVALUATION: 29, 66, 79, 170,
183, 222.
EVENING CLASSES: 1, 16, 61,
67-8, 79, 103, 177, 186.
EXAMINATIONS: 29.
EXCURSIONS: 35, 52, 74, 75, 77,
90, 140, 142, 147, 170.
EXEMPLARS: 14, 16, 57, 59, 72,
90, 92, 95, 99, 101, 106, 107,
(109-1), 153, 155, 156, 157,
160, 182, 209, 230, 231, 233,
(240).
EXISTENTIALISM: 38, 123, 216.
EXPERIENTIAL QUALITY: 12, 17,
22, 38, 46, 58, 59, 123, 175,
180, 208, 210, 215.

251

253

255

257